How to Do *Everything* with

with

Digital Photography

How to Do *Everything* with

Digital Photography

Dave Huss

McGraw-Hill/Osborne

New York   Chicago   San Francisco   Lisbon
London   Madrid   Mexico City   Milan   New Delhi
San Juan   Seoul   Singapore   Sydney   Toronto

The McGraw·Hill Companies

McGraw-Hill/Osborne
2100 Powell Street, 10th Floor
Emeryville, California 94608
U.S.A.

To arrange bulk purchase discounts for sales promotions, premiums, or fund-raisers, please contact **McGraw-Hill**/Osborne at the above address. For information on translations or book distributors outside the U.S.A., please see the International Contact Information page immediately following the index of this book.

How to Do Everything with Digital Photography

234567890 DOC DOC 01987654
ISBN 0-07-225435-1

Publisher	Brandon A. Nordin
Vice President &	
Associate Publisher	Scott Rogers
Acquisitions Editor	Megg Morin
Project Editor	Elizabeth Seymour
Acquisitions Coordinator	Athena Honore
Technical Editor	Jim Patterson
Copy Editor	Lisa Theobald
Proofreader	John Gildersleeve
Indexer	Bob Richardson
Composition	Lucie Ericksen, Tabitha M. Cagan
Illustrators	Melinda Lytle, Kathleen Edwards
Series Design	Lucie Ericksen
Cover Series Design	Dodie Shoemaker
Cover Illustration	Tom Willis

This book was composed with Corel VENTURA™ Publisher.

Dedication

This book is dedicated to Dan and Margaret Beckwith —
my in-laws by marriage, but through their love and support
over the past 30 years—my closest friends.

About the Author

Dave Huss has been a photographer for 40 years. His work has been featured in *Studio Photography & Design* magazine and Nikon's *Capture User* magazine. Dave has been seen on CNN and Tech TV, and is the author of several books including *How to Do Everything with Paint Shop Pro 8* and *Corel PHOTO-PAINT 10: The Official Guide*.

Contents at a Glance

Contents

Foreword

Inspiration.

A couple of years ago, my then eleven-year-old son ran his first marathon. I watched from the curb as he crossed mile twenty-four. Together we jogged the last few miles of the race, and when he finally saw the finish line, he sprinted toward it, leaving me behind. He made it look so easy. "Next year, Mom," he shouted over his shoulder, "we cross this line together."

I am now training to run my second marathon and my son will be running his third.

You just never know where inspiration will come from.

Back in my office at PhotoSpin, a royalty-free subscription service for photos and illustrations, I shared this story with Dave Huss, who is also a runner. Dave and I instantly became friends and he began sharing with me his stories of inspiration through his photographs.

What was most interesting to me about Dave was that he shared a lot more than the photos. He would also share the exact recipe for creating them digitally. Along with each photo he'd list out the hardware and software he'd used and special filters that had been applied to the photo. It was no surprise to me that he would write a book on how to do everything with digital photography. I think his personal goal is to inspire the world to create beautiful photos.

How to Do Everything with Digital Photography goes well beyond the camera. It is the David Huss personal cookbook on accomplishing exactly what the title offers. It just doesn't get any better than this. He'll share with you his secret recipes (not that he keeps secrets) on composition and set up. Then, once you have a digital file, Dave will show you how to import it into a computer and use filters and other techniques to enhance your image well beyond what the camera can capture. He'll make it look so easy you'll be taking pictures like a pro in no time.

At PhotoSpin, we are very fortunate to be able to offer Dave's images as part of our online subscription of royalty-free images. He has shot many series of images for us, for our customers to use. And many times, I have had customers send me examples of the graphic design work they've created. Often, those designs include Dave's photographs: pictures of colorful electrical storms illuminating brochures on energy; close-ups of the prismatic tones of oil, used as backgrounds for music websites. Like dominoes, the inspiration just moves on down the line.

That's the beauty of Dave.

Although his book may be about technique, David is all about inspiration.

Stephanie Robey, president and co-founder of PhotoSpin, and marathon mom

Acknowledgments

This is, as always, my favorite part of the book. This is the one part of the book where the secrets are kept because no one except the author and those who work with the author ever reads the acknowledgments. For example, do you want to know the truth about Area 51? It can be found in the acknowledgments section of The *Collected Recipes of the Moose Breath Cafe*. So, what secrets are hidden in these pages? Read on.

Here is a compilation of the fine folks that made this book great (these are also the people that will be blamed if it doesn't sell well). First on the list is my acquisitions editor, and friend, Megg Morin. She has the unenviable job up putting up with me, my delayed schedules, and lame excuses (not only from me but from other authors, as well). The fact that she has continued to work with me for almost 10 years could bring her state of mind into question but the fact is, she's the best. A tip of the hat goes to Scott Rogers (one of the head honchos at Osborne) who made some excellent suggestions that improved the content of this edition (oh well, there's a first time for everything, Scott). Elizabeth Seymour (project editor) has done a fantastic job of juggling multiple chapters, finding missing figures, and somehow producing a coherent book out of the sea of cumulative changes, deletions, and insertions that were scattered throughout the book during the editing process. Many thanks to my friend Jim Patterson who, as an experienced and accomplished photographer, shared his wisdom, experience, and technical knowledge while serving as the book's technical editor.

There are several others whose contributions have made this book possible. First is Steve Heiner of Nikon who loves digital photography almost as much as I do and is a wealth of knowledge when it comes to getting the most out of a digital camera. My heartfelt thanks also go to John Schwartzman (cinematographer) who taught me more about shooting in available light on a two-hour flight than I could have learned in a lifetime, and who deserves to win the Oscar for the movie, *Seabiscuit*. I also must acknowledge Val Gelineau (photographer and CEO of PhotoSpin) who reminds me how much fun photography is, and Stephanie Robey (president and co-founder of PhotoSpin), for her encouragement and acceptance of my work. My thanks also to Arlen Bartch for helping me to define and find my style of photography.

In the more important non-technical side of the book, I give thanks to my wife, Elizabeth, for putting up with long absences when I am out shooting, and for teaching me new ways to use mathematics. For example, when we got married (30 years ago this month) she was 3 years older than I was. Last week we celebrated her birthday and I discovered she is now 12 years younger than me. I'm still trying to figure out what happened there. On the bright side, by the time I am 65 years old, I figure she'll be a 28-year-old.

Did you find the secret in the acknowledgments section yet? It is that is takes a lot of talented people to put together a book like this, unlike Paris Hilton's new book which gives advice like "You should only sleep on a 600-800 count linen sheet made from Egyptian cotton." That kind of book only requires a team of publicists (a very large team).

Lastly, a thank you to Cooper Morin who is the one-year-old who keeps popping up throughout the book. Thanks, Coop.

Dave Huss, February 2004

Introduction

Digital photography is a blast. Whether you only want to take pictures to prove you have been somewhere or you are trying to capture a moment in time like a wedding, graduation, or just the pure joy of your baby enjoying a bath from mom like the one shown at right, let's face it: Photos last longer than memories.

Before digital cameras were within the consumer price range, the only choice was film; but it was still better than hiring an artist to paint a portrait. Film costs money to buy and develop; in addition, you don't know if that fantastic sunrise behind the nation's Capitol you photographed actually came out until the pictures were developed hours or weeks later—and by then it is too late to reshoot.

With digital cameras you get instant feedback on the photo you just took. You know immediately if it is out of focus, under- or over-exposed, or just right, like the little girl in the bunny costume shown here.

Not tethered by either the expense or hassle of film, a digital camera can unleash your creative potential—if only you'll let it. This book is all about learning to look at the world that surrounds you in a different way than you have before and then daring to capture what you see, using your camera. You will learn how to find the extraordinary in the ordinary and use your camera to harnass it, like the rainbow of colors in a bicycle race or the unexpected hues in a stack of drill stems waiting to ship to an oil platform.

To capture the eye candy that surrounds you takes some effort on your part. It involves a little reading (especially of your camera's manual) and a lot of practice. In this book you will discover how to compose and take a portrait like the one shown in Figure 1.

FIGURE 1 Forget paying for glamour photos. Learn to take flattering photos and use the money you save to take your spouse out to dinner.

Your digital camera is a virtual Swiss Army knife of features that includes the capability to take close-up photographs in nature, from a flower's eyeview of a butterfly, …

… to the contrasting colors and textures found in your garden,

…to a humorous angle. While the rest of the world is going wireless, this caterpillar thinks a world with wires might be a little safer.

You will also learn how to take action photos with your digital camera that will make you look like a professional.

In case you think that the ability to take good photos doesn't apply to you, and that the photos in this introduction were taken by some professionals that we borrowed from the National Geographic Society—think again. Did you like the photo of the baby getting his bath? So did I. The photographer is my friend and editor, Megg. Is she a professional? Not by a long shot. Point in fact, every photo she sends me of her baby boy has one of those fluorescent-colored time-date stamps in the corner. I have been asking her for months to turn the darn thing off and she hasn't figured it out yet.

In this book you will find out how to use the light meter on your camera so that your photos aren't either over- or under-exposed, and how to correct the colors when taking photos under less than ideal lighting conditions, like the shot of a pier in early morning, …

…or a shot of the sunset in Washington D.C., …

…and even how to shoot photos at night without a flash.

You will learn, too, how to shoot and create a panorama like the one shown in Figure 2.

FIGURE 2 This sunset panorama was made from three photographs and stitched together automatically in the computer.

You'll discover how easy it is to make a blurred shot of a moving subject like the one shown below, left.

And you will learn how to print photos or send them to friends, using popular and inexpensive photo editing software.

All of the hints, suggestions, and rules in this book are the results of over 30 years of my experience in film photography and of about five years of digital photography. My technical editor and friend, Jim Patterson, is even older than I am (egad!) and he has added tidbits and suggestions throughout the book. However, the information that is in this book will do you little good if you read it and don't apply it.

Always keep your camera handy, no matter where you go. Some of my best photographs were unplanned ones that I captured because I looked up and saw something I liked and took a picture of it—like the little girl enjoying a cup of shaved ice on a hot Texas afternoon…

…or the collapsed building with the Main Street sign leaning in the foreground shown in Figure 3. By the way, I almost didn't take this photo, thinking that I would return another day when the sun was at a better angle. Since it was a digital camera, I took several photos and made a mental note to return. I did return the next month and the Main Street sign was gone. Carpe diem.

So grab your digital camera and let's get started. The sooner you begin, the sooner you'll begin to impress your friends with your photographic skills.

FIGURE 3 The next time I went by this town, the street sign was gone.

What You'll Find in This Book

Part I – Digital Photography Basics

Working with digital cameras requires a major shift in one's thinking. Consumer film photography has been around for over 100 years and has become integrated into our lives. Along comes digital cameras and all of the familiar touchstones of film photography—film, negatives, and the local drugstore where we develop the film—are gone. The first part of the book introduces you to this digital "new kid on the block" that has invaded your lifestyle, and shows you how it is similar to, and how it differs from, film photography.

- Chapter 1: Discover the Excitement of Digital Photography

In this chapter you'll get an overview of the types of digital cameras and what they can be used for, as well as the tools that are available to the digital photographer.

- Chapter 2: Essential Equipment

Buying your digital camera is the just the first step. In this chapter you will find out which digital camera accessories are absolutely necessary and which aren't.

Part II – Take Better Pictures Now!

The second part of the book part covers all the practical information you need to know in order to take fantastic photos. No complicated theories or academic dissertations; just a lot of pages of useful advice on taking pictures.

■ Chapter 3: Learn These Essentials for Great Photos Every Time

With all of the automatic features built into the digital camera, many people believe that all you need to do is to point and shoot to get excellent photos. Cool features aside, there are still some basic photographic practices that you need to understand to allow the automatic features of your camera to produce stunning photos.

■ Chapter 4: Get the Best Lighting for Your Photos

Without getting too technical in this chapter, you will learn that the light from our friendly sun effects colors in photos depending on the time of day a photo is taken, and where the subject and photographer are in relation to it. You'll also learn some easy ways to compensate for the light when it is less than perfect (which is most of the time).

■ Chapter 5: Get Clear and Sharp Photos

In this chapter you'll discover how the auto-focus system in your digital camera works, and under what conditions it doesn't work. You will also learn several ways to focus your digital camera when the auto-focus doesn't seem to work correctly.

■ Chapter 6: Get the Right Color

This chapter teaches you the many different ways to ensure that the color in your photos is accurate or, more important, the colors that you want.

Part III – Do More Than You Can Imagine

In the preceding two parts, you will have learned basic rules to ensure that you get great photos; in this part you will discover the many things that are possible to do with your digital camera. You'll also read about other aspects of digital photography.

■ Chapter 7: Discover All Your Camera Can Do

Your digital camera has unique features that don't exist on film cameras. Some of the features do a lot of cool things than you may not be aware of. Some of the features are not apparent because their names or descriptions don't tell you what the feature can be used for. In this chapter you will discover what these "hidden" features are, and what you can do with them.

■ Chapter 8: Get Ready to Share Your Photos

After you take photos, there are so many ways to produce high quality photographs and other photo paraphernalia that it will astound you. Did you know you can have your photo put onto a cookie? This chapter provides a brief summary of the many options you have at your disposal when it comes time to share your digital masterpieces.

■ Chapter 9: Use Flash Photography to Your Advantage

The camera flash is a marvelous tool that can be used in various shooting situations. The problem most people experience with using flash is that it makes the subject appear washed out or (worse) grotesque. There is so much you can do with both the built-in flash on your camera or with an optional external one, that I dedicate an entire chapter to the subject. In the chapter you will discover tricks to get rid of red-eye when the red-eye reduction feature doesn't work (which, again, is most of the time). You will also discover a few professional but easy-to-do methods to use the flash to reduce or remove shadows on outdoor shoots, along with other exciting tricks.

■ Chapter 10: Gain a New Perspective

The position of your camera in relation to the subject being photographed is examined in this chapter. You'll find out about the power of changing the viewpoint of your camera when taking photos.

Part IV – Special Opportunities for Stunning Photographs

This part covers those specialty forms of photography that require some extra time, effort, or technique on the part of the photographer. Unlike the digital photography covered in the earlier parts of the book, each chapter in this part is targeted at a specific, specialized type of photography.

■ Chapter 11: Capture the Action

Taking action photos with a digital camera can be done—if you know how to do it. In this chapter, you will learn the cause of the problem most people have taking digital action photos. Once you know this, you'll find out how to work around it and take some great sporting action shots of the kiddos.

■ Chapter 12: Make Blurred Photos on Purpose

This chapter covers what it takes to produce photos in which part of the image is in clear focus and part of the image is blurred. Called still-motion photos, they make for great images, especially when photographing waterfalls or fountains.

■ Chapter 13: Take Great Photos of People

This chapter is all about what it takes to produce great family and group photos. It involves very little technical savvy, but lots of people skills. You will discover where and how to photograph one of the most elusive subjects on the planet: people.

■ Chapter 14: Get the Best Pictures of Babies and Small Children

If there ever was a perfect device to record photos of these precious ones, it's the digital camera. In this chapter you will discover how to photograph babies, toddlers, and small children. You'll learn how to select props, place lighting, and become part of their world so that they become unaware of you taking their photos—which is always when you get the best ones!

■ Chapter 15: Low-Light Photography: Taking Great Night Photos

When you shoot the world as revealed by the low-light of either the cool stillness near dawn or the fiery warm colors produced within an hour of sunset, you will discover common scenes take on an entirely different appearance. When you have finished this chapter you will know what equipment is necessary and how to set up your camera to get the best possible photograph with the minimum amount of digital noise (the equivalence of film grain in film photography). You will also discover how to remove or cover up that digital noise in the computer.

■ Chapter 16: Create Great Close-up Photos

Macro photography is something that most digital cameras do really well. As you will learn in this chapter, there are many uses for macro photography. Examples range from taking detailed photographs of mechanical parts to capturing detail in small collectable objects. You'll discover how to capture the incredible world of shapes and colors that exists on the smaller end of the size spectrum.

■ Chapter 17: Photograph Your Stuff Like a Pro

When it comes time to take a photo of a product or a project, be it for a science fair or for selling on eBay, you want the photos to look good—especially if you want to get a good price. In this chapter you will learn how you can set up a mini-studio with some basic materials and use it to make some very professional photographs.

■ Chapter 18: Photographing a Panorama

In this chapter you will discover that panoramas are not just for shooting photos of grand and majestic landscapes. You will also learn how simple it is to shoot a panorama. Some of equipment that you need (and some that you don't) may surprise you.

Part V – Professional Tips, Tricks and Other Stuff

All of the preceding parts of the book have focused on how to capture the best possible photo. After you have done everything to get the best picture that you can, you can further improve your photos in the computer. This chapter focuses on how to both fix goofs and create special effects using your computer.

- Chapter 19: Fixing Photo Goofs

Even the most experienced photographer uses the wrong setting or forgets something. With digital images, just about any photographic sin can be fixed (except for an image that is out of focus). In this chapter, we will discover how to correct the most common photographic goofs.

- Chapter 20: The Magic of Digital Photography

In the last chapter, we cover a broad selection of topics. The only thing that these topics have in common is that they are all done after the shoot on your computer. For example, you will learn how to remove someone or something from a photograph, using any one of several popular photo editors available for the Mac or PC.

Part I

Digital Photography Basics

Chapter 1

Discover the Excitement of Digital Photography

How to...

- Understand your own approach to digital photography
- Learn the difference between film and digital photography
- Discover the creative advantage of taking multiple photos

Digital Photography Myth Number 1: Digital photography is expensive and complicated.

Fact: Not true! Digital cameras are not just toys for "geeks" and people with too much disposable income. Digital photography is quickly replacing traditional film photography for professionals and amateurs alike, and each year sees the prices of digital cameras continue to decline. While digital cameras do contain a lot of sophisticated electronics, so do most cars coming off the assembly lines, and no one is complaining that they are too complicated to drive.

In this chapter and throughout this book, you will discover that while film and digital cameras are different, your digital camera can free you to be creative in ways you have never imagined. Whether this is your first foray into photography or you are a serious amateur making the change from film to digital, you are about to enter a whole new world of photographic fun.

Your Approach to Digital Photography

Your previous photographic experience (either film or digital) probably affects how you use your digital camera. I find people generally fall into one of the following four categories:

- **Novice** Never owned a camera and rarely used one except for the occasional disposable camera
- **Casual user** Owns a point-and-shoot camera and uses it almost exclusively for photos of family or friends
- **Amateur** Owns one or more cameras and shoots photos of a variety of subjects for the pure love of photography

■ **Professional**   Makes money taking photos for and of others

Novice or Casual Photographers

If you are a novice photographer, you have an advantage not enjoyed by those in the other three categories: because you have little or no previous experience, you have no film-related habits to unlearn. Although the casual photographer may have few ingrained film-related routines, these are generally limited to how to load the camera and where to take the film to get it developed, since most point-and-shoot cameras take care of the details for you.

Amateur or Professional Photographers

While both you amateur and professional photographers bring a wealth of photographic knowledge with you as you make the transition from film to digital, you also will experience frustration as you discover that the favorite techniques you used to get the most out of film might not work as you expect when you're shooting with a digital camera. This brings us quite neatly to the next topic—the difference between film and digital cameras.

Photography is a blend of subtleties, a combination of many things, especially technical expertise and passion. Some photographers lean more towards the technical side of perfection, others the passionate side. One photograph, while perfect in every technical aspect, may be dry and lifeless while at the other extreme, passion plays host to a multitude of technical imperfection. The masters are the ones who communicate their passion with technical expertise in a meld that simply grabs your emotions.

—*Moose Peterson, wildlife photographer*

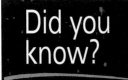

What's a Snapshot?

In the nineteenth century, the term *snapshot* was commonly used to describe a hunter who shot from the hip without taking careful aim. With the introduction of inexpensive cameras in the early twentieth century, everyone (not just professionals) began taking photos that also became known as *snapshots*.

The Difference Between Digital and Film Cameras

The most obvious difference between a digital and film camera is that the digital camera has an electronic sensor in place of film. That sounds simple enough, but for many of you, the habits you developed while you photographed with a film camera can effect the way you take photos with a digital camera.

When taking photos with a film camera, a finite number of photos are available, depending on the length of the actual film loaded in the camera. When all of the images on the roll of film are exposed, you must reload the camera with a fresh roll of film before you can continue shooting. Over the years, you develop an awareness that each time you take a picture, it costs money to develop and print. This makes most novice and casual users take photos with some degree of reluctance—you might take a single photo of a subject and hope that it will come out OK. Unfortunately, this single-shot approach to photography is a surefire recipe for disappointment when the film is developed. As a rule of thumb, the more photos you take, the more likely you'll take a good one!

With digital cameras, however, you need not buy film or pay for processing, and this frees you to take as many photos as your camera can hold. How many you photos your camera can hold is limited only by the number and size of the memory cards you use, which are covered in the next chapter. Later in this chapter, you'll learn the creative advantages offered by taking multiple photos with a small investment in some extra digital "film" (media).

Film, Digital Cameras, and Lighting

You probably know that many types of film are available—not just film for color slides and prints, but also film that is balanced for use with different types of light. For example, most film is optimized for shooting photos outdoors; this is called daylight film.

If you shoot a photo indoors illuminated by an incandescent lamp using daylight film, the picture appears reddish, as the photo shown in Figure 1-1 illustrates. Other types of film are specifically designed for shooting under particular types of lighting, but using them involves loading the film in the camera. So, for example, if you're using one kind of film in bright outdoor light, and you want to shoot in dim indoor light, you either have to finish the roll of film in your camera and load new film for the new lighting, remove the unfinished roll of film and load the new film, or just use the wrong film for the job.

However, with a digital camera, you can compensate for various types of lighting when you're shooting digitally simply by changing a setting, as you will discover in Chapters 6 and 8.

FIGURE 1-1 If you try to use outdoor film to shoot an indoor photo under incandescent lights, the photo will appear reddish.

In addition to compensating for different types of light, a digital camera can also change its *sensitivity* to light. Traditionally, the sensitivity that film has to light is defined using an ISO (International Standards Organization) number on the box, referred to as the film's speed.

Not so long ago, film speed was defined using an ASA (American Standards Association) number; today it is defined by a similar ISO number.

A film with greater sensitivity to light is referred to as *faster* film; therefore, the greater the light sensitivity, the faster the film. Fast film allows the photographer to shoot photos under low-light conditions without using a flash, as demonstrated by the photo shown in Figure 1-2.

Just as you must change film to adjust for different types of lights, so you must change film to change the light sensitivity of a film camera. A digital camera, on the other hand, can automatically change the equivalency of the camera's film speed, or the photographer can do it manually.

FIGURE 1-2 Low-light conditions require the use of faster film.

Noise

While it's possible to increase the speed of today's digital cameras to extremely high levels, taking photos at such high settings will show up as increased amounts of "noise" in the printed photo, which appears as tiny specks on the photo, similar to that shown in Figure 1-3.

If you have a background in film photography, this noise is analogous to grain in film. In Chapter 15, you will discover that all digital photos have noise to some degree or another. While high-end digital cameras offer noise reduction features, you will discover that the best way to remove this unwanted noise is to use photo-editing software in your computer. Editing software and how to use it are discussed in later chapters of this book.

FIGURE 1-3 Shooting under very low light can produce low-quality, noisy photos.

Digital Versus Film Quality Issues

When digital cameras first appeared, the quality of the prints was inferior to that of film cameras. Even photos taken by the most expensive digital camera could not match the quality of a photo taken even with an inexpensive film camera. Today, however, the quality of all but the most inexpensive digital cameras produces great photos. Nevertheless, a lot of people out there believe that digital can never replace film, just as some would passionately argue that recordings played on LPs are superior to those played on CDs.

I bring this debate up because you will encounter salesmen in camera stores, friends, and photographers who will passionately tell you everything that is wrong with digital and everything that is right about film. Passions and rhetoric aside, the fact is that digital is replacing film. In 2003, Kodak announced that traditional film photography sales were down and now provided only about 70 percent of its revenue. By 2006, the company expects this traditional side of the business will shrink to less than 40 percent of its total sales. While I believe that film will never disappear completely, I think it's fair to assume that it will become a small part of the market by 2010.

Use the Creative Advantage of Taking Multiple Shots

I could write several more pages about the differences between digital and film, but the most important two are feedback (you can see the picture immediately after you take a digital photo) and photo capacity (which is practically unlimited with digital). Almost everyone who uses a digital camera takes advantage of the instant feedback, but the most important creative tool—unlimited photos—is probably under-appreciated. This is because digital cameras act so much like film cameras that it's easy to become a victim of habit and take photos as if you were still going to have to pay for each print.

Why More Photos Are Better

What's so important about taking more photos? For one thing, it's what the pros do, and that's why they're pros. In the late '50s, the best photographers in the U.S. worked for *Life* magazine. Today, the photographers who work for *National Geographic* magazine are considered some of the best in the business. These photographers may take thousands of photos when they are on an assignment. In fact, the photos selected for use in a typical *National Geographic* article are selected from an average of 400 rolls of film!

These professionals achieve their spectacular results by trying to capture as many different views of their subjects as they can. They know that even a small change in the viewing angle, or the position of the subject, or the angle of the lighting can make a dramatic difference in the resulting photo. Because most of these photographers have traditionally used film (many of them now shoot both film and digital, however), they wouldn't normally know how the photos look until the film was developed. Shooting lots of photos is a good habit that professionals adopt that can and should become a habit with digital amateurs as well.

Whether you spend a lot of time and money traveling to some remote location or you're shooting at an important event, you don't want to chance not taking the photo that you came to get. In most cases, if the subjects are dynamic, the opportunity to take the best photo will be gone forever if you don't take it when it happens and if you don't take a lot of photos.

FIGURE 1-4 My first photo wasn't very flattering.

An Example to Consider

To demonstrate the point, I have included a series of photos I took of Michelle while I was on a photo assignment to document a company's Ethnic Diversity Day celebration. She was dressed in a traditional African outfit and asked if I could take a photo of her that she could give her husband for their upcoming anniversary. Because Michelle is not a professional model, she didn't know how to pose to highlight her best features, so it was up to me to try different angles and settings to get the best photo I could. If I had taken only one photo, the first one I shot and which is shown in Figure 1-4, she would have been disappointed with the results.

While the photo is technically accurate (correct exposure and in focus), it isn't a flattering photo. After shooting, I looked at the photo I just took in the LCD screen, adjusted my shooting angle, and then shot again. I took 14 more photos, some of which are shown in Figure 1-5.

FIGURE 1-5 Here are just a few of the many photos I took to get a single portrait that I liked.

The best one of the series was my sixth photo. The light was right, and her pose and her expression were perfect. Once I reviewed the photos on my computer (it is difficult to make an accurate assessment on the LCD screen of the camera), it only took a few moments to select the best photo, which is shown in Figure 1-6.

Summary

In Chapter 13, you will learn a lot more about taking photos. "Shoot, review, shoot again" is a theme that is repeated throughout this book. As you take more photos, you will discover that your shooting skills will improve; that's a promise.

In the next chapter, you will learn some practical information about digital cameras, computers, software, and essential accessories.

FIGURE 1-6 It took 15 photos to get it right, but this shot was worth it.

Chapter 2

Essential Equipment

How to...

■ Distinguish between digital cameras

■ Understand what's important when buying a digital camera

■ Select essential accessories

■ Make informed decisions about computer hardware and software

Digital Photography Myth Number 2: You need an expensive camera and computer equipment to get quality photos.

Fact: Not true anymore.

In the "early" days of digital photography—just a few years ago—digital cameras were insanely expensive and it took an expensive computer with an even more expensive color printer to create and print a photo that looked acceptable. Back then, a digital camera could cost upward of $20,000; today the price of a similarly featured camera is closer to $200.

Whether you're a first-time buyer or you're thinking about upgrading your existing camera, the information in this chapter will help you avoid common buying pitfalls and help you make the best decision. You will also learn what camera accessories, computer hardware, and software are absolutely necessary for the complete digital camera experience.

Types of Digital Cameras

Today, digital cameras come in all shapes, sizes, and prices. Digital cameras generally fall into one of five categories:

■ Low resolution (web cams, cell phones, and Personal Digital Assistant [PDA] cameras)

■ Combination video/still cameras

■ Consumer point-and-shoot automatic cameras

■ Semiprofessional (prosumer) cameras

■ Advanced (also called professional) or digital single-lens reflex (D-SLR) cameras

2

FIGURE 2-1 Even a low-resolution camera phone can capture the action.

Low-Resolution Cameras

The low-resolution camera creates photos that are intended for display on the Internet, the LCD displays of cell phones, or PDAs. When the images produced by these low-resolution cameras are viewed on such devices, the images that they produce are acceptable. If, however, you decide to print them at any size larger than a small snapshot, the results are disappointing. The truth is, these cameras are not intended to produce quality images. If something is happening near you and you need a quick shot, shooting with a low-resolution camera is better than nothing.

The photos shown in Figure 2-1 were taken during a typhoon in Hong Kong. These photos are low quality, and while you won't be seeing them in an issue of *National Geographic* anytime soon, they do convey the immense power of these storms—which, after all, is the purpose of a photo.

Combination Video/Still Cameras

While most point-and-shoot cameras sold today can take short bursts of video, this category is limited to digital video cameras that also advertise that they can be used as a still digital camera. The problem with these combo video cameras is that the sensor used to capture the video is designed primarily to do just that— capture video. While the camera can capture a reasonable still image, the quality is noticeably less than you would expect from a point-and-shoot digital camera. I should point out, though, that because sensor technology is constantly improving, in a few years a digital video camera may be able to take good still photos along with the excellent video it already produces.

Point-and-Shoot Cameras

The point-and-shoot camera is unquestionably the most popular type of digital camera sold today. The first consumer camera, the Kodak Brownie, which was introduced more than 100 years ago, was a point-and-shoot camera in that it had no user-adjustable settings. The quality of the resulting photos produced by the Brownie camera varied from good to horrible. Today's point-and-shoot digital cameras are very sophisticated devices that attempt to adjust all of the settings automatically so that every photo you take is a good one. While the results aren't always masterpieces, they are definitely better than the photos produced by the original Kodak Brownie.

Semiprofessional (Prosumer)

Between the point-and-shoot consumer camera and the professional digital camera is a type of camera that has too many features to be called consumer but doesn't meet the criteria of a professional camera. So a term was coined for this professional-consumer hybrid camera—*prosumer*. This is not a universally used term and you won't find it in your dictionary. Some call these cameras semiprofessional, and others just see them as very expensive point-and-shoot cameras.

Did you know?

Do Professional Cameras Take Better Photos than Point-and-Shoot Cameras?

A better question might be this: "Can I take quality photos with a consumer camera or must I buy an expensive prosumer or professional camera to get good results?" Yes, Virginia, you can take superb photos with most of the mid-level digital cameras on today's market. Can you take incredible quality photos good enough to appear on the cover of a national periodical? Probably not. Can you get great photos suitable for framing and impressing friends and family? Definitely yes.

Most of us tend to believe that a more expensive camera will produce better photos. The truth is, having a more expensive camera will no more improve your photos than buying an expensive golf club will automatically improve your golf game. The perception that point-and-shoot cameras don't take quality photos is promoted by amateur and semiprofessional photographers who don't like the idea that the automatic settings of a point-and-shoot camera could ever equal the result they achieve by carefully measuring and adjusting the settings on their more expensive cameras.

So what advantage is there to the more expensive camera? The answer is versatility. Using a professional camera, you can shoot a photo that can be blown up and put on a billboard or you can take photos on the sideline of a national playoff game and end up with a photo that can be used on the cover of a sports magazine.

Did you know?

You Can Buy Extra Lenses for a Point-and-Shoot Digital Camera

Many a digital camera owner doesn't know that even though the lens on his or her point-and-shoot digital camera is not interchangeable, the camera may allow an accessory lens to be attached. Almost all of these lenses are screw-on types and generally fall into two categories: wide angle and telephoto. They are relatively inexpensive and can greatly expand the capabilities of your camera.

What Makes a Camera Semi-Professional?

So what makes a digital camera a prosumer camera? Two features typically distinguish this type of camera: it has a comparatively large sized sensor (we'll talk more about sensor size later in the section, "The Sensor"), and it does not have an interchangeable lens. These cameras will cost several hundred dollars more than their consumer counterparts, and they offer several additional features, such as the ability to add an external flash or an electronic display in the viewfinder instead of just the LCD screen on the back of the camera.

As the competition between the camera manufacturers continues to increase, each new model of consumer camera offers more and more features; it won't be too long before the prosumer classification of digital camera disappears.

Professional D-SLR Cameras

What is the most notable difference between the consumer, prosumer, and professional digital camera? The price tag. The professional D-SLR camera is an expensive prize. Price aside, the defining feature of D-SLR cameras is interchangeable lenses. This means when you buy the camera, you buy just the body; the lenses are extra. For professional photographers, these cameras are great because they feel and act like the film cameras most longtime photographers are accustomed to. The one major difference has to do with the physical size of the sensor in the camera. Because it is typically smaller than a 35mm negative, it effects the focal length of the lens being used, often increasing the focal length by as much as 150 to 200 percent. Some D-SLR cameras have sensors that are physically the same size as a 35mm negative. They are called *full-frame cameras,* and because the sensor is the same size as the film negative, the focal length is unaffected.

How a Digital Camera Works

In place of film, the digital camera has a *sensor* like the one shown here, positioned behind the lens. When you press the shutter button, the sensor measures the light striking it and creates a digital image much in the same way a photocopier makes a copy of a document. This image is stored on digital film (correctly called *removable media*) from which you can, through a multitude of ways, move these images to a computer.

Photo courtesy
of Foevon Corporation

The Sensor

Two kinds of sensors can be used in digital cameras, CCD and CMOS, acronyms that stand for the type of semiconductor used to make the sensor: charged-couple device and complementary metal-oxide semiconductor, respectively. The sensor in most consumer cameras is a CCD sensor, and CMOS is used in PDAs and cell phones, plus very high-end professional digital cameras.

The important feature of a sensor is not whether it is a CCD or CMOS, but rather its physical size. The larger the sensor, the larger the digital image it produces, and CMOS sensors are generally larger than CCD varieties. The size of the sensor is typically described by the total number of pixels it produces. For example, one of the cameras I use has a 4.0 megapixel sensor, meaning the camera can take a photo with more than 4 million pixels. The sensors in digital cameras sold today range from 2 to 5 megapixels.

Pixels: The Foundation of Digital Photos

So what's a pixel? Pixels are the building blocks of digital pictures. Just as different colored squares can be placed in such a way to produce an image in a mosaic, in much the same way pixels produced by a camera sensor are arranged in a digital file to produce a photo. Later in this chapter, in the section "Sensor Size: How Big is Big Enough?" you will learn more about pixels when we consider what size of sensor is best.

What Features Are Important?

Look at any digital camera advertisement and you will discover more technical information than you ever wanted to know—or need. Like all electronic devices, a lot of technical information has been printed (usually in fine print) about the device. You don't need to know most of it to use the camera, just like you don't need to know all the functions of the parts under the hood of your car to drive it.

Three features are important considerations when you're looking for a digital camera:

- Sensor size
- Zoom factor
- Digital "film" type used

In the following sections, you will discover what is most important and what is not so important when it comes to digital cameras.

Sensor Size: How Big Is Big Enough?

The one feature that is advertised first for all digital cameras is the size of the sensor. If someone tells me they bought a digital camera, usually the first question I ask is "How big is the sensor?" Many people buying digital cameras believe that buying a camera

As the official photographer for Austin-tatious Red Hat Society, I go around before the meeting and close all the blinds on the windows in the restaurant. If I don't, I spend hours with my photo-editing software dodging and burning to darken the background and lighten the foreground. Don't delete those pictures where your flash overexposed the closest object and left you with a dark background. Remember that a dark photo may still have all the detail in it; all you have to do is use the dodge and burn tools of your photo editor to bring the detail out.

—*Pat Gibson, Web mistress, Austin-tatious Red Hat Society*

with a larger sensor means it must take better photos, but this is absolutely not true. At the moment, consumer digital cameras range in sensor size from 3 to 5 megapixels. The most popular sized sensor of digital camera being sold as I write this chapter is 4 megapixels.

The size of the sensor effects how large you can enlarge the resulting photo. If you take only the standard 4×6 or 5×7 inch photo (which accounts for more than 96 percent of all photos processed in the U.S.), any camera with a sensor greater than 3 megapixels will work fine. If you were to take a color photograph of a scene with three cameras with different-sized sensors (3, 4, and 5 megapixels), the 4×6 and 5×7 inch prints would appear to be the same quality. But if you wanted to make an 8×10, sensor size matters. For other than wedding, school, and graduation photos, when have you ever had or even wanted an 8×10 photo? Most amateur photographers rarely need to produce photos that large. If you do want to make 8×10 photos, you should be shooting with a 4 or 5 megapixel camera.

Optical vs. Digital Zoom Factor

All consumer and prosumer digital cameras have built-in zoom lenses. A zoom lens allows you to control how much of the scene is captured by the camera. A camera's zoom factor is usually printed using large letters on both the camera box and on a sticker on the camera body. Zoom factors tell you the amount of zoom that is possible using the lens. So, for example, a camera that advertises a 6X zoom factor is saying the subject being photographed will appear six times closer when the zoom lens is fully extended as compared to when it is fully retracted.

Two different zoom factors are used with digital cameras: optical and digital. The optical zoom factor describes the amount of enlargement that is produced by the camera's lens. The digital zoom factor is the amount of enlargement that is created by electronically magnifying the image. Of the two, optical zoom is the most important; keep reading to find out why.

On many cameras, the zoom factor appears in large type, with other information in smaller type under it, like that shown

A new wrinkle with the digital zoom involves a name change. I am using an excellent camera loaned to me by Sony, and it took a little time to figure out that Smart Zoom was Sony's name for digital zoom. Different name, same problem.

FIGURE 2-2 Zoom factor labels can be misleading; read the fine print.

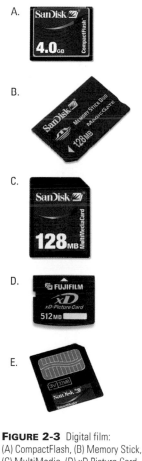

FIGURE 2-3 Digital film: (A) CompactFlash, (B) Memory Stick, (C) MultiMedia, (D) xD Picture Card, and (E) SmartMedia

in Figure 2-2, a photo of the label attached to a popular digital camera. It appears that the camera has a 6X zoom factor, but if you read the fine print, you'll discover that the camera has a 2X optical zoom lens and a 3X digital zoom feature; when multiplied together, this produces the advertised 6X zoom factor.

The problem with using digital zoom is that it degrades the quality of the image by literally cropping from the center of the sensor. While someday camera manufacturers will improve the quality of digital zoom, it remains a feature that you should turn off as soon as you unwrap the camera.

When considering a digital camera, you should always try and get the greatest optical zoom factor that you can afford. This is especially true if you will be photographing children or wild animals (no relation), because the farther you are away from them, the better your chances are of getting good candid photos without them being aware of it.

Media Storage (Digital Film) Choices

At one time, the type of media used by the digital camera was a factor in deciding which camera you selected to buy. When digital cameras first came out, the choices were CompactFlash and SmartMedia. Today, most digital cameras use CompactFlash cards and MultiMedia cards, although some Olympus cameras still use SmartMedia. Most Sony cameras use Memory Sticks (and a few of their cameras store images on CDs and disks). Newer Olympus cameras and Fuji cameras use a proprietary media called an xD Picture Card.

Figure 2-3A-E shows all of the media currently being used in digital cameras.

Today's primary reason for considering the type of media used by the camera is the cost of buying additional media. The following summary of the memory types should provide an overview of the advantages or disadvantages of each type of media.

- **CompactFlash**   The most popular card, many companies manufacture them and you can get some good bargains.

- **Memory Sticks**   Several manufacturers make Memory Sticks, so the pricing is quite competitive.

- **MultiMedia cards**   Approximately the size of a postage stamp, the MultiMedia card (MMC) is gaining in popularity in newer digital cameras designs because it can be used in PDAs and MP3 players as well as digital cameras. Their only disadvantage: smaller memory cards are much easier to lose than larger ones.

- **Secure Digital cards**   These cards are the newest generation of MMC cards that offer faster data transfer rates and the ability to protect the information on the card from being read by an unauthorized user, which is excellent for PDAs but offers no advantage for the digital camera user.

- **SmartMedia**   A medium that is no longer being manufactured by many memory vendors. As a mostly discontinued product, there are bargains to be had.

- **xD Picture Card**   Because FujiFilm is the only manufacturer, additional memory is quite expensive when compared to CompactFlash or Memory Stick.

Which Brand of Camera Is Best?

No true answer to this question is possible, since everyone has an opinion. If you ask the clerk at the camera store, her answer will be based either on personal experience or on which brand the store is trying to move. When I have a choice, I shoot with Nikon cameras because I have used Nikon cameras for both film and digital photography for almost 40 years (egad, am I that old?) and I am familiar with how the features in their cameras work. Had I shot Canon or Olympus cameras over that same time span, I would feel strongly about their brands of cameras as well. All of the name brand cameras on the market today, like those shown here, are capable of producing quality photos. The same cannot be said for some cheap imports that are beginning to appear. If you bought a Happy-Sun-Moon brand digital camera because it was cheap, good luck—you'll need it.

I have found that working with a new camera is like breaking in a new pair of shoes. It is uncomfortable at first but eventually the shoes and the feet get used to one another and the shoes feel great. Likewise, with any new camera, it takes a while to learn where all of the buttons

2

are and what they do. Keeping with the shoe metaphor, the shoes won't become broken in unless you wear them as often as possible, just as the camera won't become comfortable unless you spend time shooting with it. So the real answer to the question is this: The best camera for you is the camera that you learn to use and become comfortable with.

Essential Digital Accessories

Once you get the camera, you *must* acquire certain accessories as well:

- Rechargeable batteries
- Battery charger
- Extra media (film)

Buy Plenty of Batteries

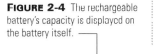

FIGURE 2-4 The rechargeable battery's capacity is displayed on the battery itself.

Digital cameras can drain the bunny out of your typical alkaline battery faster than you can say "it keeps going and going." Seriously, that LCD screen on the back of your camera and the zoom motor for the lens need lots of juice to operate.

If your camera uses AA size batteries, you need to invest in at least two sets of rechargeable batteries so that you have one set in the camera while the other set is recharging. Radio Shack is a great place to purchase such batteries. Look carefully at the label on the pack of batteries for the battery capacity, listed in milleampere hours (mAH). The battery with the largest mAH value will hold the greatest amount of charge, which translates into more time between charges. The capacity range of an AA battery is typically from 1100-2200 mAH. The battery shown in Figure 2-4 is a pretty large capacity battery at 2000 mAH.

Most of the newest digital cameras use a proprietary high-capacity Lithium Ion (Li-Ion) battery. The Li-Ion battery is much lighter than rechargeable AA batteries and holds a comparatively greater charge. Because these batteries are proprietary in design, you can't just go to the corner store and buy a replacement. When I go on extended trips I always take two, or sometimes three, batteries with me—just in case.

Tip *If you can, buy third-party brand batteries rather than the official camera brand batteries for your camera. Save some money.*

Choose the Best Battery Charger

Many newer digital cameras now come with their own battery chargers. If your camera uses AA batteries, it probably doesn't include a charger. When buying a battery charger, you should always pay a little extra to get a rapid charger as opposed to the regular chargers that can take an average of 13–15 hours to charge a battery.

If you are going to be traveling by car (yours or a rental), consider buying a power inverter. These marvelous yet inexpensive devices, like the one shown in Figure 2-5, plug into the cigarette lighter of a vehicle and provide AC power, allowing you to plug your battery charger into it and charge your batteries while you're driving.

FIGURE 2-5 A power inverter is handy when traveling.

Tip

If you travel outside of the U.S., make sure that your charger works on both 60Hz and 50Hz (as well as 110/220 V). Plugging a charger rated for 60Hz into a 50Hz supply will destroy it.

Get Lots of Digital Film

The best feature of a digital camera is that you can take photos without the need to buy film and pay for developing the prints. The number of photos that you can take is limited only by the size of the memory card in your camera. The memory cards that ship with every digital camera I have ever worked with are too small to be of any practical use. Rather than try to change the quality settings on your camera to fit more images onto a smaller card, buy additional cards.

Unless your camera uses xD Picture Cards, memory cards for digital cameras are inexpensive. When buying a memory card, check the pricing on 128MB, 256MB, 512MB, and 1GB (gigabyte) cards. As you check the pricing, you will discover that at some point, doubling the capacity more than doubles the price. To save money, you can buy the largest card below that breakpoint. For example, as I am writing this chapter, the average price for the CF cards is as follows:

- **128MB** $39
- **256MB** $70
- **512MB** $159
- **1GB** $200

You can see that buying two 128MB CF cards (total of 256MB) costs more than buying a single 256MB card, but buying two 256MB CF cards (total of 512MB) costs less than buying a single 512MB CF card. Therefore, the best bargain (at the moment) is the 256MB card.

Memory card pricing is very volatile. The values discussed here are for illustrative purposes only and will have changed before this book is even printed, so check you favorite online retailer or eBay to get current pricing and the best bargains.

Keep in mind that memory cards can be susceptible to damage and loss of data if not handled carefully. Many photographers favor buying several smaller capacity cards over putting all their image eggs into one big (say a gigabyte) card that might fail.

Did you know?

Do I Need Fast Camera Memory Cards?

When you go to buy a CF card, you will discover that many CF cards advertise that they read and write faster than a typical card—examples are 4X, 8X, and even 24X speeds. Is it worth the extra money for the faster card? Unless you are using a professional D-SLR camera, you won't notice any difference in the speed of the card. Regardless of how fast the card is, consumer cameras and even most prosumer cameras cannot take advantage of the card speed. Quite literally, the faster cards are much faster than the camera's ability to write data.

Nonessential Accessories

You might choose to buy a lot more accessories to enhance your digital photography experience, but if you have obtained the items mentioned earlier in the chapter, the rest, as they say, is details. Other equipment, such as a tripod, filters, and other accessories, are discussed in individual chapters throughout this book.

How Much Computer Do You Need?

Now that we've covered the camera, let's talk briefly about what other hardware you might require. These days, it is possible to have and use a digital camera and not even own a computer. I can shoot photos with my camera and then take my memory card to my local photo developer (like the one shown in Figure 2-6), stick the memory card into the in-store computer, and get my prints made for me. The fact is, most of us own a computer and want to be able to look at the photos we have taken in the privacy of our own home, where we have the time to sort, edit, and otherwise browse through them. How much and what type of computer you need is another variable factor.

FIGURE 2-6 Developing kiosks like this make owning a home computer unnecessary to enjoy digital photography.

Which is Better: PC or Mac?

The best computer for working with your digital photos is the computer you are accustomed to using. Both platforms have their advantages and disadvantages, making neither the obvious or superior choice.

If you are using a Mac, you should be using at least a G3 processor with 256MB of RAM. The OS can be either 9.x or OS X, but be advised that most newer Mac applications are no longer supporting OS 9.x, so if you intend to stay with the Mac, you are going to have to change eventually.

If you have a PC, you should be running Windows Me at the minimum, with Windows XP preferred. While Windows 98SE supports universal serial bus (USB) cables and other necessary features used with digital photography, you'll probably need to install additional software to get what you need. Like the Mac, your PC should have at least 256MB of RAM.

The Importance of RAM

Despite all of the press written about the speed wars between processor companies and platforms, the speed of your processor is not nearly as important as the amount of Random Access Memory (RAM) available for the program to use.

RAM memory is the temporary storage area in your computer that holds your program while it is running. If the amount of RAM available for running applications gets low for any reason (for example, you have opened many large photos), the computer is forced to use area on the hard drive as if it were RAM—very slow RAM. With current RAM prices being quite low, it doesn't take that much money to add an additional 256MB or even an additional 512MB to your system (assuming that the total doesn't exceed the maximum allowed by your hardware). In most cases, you will experience a noticeable improvement in the performance. If your machine is still sluggish, you might be running out of space on your hard drive and you should consider adding additional hard drive space.

Add Hard Drive Space

If you use a digital camera for a while, you will discover that it can quickly fill up your existing hard drive. In times past, installing a newer, larger hard drive was expensive, complicated, and the stuff that even computer geeks avoided if they could. Today installing an additional hard drive is relatively simple and inexpensive.

You can add a drive in two main ways: you can open your computer case and install an internal one, or you can plug one of the new portable hard drives (shown in Figure 2-7) into a USB or FireWire (IEEE-1394) port.

Add Archival Storage

An alternative to storing digital photos on your hard drive is to archive them to CDs or DVDs. Portable CD recorders (called burners) and DVD burners can easily attach to your computer and allow you to store more than 700MB of photos on a CD and 4.7GB on a DVD. Many new computers even ship with CD or DVD burners installed in the case. At the moment, you can buy blank CDs for less than 4 cents each. Blank DVDs still are a little more expensive than CDs, but prices are falling rapidly.

FIGURE 2-7 A portable hard drive

LCD Monitors vs. CRT Monitors

As of late 2003, LCD monitors were outselling CRT monitors. LCD units are physically smaller and lighter and have a higher contrast than CRTs. This means that your photos appear brighter and more brilliant on a LCD monitor than they do on a CRT. If there is a downside to LCD monitors, it may be the fact that prolonged viewing of this high-contrast beauty may be a little hard on your eyes. As CRT monitors become less popular, though, you can pick up some great bargains on large-screen monitors.

Which Photo Editor Is Best?

A lot of software choices (like the ones shown here), are available to you when working with digital photos. They generally fall into one of three categories:

- Professional
- Consumer
- Promotional/freeware/shareware

While some will argue this point, the industry standard software for photo editing is Adobe Photoshop. The newest version is Photoshop CS (Creative Suite). It is expensive and available on both Mac and Windows platforms. So, if Photoshop is the best program, should you be using it? If you are not doing professional photography, you don't really need the top-of-the-line software, because several excellent consumer photo-editing programs cost must less than $100. But for professionals, Photoshop is *it*.

The following programs are top sellers:

- **Adobe Photoshop Elements (Windows/Mac)**
  http://www.adobe.com
- **Microsoft Picture It! (Windows)**
  http://www.microsoft.com
- **Jasc Paint Shop Pro (Windows)**
  http://www.jasc.com

With the exception of Picture It!, free 30-day evaluations of these programs can be downloaded from the manufacturer's web site. I recommend that you visit the sites, study the program description, download one of them, and try it out for a while.

The software that comes with your digital camera may be a limited version of one of these programs or a proprietary software photo editor, such as Epson's Film Factory. The usefulness of these programs varies from excellent to a waste of space. Don't feel obligated to use the software that comes with your camera. It wasn't included necessarily because the manufacturer thought it was the best software for the camera; it may have been included because it was the cheapest product, had the best-looking package, or because the software company had the smoothest-talking salesperson.

Part II

Take Better Pictures Now!

Chapter 3

Learn These Essentials for Great Photos Every Time

How to...

- Use the simple steps necessary to take good photos
- Prepare your camera for taking photos
- Set up the subject and compose the shot to make the best photo
- Choose the best lighting
- Ensure that you get sharp and clear photos

Digital Photography Myth Number 3   Only a professional photographer with years of training and experience can take the kind of photographs that appear in National Geographic Magazine.

Fact   Absolutely not true. The fact that you are shooting with a digital camera gives you an advantage over some of these industry-revered professionals. Many professional photographers still shoot an enormous number of photos with film, which gets pretty costly. But you can shoot as many photos as you want for free—well, almost.

In this chapter you will learn the fundamentals of taking darn good pictures the first time by avoiding the most common photo-taking mistakes.

Know the Steps to Taking a Good Photo

Many rules for lighting, composition, and camera settings are accepted as standards in photography, but if you take the time to learn all of these photographic commandments and carefully follow them each time before you squeeze the shutter, I can guarantee that by the time you are ready to take a photo, the opportunity will have passed. For example, the photo captured in Figure 3-1 occurred as I was walking through a kid's carnival. It was over in a moment. If I had attempted to compose or set up the shot, the moment and the photo would have never happened. Technically, the photo is slightly overexposed and a little out of focus, but these details don't prevent the photo from being a great moment in time that has been captured forever.

FIGURE 3-1 Sometimes you have to take the photo, and not worry about the settings.

I always keep my camera in my purse because I never know when my two-year old will do something adorable or silly.

Barbara Hedgesworth, accountant

This chapter is all about the simple steps that you should know about, but that you should not necessarily be controlled by, for preparing your camera and taking photos. The first step is preparation—in other words, having your camera set up and ready to do the job. The following preparations take about 10 minutes to read but only a few seconds to accomplish.

Before any commercial airline pilot takes off, she and her copilot go through a checklist to ensure that the aircraft is ready for takeoff. Everything on the checklist is patently obvious to both of the pilots, yet they still go through the checklist every time prior to leaving the gate. Likewise, when you head out the door with your camera, you should check a few things as well to make sure that your camera is ready to take a photo when you need it.

Is There Film in Your Camera?

Of course, your digital camera doesn't have film, exactly; the *removable media* in your camera is your "film." So a better title of this section might be "Does your camera have a memory card installed?" If you own several media cards, make it a habit to open the media card compartment of your camera, like the one shown in Figure 3-2, and pull out the card to check the size of card that is installed.

If you do have a memory card in your camera, the next question is, Are there any more exposures left on your memory card? In most cases, this means that you must turn on the camera and look at the image counter displayed on the LCD screen to see how many images remain.

I can't overemphasize the importance of this question. Here's a case in point: A few years ago I was in Los Angeles to teach at a Photoshop conference. It was early on a Saturday morning and I left my hotel a little early so I could take some shots as I walked to the conference center. I checked my camera

FIGURE 3-2 Always check what media card is installed in your camera.

and saw that I had forgotten to download the images I had taken the previous evening, so only a few more shots would fit on the card. It was only two blocks to the conference center, where I had all of my extra memory cards—no sweat, I thought. How much can happen in two blocks?

Within a block, I saw that a production crew had set up to shoot a scene for the movie *Rush Hour 2*. I had just taken the photo shown in Figure 3-3 when the stars appeared briefly in front of their chairs. I squeezed the shutter and nothing happened. I looked at the indicator on the camera to see the word *FULL* flashing on and off. I quickly reviewed the existing photos on the card, deleted two of them, and looked up, but the actors were gone. Lesson learned.

FIGURE 3-3 A missed opportunity, all because of a full memory card

Are Your Batteries Charged and Is Your Lens Clean?

Is your battery charged? The LCD screen and zoom lens on digital cameras use a lot of power and can suck a battery dry pretty fast. Most digital cameras display an icon like the ones shown in Figure 3-4 on their LCD screen to indicate how much charge remains on the battery. Some cameras even display an estimation of how many minutes of charge are left. The accuracy of these indicators varies between manufacturers.

For example, on one of my older cameras the battery charger symbol would change from solid to a partial charge symbol when the battery was almost exhausted and there was only enough energy for one or two more shots. Most of the charge indicators today give you fair warning as the battery charge begins to diminish. After you have some shooting experience with your camera, you will become familiar with just how much charge remains based on the battery icon displayed.

FIGURE 3-4 These icons indicate various stages of battery charge.

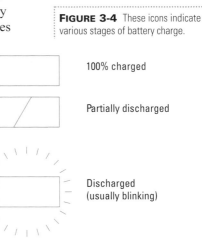

100% charged

Partially discharged

Discharged (usually blinking)

Many battery charge indicators appear solid (fully charged) even though the battery is partially discharged.

3

FIGURE 3-5 Automatic lens covers help keep your lens clean.

Automatic lens cover

If your battery is charged, your next question is, Do you have a spare battery? Newer digital cameras have proprietary batteries that are a bit expensive, but it is important that you carry a spare (fully charged) battery with you at all times.

Next ask yourself, Is the lens on the camera clean? Many of the newer digital cameras are small enough to fit easily into a shirt pocket or a purse. This makes them easy to use—and easy to get dirty. These same cameras usually have an automatic lens cover similar to the one shown in Figure 3-5 that closes to protect the lens whenever the camera is turned off.

Don't worry if you can see a little dust on the lens— just make sure that no big, greasy thumbprint or food is smeared on it. I recommend purchasing and carrying around one of the new microfiber lens cleaning cloths. (They're great for cleaning your glasses as well. And note that these miracle cloths do need to be washed now and again. Follow the directions that come with the cloths.)

What Are the Quality Level Settings?

The number of photos a film camera can take is dictated by the number of exposures on the roll of film that is used. With digital cameras, the number of exposures that will fit on a memory card is controlled by the following factors:

- **Sensor Size of the Camera**   Larger sensors produce bigger images and fewer photos per memory card.

- **Resolution**   Some digital cameras allow you to change the physical dimensions, or resolution, of the images created by the sensor.

- **Type of Image**   In addition to the JPEG (Joint Photographic Expert Group) format, some cameras can save images as TIFF (Tagged Image File Format) and some cameras now offer the ability to save the unprocessed data from the sensor in a proprietary format unique to the manufacturer. This format is generically referred to as raw images.

- **Quality Levels**   On most consumer cameras, the quality setting determines how much the image is compressed when it is stored on the media.

Note *You'll learn more about TIFF and raw images in Chapter 7. The JPEG format is covered a bit later in this chapter in a "Did You Know?" sidebar.*

While all four factors affect the number of photos that your media card can hold, your camera's quality level setting is the one that is most often changed. The quality level setting controls how much each image is compressed before it is stored on the camera's media. The quality level settings are usually controlled through one of the many menus on your digital camera's LCD screen like the one shown in Figure 3-6.

The names used to describe the amount of compression vary between camera manufacturers. Table 3-1 lists some of the names used by popular camera manufacturers.

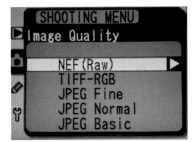

FIGURE 3-6 Quality level settings are often selected using the menu.

The Tradeoff Between Quality and Quantity

Increasing the amount of compression means that you can store more images on your media card, but there's a catch, because as the compression increases the quality of the resulting photo decreases.

A coworker of mine took a family vacation to Hawaii and for the first time he took a digital camera. When he got back home, he was disappointed with the shots he took. Assuming that something was wrong with his camera, he brought the CompactFlash card with the images still stored inside for me to look at. I immediately noticed that this was the 16MB card that came installed with the camera, and it had almost 100 images stored on it! No wonder his image quality was disappointing!

Figure 3-7 shows a photo of my friend's grandson, and the insert zooms in on his face to show the effects caused by the heavy compression setting that the photographer had used.

FIGURE 3-7 The effects of low-quality level settings aren't very pretty.

Amount of Compression	Photo Quality	Nikon	Sony	Olympus	Kodak
Minimum	Best	Fine	Fine	Super High	Best
Moderate	Average	Normal	Not available	High	Better
Maximum	Least	Basic	Standard	Standard	Good

Table 3-1 Comparing Quality Brand Name Cameras

Tip *Be wary of an advertiser's claims that you can make hundreds (thousands) of images on a single memory card. Although you can do this, the image quality will be suitable only for onscreen use or tiny snapshots.*

3

Determine Which Quality Level Setting Is Best for You

When I teach digital camera classes, I have discovered that some students automatically assume they must set their cameras to the maximum quality JPEG setting. While there is nothing wrong with doing that, it isn't always necessary. If you ask yourself the following questions, you can determine the most appropriate settings for your needs:

- **Are the pictures for print or the Web?**   If you plan on shooting photos only for attaching to e-mails or posting on a web site, you can (in most cases) use the lowest possible quality setting (for the maximum number of exposures). However, if you want to use your images for printing photos you'll need to use the next to highest setting.

- **What is the normal size of photo that you use?**   If most, or all, of your printed photos are the standard 4×6 size, a moderate or average (not the best) setting is more than sufficient. However, if you want your images to be larger, use the highest quality setting. Even though this results in fewer exposures per card, the improvement in quality when the photo is printed as a larger photo is worth it.

- **How big is the sensor in your camera?**   If you have a camera with a large sensor (4 megapixels or larger), you can still use a moderate or average setting without noticeable loss of picture quality. However, if your sensor is smaller than 4 megapixels, you should use the highest or at the very least the second highest quality setting to ensure a photo that can be enlarged when printed.

Tip *If you are almost out of exposures on your media card and you don't have a spare, you can lower the quality settings and get additional exposures.*

If you are shooting photos with a lot of detail or high contrast edges in them (such as the Eiffel Tower or a lace tablecloth), you should always change the settings to maximum quality for those shots, as the effects of compression are always most noticeable on the edges of the subjects in these photos.

Did you know?

What Is a JPEG Image?

Color images result in large image file sizes. JPEG compression can drastically reduce the size of these color images so more images can fit onto your media. The problem with JPEG compression, however, is that image quality suffers when it is used. At the lowest compression levels, the quality loss is so small that it's undetectable; at higher levels of compression, the deterioration becomes more apparent in what appears to be tiny, random pixels, especially near high contrast edges. These random pixels are called JPEG *artifacts*.

A similar type of compression used on video is called MPEG (for Moving Picture Experts Group), which comes in several versions: MPEG, MPEG-3, and MPEG-4. I mention it here because some clever person figured out that if MPEG-3 was good at compressing movies and their soundtracks, it could probably be used to compress music, which explains the name *MP3* for the popular audio players.

What Are the White Balance (WB) Settings?

The light source used to illuminate your subject has a color *temperature* that effects the colors in the final photo. If you've taken photos with film cameras, you probably shot with "daylight-balanced" film. If you took indoor pictures of your office workers without a flash, you may have noticed that they had a green tint from the fluorescent lamps; or if a subject was illuminated by an incandescent lamp or candlelight, he or she tended to have a reddish color like the photo of the boy shown holding a candle in Figure 3-8.

FIGURE 3-8 The color temperature of the light source effects how the colors appear in the photo.

Tip *When you change your WB setting to anything other than Auto, remember to return it to Auto when you have finished shooting, or you may find that the colors in your next photo are incorrect. Make a good habit of checking all of your adjustable camera settings before your next shoot to avoid making bad images.*

A.

B.

C.

D.

FIGURE 3-9 White balance settings effect the colors in your photos. The same subject was photographed using (A) Auto, (B) Incandescent, (C) Fluorescent, and (D) Cloudy.

Your digital camera attempts to detect and balance its colors automatically using a feature called *Automatic White Balance* (AWB). Although we will be visiting and revisiting this topic throughout the book, for now the important part to know is that you should either leave the white balance (WB) set to automatic (the default) or, if you are shooting somewhere other than outdoors, change the setting to match the type of light source.

Figure 3-9 shows the same image taken using four different white balance settings to demonstrate the effect that different settings have on the resulting photo. The WB settings are usually made using the menu in the camera's LCD screen. Some cameras have a large number of presets, but until you learn more about these settings, I recommend keeping it set on Auto unless you are shooting inside, and then change the setting to Incandescent or Fluorescent, as appropriate. While most cameras offer a flash setting, keep the WB setting on Auto. The camera is smart enough to know when it is using its own flash.

Shooting the Picture

With your camera ready, it's time to take a picture. The remainder of this chapter offers suggestions and guidelines that will help you produce noticeably better photos using either digital or film cameras.

Fill the Frame with Your Subject

A great American photographer, Robert Capa, summed it up back in 1944 when he said, "If your pictures aren't good enough, you're not standing close enough." Getting close to your subject is more difficult with a digital camera, because for technical reasons a digital camera must use a wider lens than an equivalent film camera. With a wider lens, you have to stand closer to shoot than you would normally need to. Figure 3-10 shows the difference that getting closer to your subject can make. (In case you were wondering, she is waiting to catch a water balloon.)

Use the zoom feature of your camera to get closer whenever possible to reduce the distortion caused by a wide angle lens (called *barrel distortion*), which pushes out the middle and bends the lines on the edge, as shown in Figure 3-11 (the doors of the U.S. Supreme Court). This problem is worse when photographing people, because barrel distortion makes their faces look much larger and rounder, with exaggerated noses.

A.

B.

FIGURE 3-10 (A) The subject is lost in the center of the photograph. (B) The photo is zoomed in, making her the focus.

FIGURE 3-11 An example of barrel distortion

See the Whole Picture, Not Just the Subject

When composing a photo, you need to view the entire picture area rather than focusing your attention only on the subject matter. How the subject fits in with the background is just as important. You want to consider all of the parts that make up the image, not just the subject that is the focus of the photo. Figure 3-12 shows an example of an image to demonstrate this point: a painter in San Diego's Balboa Park.

FIGURE 3-12 This photo has captured the painter and the surrounding area.

3

FIGURE 3-13 Getting closer to the subject fills the frame with her and her painting.

In Figure 3-13, I filled the frame with her and her painting, which brings the viewer closer to her work, so you can see some great details, like her paint-spattered gloves.

Finally, I thought about including the subject of her painting in the photo, making the final photo a completely different composition, as shown in Figure 3-14. The painter is no longer the subject; now her painting is the focus, with the slightly out-of-focus scenery in the background.

Which photo is the best one? All of them. Here's why: The first photo features good composition, with the painter anchoring the side (and not the center) of the photograph. I like the second photo because it fills the frame and provides much more detail that becomes apparent as you look closer. The last photo is a classic "picture within a picture."

Change Your Camera Position

When you come upon a photo opportunity and raise your camera to shoot, you are not compelled by any state or federal law to remain in that position. Sure, the subject may look good from the first position that you choose to shoot it, but it may look even better from another angle, so why not try it out? For the car photograph shown in Figure 3-15, I quickly shot a photo while the street behind the car was empty.

FIGURE 3-14 Changing camera position changes the entire composition and you can see her painting and what she is painting.

FIGURE 3-15 Cool car and an OK photo

Next, I stepped out into the street and saw what the curb prevented me from seeing—big old balloon tires with really wide sidewalls, as shown in Figure 3-16.

As I got out of the street (because the light was about to change), I saw my favorite shot: the hood ornament shown in Figure 3-17, looking so elegant and aloof, reflected in the shine of the hood. The point here is that if I had not taken the time to look at subject from several different angles, I would have never gotten my favorite shot.

FIGURE 3-16 A view of the car from the street looked even better.

Surefire Rules of Composition

While the subject of composition is covered throughout the book, here are some simple, surefire rules of composition. Whenever possible, do not place the subject in the center of the photo; rather, place it off-center. This is especially true when taking photos of people. The only two types of photos that have the subject in the center staring at the camera are found on passports and driver's licenses—and we all know how good those photos look.

A popular guideline used by photographers and other artists is called the "Rule of Thirds," and with it imaginary lines are drawn dividing the image into thirds both horizontally and vertically, as shown in Figure 3-18.

When composing a photo, you should try and place important elements of your composition where these lines intersect. While not a hard-and-fast rule, using the Rule of Thirds can help you make your portraits look more professional. You will find several examples showing how to use the Rule of Thirds throughout the book.

Another important consideration before you press the shutter button is the background. Is it so cluttered

FIGURE 3-17 My favorite shot was not of the entire car but just the hood ornament.

FIGURE 3-18 The imaginary lines of the "rule of thirds" are helpful in composing your photos.

This rule is so important that many professional cameras feature a grid in the viewfinder to set this up.

that it will compete with the subject of the photo? Do background objects conflict with the subject, or do they appear as distractions rather than backgrounds? Many times, you can change a background, and improve a composition, simply by shifting your position a few feet one direction or another.

Know Where the Light Is Coming From

While your camera will try and change its settings automatically so that your photo will be properly exposed, the metering system in the camera can get "confused" under certain light conditions. For best exposure, avoid having the sun or another light source coming from behind the subject (backlighting) or from behind the photographer (unless you like photos of people squinting).

Having the light directly overhead is not good either, as it can cast harsh shadows on the faces of the subjects. Your best lighting comes on overcast days, but when that isn't available and you're faced with a backlit situation, try turning on your flash to act as a *fill flash*, which will allow the background and the subject to be correctly exposed.

The guide at Pioneer Farms, shown in Figure 3-19, standing outside on a sunny Texas summer afternoon would have had deep shadows on his face because of his hat were it not for using the flash as a fill flash to prevent the shadows. See Chapter 9 for more information about using your flash as a fill flash.

Sometimes you can use a fill flash on a heavily backlit subject to create a cool effect like the photo of a gold star on an iron fence shown in Figure 3-20.

FIGURE 3-19 Using a fill flash allows you to take a photo of someone who would have had dark shadows produced by headgear.

FIGURE 3-20 Using a fill flash on a strongly back-lit subject produces stunning effects like this one.

Ways to Ensure Proper Focus

All digital cameras have auto-focus, and they all work in essentially the same way. Sometimes the auto-focus doesn't work as advertised, so here are some quick tricks to tackle auto-focus problems:

- Find a high contrast subject roughly the same distance from your camera. Focus on it by pressing and holding down the shutter button half way (this produces a focus-lock). While still holding the button, turn the camera to face the original subject and press the button the rest of the way.

- If you are too close to the subject, either back away and try zooming in or change the camera to macro mode (if it has one).

- For situations in which the light is too low for the auto-focus to work properly, I recommend that you use a *focus* light (which sells for about $10) to illuminate your subject while you press down the shutter button to get the proper focus.

Simple Ways to Steady Your Camera

A common error many a photographer makes is to move the camera when he presses the shutter button to take a photo. The resulting blur in the image is thought to be a focus problem; however, it may have been caused by camera movement. Gently squeezing the shutter button instead of pressing it eliminates a lot of this unintended camera movement. Keep in mind that if you are shooting with the zoom set at its maximum magnification position, any camera movement is greatly magnified. Remember that if there isn't enough light for the auto-focus to work during a shot, you will probably need to use a tripod or something else to stabilize the camera.

In addition to traditional methods of steadying a camera, such as a tripod or monopod, you can use several other stabilization methods. For example, when I am out in the field without my large (heavy) tripod and I need to take a low-light photo, I find a stable base (a log, fence post, or bench), and cradle the camera in my felt hat. You can also use a small beanbag if you don't have a hat.

After the camera is stable, make all of your settings. Once the camera is set, use the self-timer to take the photo so that you don't accidentally move the camera while the photo is being shot. Figure 3-21 shows the interior of a California mission, taken while the camera was nestled on my backpack, which was placed on a pew. Because there wasn't nearly enough light to take a hand-held photo, I wedged the camera onto the backpack and set the timer.

FIGURE 3-21 This low-light photo was taken while the camera was wedged onto a backpack to hold it steady.

Chapter 4

Get the Best Lighting for Your Photos

How to...

- Understand camera metering systems
- Match the metering system to the lighting
- Use exposure values and auto bracketing
- Use available lighting to your advantage

Digital Photography Myth Number 4:
You can get the best outdoor people photos around noon or when the sun is directly overhead.

Fact: False. Of course, this could be true if you wanted your subject to look washed out and bluish, with dark shadows cast under the eyes.

Without getting too technical, this chapter will show you how light effects the photos that you take. You probably already know that you need enough light to prevent underexposed photos, and you can't have too much light or the picture will be overexposed. What you may not know is that sunlight effects colors in your photos depending on the time of day they are taken and where the subject and photographer are located relative to the sun. The photos in Figure 4-1 show how the wrong exposure setting can even effect the resulting colors in the finished image.

In this chapter, you will learn how your camera measures light and why its wonderfully sophisticated automatic metering system can sometimes choose the wrong settings. You will also discover some features in your camera that allow you to work with troublesome lighting and some easy ways to work around common lighting problems.

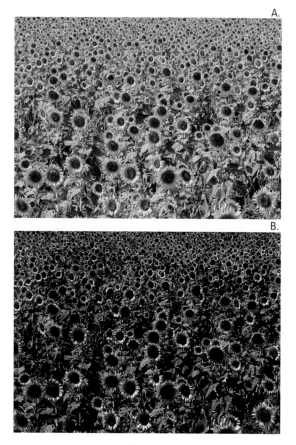

A.

B.

FIGURE 4-1 (A) This photo was overexposed, washing out the colors while this one (B) was correctly exposed.

Getting the Correct Amount of Light

Along with focus, the most important factor in getting a good photo is to have the proper amount of light to achieve the proper exposure. Back in the early film days, getting a proper exposure meant guessing at the amount of light on the subject or reading a hand-held light meter and using that data to adjust the camera settings. When manufacturers began building cameras with built-in light meters that measured the light through the lens (called TTL meters), photographers were thrilled. Over the years, the built-in light meters (called metering systems) have improved dramatically.

Caution   *Never point your camera directly at the sun, as it can damage your eyes, the camera sensor, or both. However, at sunrise or sunset the light from the sun is usually diminished because it is traveling through so much atmosphere near the earth's curvature.*

How Your Light Meter Reads an Image

The sensor used to measure light in a camera is composed of many separate elements that allow the metering system to measure how much light is illuminating the subject in different parts of the framed image.

FIGURE 4-2 A single image like this one can show many areas of extreme differences of lighting.

The photo in Figure 4-2 illustrates how areas of a single photo can radically differ in the amount of light that they contain. In the photo, the morning sun has risen sufficiently to be partly shielded by the low clouds, but it still produces an intensely bright area in the frame. The second brightest area is the reflection of the sun on the water. The unlit water is darker still, and the pier (being in silhouette) is black.

The light sensor in your camera can read the different parts of a

scene like that shown in Figure 4-2. Each camera has its own way of dividing up the image area into zones, and exactly how it is accomplished isn't important. How the camera uses the light reading from these different zones to calculate the correct exposure is determined by the metering system you select, and your selection is an important factor in getting a good shot.

Automatic Metering Systems

The automatic metering systems used in digital cameras are similar to those found in film cameras. Depending on the camera you own, you can switch between three basic metering settings using the camera menu or a switch on the camera body: center-weighted metering, matrix metering, and spot metering. Knowing what metering methods to use for specific lighting situations will noticeably improve many of your photos, as the two photos in Figure 4-3 illustrate.

These two photos of a water lily were taken within moments of one another. Using the same light source and same subject, different metering methods were used. Obviously, the (A) shot was overexposed because the wrong metering method was selected. The meter measured the light from the shadow reflection in the water and it resulted in an overexposed photo. The (B) photograph used spot metering to measure the brightest part of the flower, resulting in a proper exposure of the flower. While the background of the photo is a little dark, it's an acceptable compromise.

FIGURE 4-3 Your selection of metering systems affects the quality of your photos.

A.   B.

Not all digital cameras offer all three types of metering systems, and they often use different names for their metering systems.

Center-weighted metering

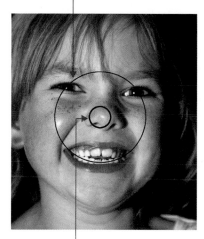

Spot metering

FIGURE 4-4 Some cameras have markings to show the areas being measured by different metering systems.

FIGURE 4-5 Use center-weighted metering to capture back-lit subjects.

Some cameras display small circles in the center of the LCD screen, like those shown in Figure 4-4, so that you can see the area that is being measured by the metering system. The small inner circle indicates the area being measured when using spot metering, while the larger circle shows the part of the frame that is being used to measure the light for center-weighting.

Center-Weighted Metering

This metering system is found in nearly every digital camera, especially in cameras that offer only one metering system. *Center-weighted* describes a metering system that measures the light in the entire scene and averages the exposure of the scene, giving extra weight to the light readings in the center of the frame. Center-weighted metering assumes that the subject is in the center of the frame and therefore uses the light measured from the center to influence the overall exposure of the photo. Center-weighted metering works best when the light source is behind the subject or when the subject is white or very light.

The image shown in Figure 4-5 was taken of a contented cat that was back-lit by the light streaming in from the window. If center-weighted metering had not been used, the light from the window would have dominated the exposure calculations, resulting in a properly exposed photo of the window with the cat being so underexposed that it would have appeared as a silhouette. By using center-weighted metering, the camera measured the darker area in the center of the cat's smug expression and used that reading to get a proper exposure of the cat at the expense of the window being overexposed—which does not affect the overall quality of the photo.

When shooting with center-weighted metering, remember that the camera is measuring

the light at the center of the image, so if your subject is off-center, you will need to use exposure lock to read the light on the subject before composing the photo. For more information about exposure lock, see the Did You Know box topic "Discovering Exposure Lock," later in this chapter.

You can also use center-weighting when the subject is white or a very light color. Using center-weighting will prevent or reduce blowouts and loss of image detail. See the Did You Know box "Blowouts and Digital Cameras," later in the chapter.

 Most camera manufacturers use the term center-weighted to describe this metering method, although the feature is sometimes called average metering.

Matrix Metering

Matrix metering represents the most complex metering mode, and how it works differs among camera brands. Matrix metering breaks up the image into a matrix of metering zones (as many as 200); each zone is evaluated to determine the best possible exposure. For example, one camera manufacturer's meter measures the upper zone of an image, and if it finds it to be

Did you know?

Blowouts and Digital Cameras

A *blowout* is an area of a digital image that has gone 100 percent white. Any detail in the blowout is lost and cannot be recovered, even by photo-editing software. Blowouts can be caused by many different factors. Some of the common causes include light reflecting off of a shiny object, taking a flash photo too close to the subject, and incorrect exposure settings. Some blowouts are expected—think of the reflection off the 300 pounds of chrome on a motorcycle. For the blowouts that shouldn't be there, such as a bride's white gown, you can use several methods to avoid them—you can use the optimum metering system, use a bounce flash (see Chapter 9), or slightly underexpose the subject.

If you are an experienced film photographer, it is important that you understand that blowouts are more likely to occur with digital cameras than with film because film has a greater tolerance to overexposure than does the sensor in a digital camera.

When it comes to digital images, you can almost always recover detail from an underexposed area, but you never can recover detail from a blowout.

brighter than the rest of the frame, the meter assumes it is the sky and will pay less attention to it when it comes to calculating the exposure settings.

In most shooting situations, you *should* use this metering system—it's usually the default setting of your camera. The only downside to using matrix metering is that it automatically calculates an exposure setting and attempts to capture as much detail as possible, and this can be a problem if the background or subject is either exceptionally bright or dark. In such situations, the meter will include the light information from these bright or dark areas in its calculations, even if these areas aren't important to you; the resulting compromise may be a photo that is either overexposed or underexposed.

FIGURE 4-6 Using the matrix metering method preserved all of the detail in this photo.

If everything in the frame is important to you, using matrix metering can produce a photo that doesn't show all the detail in either the highlights or the shadows—as shown in the sundown in Figure 4-6, which loses some of the delicate detail in the clouds. The resulting compromise can sometimes result in an exposure setting that is the best possible for the image.

Note *Of the three metering methods, every manufacturer uses its own name for the matrix method. Other popular names for this type of metering include multi-segment metering, evaluative metering, multi-zone metering, and pattern metering. Regardless of the name uses, they all do they same thing.*

Spot Metering

Spot metering allows you to measure the lighting at the center of the image. Like center-weighted metering, the most common use of spot metering is when the light source is behind the subject. Spot metering is also used when the subject is much brighter than the background, to prevent blowout. In Figure 4-7, the Washington Monument is a bright subject, and the only way to keep this light obelisk from turning solid white was to use spot metering while shooting.

Using normal matrix metering on a subject with a dark background results in the details of the white flower being completely blown out, as shown in the image on the left in Figure 4-8. When the same photo is taken using spot metering on the brightest spot of the flower, the details are preserved, although the background is underexposed, as shown in the image on the right.

Create Dark Backgrounds with Spot Metering The background of a photo is sometimes not at all important to the content of the photo, and at those times, you may want to emphasize a subject by making the background darker. The photo shown in Figure 4-9 is an example of this. The sunlight coming through the trees lit the aquatic plant hanging over the edge of a small pond, but little else was lit.

When I was shooting this photo, I could easily see the plant and the rest of the background. That's because the human eye has an incredible dynamic range that far exceeds

FIGURE 4-7 Using spot metering on the monument ensures that the subject is correctly exposed.

FIGURE 4-8 Matrix metering overadjusts for the dark background, causing details in the flower to be lost (A), but spot metering properly exposes the flower (B).

A.

B.

what your camera can see. In this case, however, the camera's limited range works just fine. Using spot metering, the camera adjusted its meter settings to expose the brightly lit plant properly, and the background goes almost solid black. It works to create a remarkable image.

Using a Photo Editor to Capture the Entire Image

If you study the flower images from the last section, it might seem that you have a choice of either preserving the detail of the subject and losing a lot of the background or getting most of the photo properly exposed but losing the details on the subject. But there is a third alternative: you can use both exposures. Take two photos of the same subject using spot and matrix metering, and then combine the photos in a photo editor. Figure 4-10 shows how this might look. You'll learn how to do this in Chapter 20.

FIGURE 4-9 Using spot metering can make the background go solid black for a stunning effect.

FIGURE 4-10 Combining the two photos preserves the flower details while retaining the background.

Shoot, Review, Adjust, and Shoot Again

All this information about metering systems won't do you much good if you don't take advantage of it. After you take a photo, evaluate the photo you just took using the LCD screen on the camera. Does the photo appear to be properly exposed? Does it appear washed out? Granted, viewing the LCD screen on a digital camera on a bright sunny day is nigh impossible, but you can still determine a few general details about the quality of a shot.

The best way view the image is to step into a building or into a shaded spot, let your eyes adjust to the light, and then view the photo you just shot. If no building or shade is available, hide under a coat or some other covering. (Don't be concerned about what people think when they see you standing with a blanket over your head. You're a photographer!) On a hot August day in Texas, I never seem to have either a jacket or a blanket on me, so I resort to a technical evaluation—a histogram.

Evaluate Using A Histogram

A *histogram* is a complicated looking bar chart that shows the distribution of all of the shades of pixels in an image. The left side of the chart represents the darker pixels (shadow) and the right side of the chart represents the brighter pixels (highlights), like the one shown in Figure 4-11. It used to be that a histogram display was available only on professional cameras, but that's not the case anymore.

While not all digital cameras provide histogram displays, they are beginning to appear in the mid-level cameras. Unfortunately, the histogram that is displayed in a digital camera's LCD screen is very small and lacks detail. Even so, while a wealth of information is contained in that frightfully complicated looking chart, you need to determine only whether lots of pixels are bunched up near the extreme edges of the chart.

For purposes of illustration, the histogram for the image shown in Figure 4-12 was captured from a photo-editing application and displays the same information found in the camera's histogram—except in greater detail (and size). Notice how the levels are very low at both ends of the chart, indicating that few pixels in the photo are either very dark or very bright. Many of the pixels are concentrated near the highlight region, because of the large amount of white present in the image.

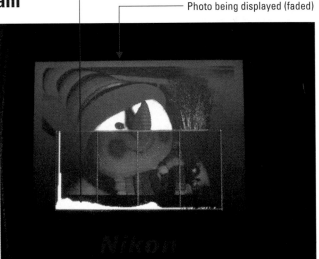

Histogram of the image

Photo being displayed (faded)

FIGURE 4-11 A histogram is a quick visual indicator of a proper exposure.

A.

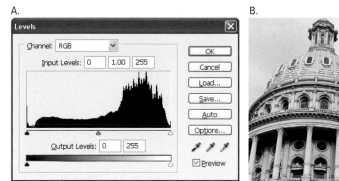

B.

4

FIGURE 4-12 The histogram (A) shows that this photo (B) has no pixels that are either too dark or too light.

FIGURE 4-13 The histogram for the overexposed photo in Figure 4-3 shows a concentration of pixels in the highlight region and clipping.

Now look at the histogram shown in Figure 4-13. This is the histogram for the overexposed water lily photo shown back in Figure 4-3. You can see how the pixels are crowded on the right side of the chart. This means that most of the pixels are bright. Also notice that the pixels don't slope off as they approach the right. When lots of pixels appear at the extreme edge of a histogram, it is called *clipping*. Clipping in the highlight region means that the image is overexposed, resulting in blowouts in the photo.

The last histogram shown in Figure 4-14 is of the photo of the flower made using spot metering and shown in Figure 4-8B. Most of the pixels are in the shadow region, and many are clipped— any detail in the shadows can't be recovered by a photo-editing application on the computer.

 A trend in mid-level and higher priced digital cameras is a pre-exposure histogram which is a preview created by the camera predicting what the final histogram will look like. Reliance on such a feature can lead to target fixation, a tendency for the photographer to concentrate on the graph rather than the elements that will make a good image.

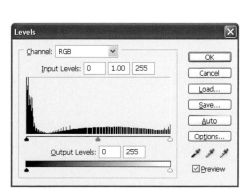

FIGURE 4-14 The histogram for Figure 4-8B shows a concentration of pixels in the shadow region and clipping.

Did you know?

Discovering Exposure Lock

What happens if you want to use spot or center-weighted metering but the subject is not in the center of the frame? Almost every digital camera has a neat feature called auto exposure lock (AEL).

To use it, point the camera at the subject that you want to use to determine the exposure, and press the shutter button halfway down; this locks the exposure settings. Compose the photo, and then press the shutter the rest of the way, and the locked-in exposure setting will be used for the shot. Note that some cameras will also *lock* the focus at the same time, so make sure the subject you are measuring is the same distance from the camera as the subject that you want in focus.

Understand Exposure Values

The amount of light that strikes the camera's sensor is controlled by two factors: how much light is let into the camera (via the aperture) and how long the light is on the sensor (shutter speed). Your camera calculates these settings for you automatically, but at times you may want to override these settings. For example, if the digital camera reads the scene incorrectly and overexposes an image, you'll want to correct the settings and reshoot. To compensate for this potential problem, most digital cameras offer a setting called Exposure Value (EV) that lets you make small changes to increase or decrease the exposure of the photo.

The EV is measured in decimals or whole steps. Positive steps such as +.5, +.7, +1, and +1.5 increase the exposure, making the resulting photo lighter with each increase; negative steps such as −.5, −.7, −1, and so on, make the exposure darker with each decrease. The decimal settings produce a small change in the overall exposure, while a setting of 1.5 or 2 will significantly change the exposure.

When I am shooting outdoors on a bright Texas day, I usually have my camera's EV set at −.5, since I prefer to underexpose my photos slightly to ensure rich saturated colors. The photos in Figure 4-15 show the difference between the effects of the camera's automatic setting and the effects of using different settings of EV.

FIGURE 4-15 The effect of different EV settings on the finished photo

EV = 0

You can use the EV Compensation feature of your camera to increase the exposure for backlighting. Try a +1 EV or even +1.5 while metering on the subject's face. Some cameras with scene presets even have a backlighting mode that does this automatically.

On most cameras, the EV setting is buried in the menu system, which makes changing it somewhat of a pain. You will need to read your manual to find out how to do this, since the odds of your finding it without help is pretty remote.

4

For more about exploring your camera's features, see Chapter 7.

Finding the Best Exposure with Auto Bracketing

A quick and easy way to ensure that you get the best exposure is to use *auto bracketing*. More and more cameras are now

EV= +.5

EV= −.5

EV= +1.5

EV= −1.5

offering an auto bracketing feature that automatically changes the settings each time you take a photo. Generally, auto bracketing can control the EV or the white balance settings. (You will learn more about white balance settings in Chapter 6.)

With auto bracketing turned on, each time you press the shutter, the camera will take the photo at a different EV setting—for instance, the shot may be taken at −.5, then normal, and then +.5. The number of EV steps that the camera offers and the range of EV settings used is selectable in the camera's menu, which is also where you turn on the auto bracketing feature.

Exposure auto bracketing can be used for static subjects, such as landscapes. It shouldn't be used when photographing a moving subject, because you may end up with the perfect shot either overexposed or underexposed because you took it when auto bracketing was set to one of the extreme EV settings.

 In some cameras, exposure bracketing remains on until it is disabled, so be sure to check your camera settings before attempting to shoot an unbracketed image.

Making the Best of Available Lighting

You've learned about the light metering problems created by backlighting, so now let's talk about some advantages of backlighting. Face it, when you are on vacation and you want to take the classic "we were there" photo in front of a recognizable monument, the sun always seems to be in wrong place. If, for example, the sun is behind the subject, nobody will be squinting their eyes, nor will hats, brows, noses, or other body parts cast odd shadows across their faces. For all of these pluses, however, the downside is that their faces are not lit and may be underexposed.

Several simple workarounds are available for this type of situation—of course, the easiest solution is to turn on your flash. Several flash settings are available on your camera (other than Auto). When you change the flash mode to Always On, it will fire every time you press the shutter button. When the flash is used in this way, it is called a *fill flash,* and your camera automatically compensate for the additional light provided by the flash. You'll learn more about fill flash in Chapter 9.

Professional photographers often use reflectors to illuminate a back-lit subject. Go on any movie set and you will see several large reflective panels that flood the actors' faces with soft, diffused light. Obviously, you can't drag one of these 400 pound reflectors with you on your vacation—and you don't need to. The quickest and easiest reflector you can use when the light is behind your subject is your own body. If you are wearing white clothes (tee-shirts work great), you can become a natural reflector.

 *Be careful when photographing a subject standing near a brightly colored wall, because like a reflector, the light reflecting off of the wall may add unwanted color to your photograph.*

FIGURE 4-16 I used my white tee-shirt as a reflector to prevent shadows.

The photo in Figure 4-16 shows a young girl sitting on a bench. Without compensating for the back-lighting, this shot would have been ruined by a dark shadow cast across her face. I didn't want to use a fill flash because it would have interrupted her daydreaming. So I positioned myself so that my white tee-shirt acted as a reflector.

Another reflector you may have handy is a car windshield sun shade. Here in Texas, sun shades are a vital part of your car gear; the one I own is made of some synthetic material, and it collapses down to the size of a hubcap. One side of the shield is shiny silver and the other side is white. The disadvantage of using such a big shield is that you will probably need someone to hold the reflector for you.

Block the Sun to Get the Shot

Suppose you want to take a photograph of a scene, but the sun is low on the horizon staring back at you. If you try and take the photo with the sun in it, the camera's metering system will react to the sun's extra light, resulting in a black photo with a bright spot where the sun is. To take a photo under such conditions, you can find some object in the foreground that you can place between you and the sun.

When I was trying to photograph the clouds of a Galveston sunset from the seawall last week, the sun (which up until that point had been behind some clouds) broke out and prevented me from taking the photo. I quickly moved further down the seawall so that a traffic signal was in a direct line with the setting sun. The signal was large enough to block the light and allowed me to take the photo shown in Figure 4-17.

Block the Sun for Special Effects

On occasion, using a foreground object to block a light source can be used to produce cool effects. One morning in the Shenandoah Valley, the sun had already been up for several hours by the time it came over the ridge where I was shooting, so it was quite bright. I positioned myself so the tree in the center of the photo blocked the sun, which produced the photo shown in Figure 14-18.

Summary

After all that we have discussed in this chapter, you should know that one of the most important things you can do when taking outdoor photos is to match the metering system selection with the lighting situation. Do that, and I promise that your photos will improve.

In the next chapter, you will learn how to ensure that your photos are sharp and in focus.

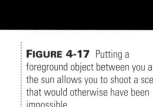

FIGURE 4-17 Putting a foreground object between you and the sun allows you to shoot a scene that would otherwise have been impossible.

FIGURE 4-18 Blocking the sun with a foreground object can produce stunning effects.

Chapter 5

Get Clear and Sharp Photos

How to...

- Determine the cause of blurred photos
- Prepare your camera for taking photos
- Understand auto-focus
- Understand depth of field
- Eliminate camera movement
- Ensure you get sharp and clear photos

Digital Photography Myth Number 4:   If the photo is blurry you can always fix it in the computer.

Fact: False. Only in the movies can the fuzzy photo of a license plate on a computer monitor be wondrously restored to a sharp image by someone saying to a technician, "Now, enhance it."

Because you can't fix fuzzy photos in the computer, you need to understand how to ensure that the photos you take with your digital cameras are sharp. In this chapter you'll discover what causes photos to be blurry (which may surprise you), how the auto-focus system in your camera works, and under what conditions it doesn't work. You will also learn how to prevent the most common causes of those unacceptably "soft" photos.

Reviewing Your Fuzzy Pictures

Blurred photos have been around since the first photos were taken with the first cameras. With film cameras, you didn't know your pictures were blurred until you got them back from the developers. With digital cameras, though, you can see your pictures right after you take them by viewing them on the LCD screen on the back of the camera. With this instant feedback you shouldn't have any blurred photos, right?

 If your photographs are important to you, make a habit of carefully examining the images in the LCD screen before you move on.

Unfortunately, that's not necessarily the case. The photo shown on an LCD screen is typically about an inch and a half wide, and

even if a photo is out of focus, the small size of the LCD screen adds a perceived sharpness that makes blur detection difficult. The image appearing the in LCD screen can look much better than the actual photo, as shown in Figure 5-1.

Fortunately, many cameras have a feature that allows you to magnify the image on the LCD screen, making it easier to detect faulty focus—but that works only if you take the time to use it.

FIGURE 5-1 The photo in the camera LCD screen doesn't reflect how blurry the actual photo is.

The Out-of-Focus Experience

Even though all digital cameras have an auto-focus feature, you can still end up with blurred photos. Knowing what causes them can help you avoid them. Most of the time, a photo ends up blurry for one of two reasons.

- The lens isn't properly focused.
- The subject or camera moved during the exposure.

Regardless of the type of camera you use, the auto-focus feature works in the same way: the camera takes information from the camera sensor and moves an internal focus motor to focus the lens on whatever the camera lens is pointed at until the subject appears to be in focus.

Auto-focus systems are classified as being *active* or *passive,* as shown in the illustration in Figure 5-2, and some cameras use a combination of both. Active systems beam pulses of invisible infrared light at the subject to determine the distance to the subject and control the focus.

A passive auto-focus system looks for contrast in the subject by comparing contrasting pixels in the focusing area and moving the focusing motor in and out while measuring the amount of contrast. When the contrast is at its greatest, the image is in focus (at least it's supposed to be). (See the Did You Know Box "How Passive Auto-Focus Works" for a more detailed explanation.)

FIGURE 5-2 Two types of auto-focus systems are found in digital cameras.

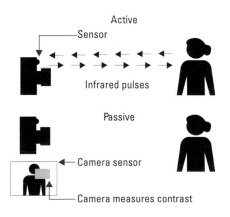

Which Auto-Focus System Does You Camera Have?

If your digital camera is a point-and-shoot model without interchangeable lenses, it probably has an active auto-focus system. If your camera is a single-lens reflex (SLR) type with interchangeable lenses, it probably is a passive system. Here is a quick way to confirm what type of system your camera uses:

1. Point your camera at a patch of cloudless sky. Look at the LCD to make sure that nothing else is in the frame that your auto-focus can focus on. Press the shutter button halfway down.

2. If the focus indicator on your camera quits flashing, which indicates that it is in focus, you probably have an active auto-focus system. The infrared pulses didn't return and your camera's auto-focus system focused to infinity.

3. If the focus indicator continues to blink, indicating that it has not achieved focus, it's a passive auto-focus system. The camera sensor couldn't find any contrasting pixels in the solid blue sky and after a few moments it usually sets the lens to infinity, but unlike the active system, it's not sure whether it is in focus or not.

Regardless of which auto-focus system your camera uses, in most cases they work fine and the subject is in focus. Digital cameras and their auto-focus systems are constantly improving. Several cameras actually scan the entire frame and automatically determine where the subject is within the frame and then use that distance for focusing; others have a feature that will focus on the closest subject in the frame. Isn't technology grand?

For all the technical whiz-bang stuff, the auto-focus system in your camera is *not* foolproof, and some conditions can trick the camera's auto-focus.

When Auto-Focus Doesn't Work

Most digital cameras have an indicator light that flashes (some change color and flash) while the auto-focus is attempting to determine a correct focus. When your camera *thinks* that the scene is in focus, the indicator light stops flashing as shown in the illustration. Of course, your camera can't think, but the auto-focus mechanism can be "tricked." For example, when

Flashing indicator is a warning that the auto-focus is not in focus.

you're taking a picture through a window, the auto-focus will often attempt to focus on the glass, rather than the scene on the other side of the window.

Tip *To shoot a photo through an airplane window, set the camera to manual focus and choose the infinity setting. Even with this setting, don't expect quality images, because the Plexiglas windows are usually dirty and scratched—and Murphy's Law dictates that the light will always come from the wrong direction.*

Even with the newest auto-focus systems, some common elements may confuse your camera's system, resulting in a fuzzy picture:

- **Open flames**   Candles and fireplaces produce a great amount of infrared energy that can overwhelm the infrared sensor of a camera with an active auto-focus system, making it difficult for the camera to read the returning pulses. Of course, if the subject is the flame, it will work fine.

- **Low-contrast subject**   A problem for passive systems is large areas of solid or similar colors that have little or no contrast. When the colors in the subject are all the same or similar colors (such as a flat wall), the auto-focus mechanism may not be able to determine whether the subject is in focus.

- **Black or dark colors**   Some materials (especially dark colors or black) can absorb the infrared pulses, confusing an active auto-focus system.

- **Low light**   Even though infrared signals can work in the dark, if your camera uses a passive auto-focus and you are shooting a low-contrast subject in dim light, the camera may have difficulty determining the correct focus.

- **Subject too close**   All cameras have a minimum focusing distance, and if you are closer than the minimum distance the focusing motor will try several times to focus before stopping (to save the battery).

- **Wrong subject**   The auto-focus can be fooled by something that is either farther or closer than the subject you intended to be in focus.

Note *It is not uncommon for a camera's auto-focus to "think" it isn't in focus when it actually is. This condition usually occurs when the camera has attempted to focus (and got it right), but the auto-focus hasn't met some internal threshold for the camera's electronics long enough to stop the focus indicator from flashing.*

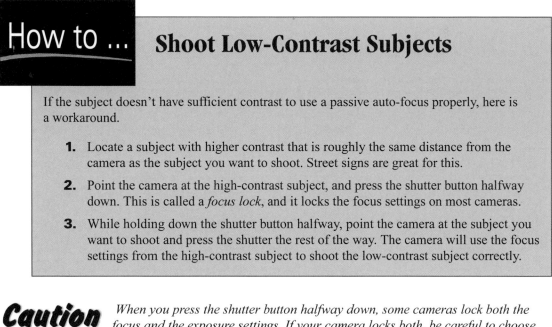

How to ... Shoot Low-Contrast Subjects

If the subject doesn't have sufficient contrast to use a passive auto-focus properly, here is a workaround.

1. Locate a subject with higher contrast that is roughly the same distance from the camera as the subject you want to shoot. Street signs are great for this.

2. Point the camera at the high-contrast subject, and press the shutter button halfway down. This is called a *focus lock*, and it locks the focus settings on most cameras.

3. While holding down the shutter button halfway, point the camera at the subject you want to shoot and press the shutter the rest of the way. The camera will use the focus settings from the high-contrast subject to shoot the low-contrast subject correctly.

Caution *When you press the shutter button halfway down, some cameras lock both the focus and the exposure settings. If your camera locks both, be careful to choose a focus subject that has roughly the same lighting as the actual subject.*

Workarounds for Low-Light Conditions

Low-light conditions affect passive auto-focus systems the same way that low-contrast conditions do. Most active systems can focus in dim light. If there's not enough light for your camera to see the subject clearly, a passive auto-focus mechanism cannot function properly.

Some cameras have built-in features that work great for focusing in low-light situations. Some of the higher end Sony cameras have a visible infrared light that actually reads the image and calculates the correct distance. Other cameras offer an auto-focus assist lamp that turns on momentarily to allow the camera to find the focus. When this lamp lights up, it sometimes confuses the people you are photographing, since it is bright—but it isn't as bright as a flash.

Because many digital cameras don't have these features, you can use a few tricks to get a sharp focus under low-light conditions. A hand-held focusing light, like the one shown in Figure 5-3, is a handy little lamp that attaches to your keychain (I wear mine on a lanyard). It costs around $10

FIGURE 5-3 This tiny light attaches to your keychain and outputs more than sufficient light to achieve a sharp focus.

Photo of Photon Micro-Light courtesy of LRI

How to ... **Estimate Distance**

Here's an easy way to estimate distance for manual focusing: Imagine yourself lying flat on the ground between where you stand and the subject you want to shoot. You can guess the distance by guessing how many of your body lengths would fit between you and the subject. If, for example, two of your body lengths would fit between the camera and the subject and you're 5 feet tall, you could estimate a distance of 10 feet. It's rough, but effective.

5

and comes in white and red light (not to be confused with the laser pointers that were so popular awhile back), among other colors. The red light is the best choice for photographing creatures at night that might be spooked by a white light, and it's helpful for maintaining your night vision.

When all else fails, most digital cameras allow you to turn off the auto-focus and use manual focus. The problem with manual focus, however, is that, unlike with SLR cameras, you cannot view the subject and rotate the lens until the subject appears in focus. With digital cameras, you must go to the menu and select the distance to which you need to focus (which implies that you actually know the distance).

FIGURE 5-4 The auto-focus focused on the wrong subject.

When Auto-Focus Doesn't Focus on the Right Subject

Incorrect subject focusing is a common problem with auto-focus systems. In Figure 5-4, as the girl was running toward me, the AF auto-focus got confused and focused on the silk flowers and the teenager standing behind the running girl.

A subtle example of the auto-focus focusing on the wrong subject is shown in Figure 5-5. This Halloween photo was auto-focused under low-light conditions, and the object the auto-focus locked onto wasn't the subjects (the young women), but the chandelier that was right behind them. Even though my camera uses a combination passive/active auto-focus system, it locked on to the highest contrast object in the frame and focused on it, bringing out the detail of the chandelier but leaving the details of the women a little soft.

Some digital cameras allow you to control which part of the frame the camera uses as a point of focus. My camera allows me to move a cursor to one of five areas of the frame, which tells the camera where to focus. So, why didn't it work here? I had changed the auto-focus settings for an earlier photo and forgot to change them back.

Using Focus Lock for Sharp Focus on the Correct Subject

If your digital camera focuses only on the center of the frame (and many do), to take a well-composed photo with the subject off-center requires the use of the focus lock feature of your camera. For example, the subject in Figure 5-6 is out of focus because the camera is trying to focus on the grass. On most cameras, the focus lock works by depressing the shutter button halfway.

FIGURE 5-5 A subtler example of auto-focus locking on the wrong subject creates a lack of focus of the true subject.

FIGURE 5-6 The subject is out of focus but the background isn't, because the auto-focus is locked on the background and not the subject.

Here is how to use focus lock to compose a picture:

1. Move the camera right or left so the square brackets in the center of the viewfinder are over the actual subject, as shown in Figure 5-7.

2. Press and hold the shutter button halfway down so the camera focuses on the subject. Keep your finger on the button.

3. Slowly move your camera to compose the shot. Gently squeeze the shutter button all the way down. The background should now be out of focus, while the subject is in focus, as shown in Figure 5-8.

FIGURE 5-7 Repositioning the center of the camera allows the auto-focus to focus on the subject.

FIGURE 5-8 Focus lock prevents the auto-focus from refocusing on the background.

To get the best results from your camera's auto-focus system, be sure that a clear path lies between you and your subject, and be sure that no objects are close by that might reflect the infrared pulses, focusing the lens on them and not your subject. Most camera auto-focus systems are designed based on the assumption that the subject will be in the center of the frame; if your subject is off-center, you need to accommodate for that using the tricks discussed in this chapter.

When photographing kids who move a lot, it is best to have some sort of object that keeps them in the same relative position (a bench or chair). Then it's best to pre-focus, usually by pressing down the shutter halfway. When the expression is just right, the click to take the picture is decreased and your odds of a great picture increases.

Nancy Peterson, QA engineer and mother of three

Did you know?

How Passive Auto-Focus Works

Most digital cameras send an infrared signal from the camera to determine the distance to the subject. The effective range for most auto-focus mechanisms is from 18 to 22 feet from the camera. If the subject is out of range of the auto-focus system (such as a distant mountain range), the camera focuses the lens to its maximum setting (which is called infinity).

When you take a photo, a lot is going on inside your digital camera. A beam of infrared pulses travel out from your camera, the subject reflects part of these infrared signal back to the camera, and the camera compares the two pulses to determine the time difference and therefore the distance to the subject. Using this information, the camera drives the focus motor to move the lens. This focus process repeats over and over while the camera shutter button is pressed halfway down.

Be Aware of Your Minimum Focus Distance

Your camera lens has limits as to how close it can focus, called the *minimum focus distance.* Anything that is closer to the camera than the minimum focus distance will not be in focus. In the image shown in Figure 5-9, the flower was too close to the lens and as a result it blurred badly.

A special setting on many digital cameras, called *macro*, allows you to photograph a subject at amazingly close distances. In Chapter 16, you'll learn a lot about how to use the macro setting of you camera to get great close-ups.

FIGURE 5-9 If the camera is too close, the camera cannot focus.

A Moving Experience

While focusing is important, most of the soft photos I see usually result from the camera, the subject, or both moving

FIGURE 5-10 Hand-held photos taken at low shutter speed are a recipe for blurry photos.

FIGURE 5-11 Low light and slow shutter speed produce blurry photos of a moving subject, even though the camera was mounted on a tripod.

when the photo was snapped. Here are some classic examples. Figure 5-10 is a photo of some fresh cigars taken at a cigar factory. I didn't have a tripod and I wanted to take the photo using available light so that the colors of the tobacco wouldn't be washed out by a flash. Holding my breath, I took this photo at a very slow shutter speed (1/8 of a second). Result—cigar-shaped blurs with lovely warm colors. Cause: I moved.

In the image shown in Figure 5-11, the camera was mounted on a tripod so it couldn't move, but I was shooting with available light (the subject was too far away to use flash). The performer's movements blurred the photo in this case.

At times, everything works to ensure that the resulting photo is almost unrecognizable. Figure 5-12 is a classic wedding shot—the bride dancing with her father. Low light gave the auto-focus of the camera the fits trying to focus. The flash didn't go off, and I ended up with a combination of a soft focus, shaky camera, and moving subject—making me thankful I wasn't the official photographer for the wedding!

FIGURE 5-12 Sometimes both the subject and the camera move, producing a colored blur.

Note *Telltale signs that the camera was moved during an exposure are small trails behind a light, such as the little curly patterns of the lights in Figure 5-12.*

Depth of Field and How It Effects Focus

When you focus your camera on an object, you can be certain it will be in focus, but the rest of the image may not be. The range in a photograph, from near to far, that appears to be in focus is called *depth of field*. In a *narrow* depth of field, only a short distance in front of and behind the subject is in focus. A *wide* depth of field means more distance in front of and behind the subject is in focus.

Because the size of the sensor in digital cameras is smaller than a 35mm negative, digital camera manufacturers must use a very wide lens on most consumer digital cameras. (The reason for this has to do with the physics of the optical lens and a lot of mathematics that we won't get into here.) These wide lenses mean that your digital camera may have a very wide depth of field. Producing a blurred background with a very wide lens due to a narrow depth of field is a pretty unlikely occurrence.

However, using a few tricks, you can take photos with narrow depths of fields. Figure 5-13 is a photograph taken of some construction steel with a narrow depth of field. Notice that the

FIGURE 5-13 A narrow depth of field causes the foreground and background of this photo to be out of focus, while the center is in focus.

parts of the steel nearest the camera and those far away are both out of focus. (If you are interested in learning more about what controls the depth of field in your camera, see the Did You Know box "Controlling Depth of Field.")

Controlling the depth of field can enhance a photo or create a cool effect. A narrow depth of field can make the subject stand out, as shown in the photograph of a butterfly in Figure 5-14. Because the camera has such a narrow depth of field, the background is completely blurred, which makes the butterfly the center of attention; if the background had also been in focus, the butterfly might have gotten lost in the swirl of garden colors.

In Figure 5-15, a very narrow depth of field caused the tips of this plant to be in focus and nothing else, creating an artistic effect.

FIGURE 5-14 A narrow depth of field produces a soft blurred background and a brightly focused subject.

FIGURE 5-15 Focusing on the tips of this flower and using a narrow depth of field produces another cool effect.

Eliminate Camera Movement

The examples of camera movement shown earlier in this chapter are pretty gross. In fact, small amounts of camera movement will cause an image to appear a little soft but still in focus. Many things can make your camera shake and thereby soften your photos.

Did you know?

Controlling Depth of Field (DOF)

Without getting too terribly technical, the DOF of a photograph is controlled by the distance the subject is located from the camera and the aperture of the lens (measured in f-stops). Although several other factors control it as well, distance and f-stop have the greatest effect on DOF. The farther the subject is from the camera, the greater the DOF. As the lens focuses out to infinity, the DOF also becomes infinite. For closer work, the f-stop narrows or widens the DOF. As the camera lens is opened up (the f-stop setting decreases), the DOF narrows. As the aperture is closed down (the f-stop setting increases), the DOF also increases.

On most digital cameras, the aperture and shutter speed settings are controlled automatically, but on some cameras, you can take control of one or both of these settings. By changing the camera to aperture priority, you can increase or decrease the aperture setting and the camera will automatically adjust the shutter speed to ensure a correct exposure.

Another way to decrease the DOF is to zoom out the lens to its maximum setting. As we zoom out to a longer focal length—telephoto—the apparent depth of field decreases. For this reason, a telephoto focal length is often desirable for shooting portraits with out-of-focus backgrounds.

Push the Button Slowly

Probably one of the greatest contributors to camera movement is pressing the shutter button. (In fact, the National Photofinishers Association estimates that this type of camera movement results in approximately 80 percent of refused prints.) You should always try and *squeeze* the shutter button smoothly and not jab at it. Shutter button bounce has become a greater problem with the newer cameras that are small and light; it can be difficult to hold the camera still and not have the pressure of your finger on the button move the camera.

To take a photo in low-light conditions without moving the camera when you push the shutter button, place the camera on a table or some other nonmoving surface and use the camera's self-timer.

How Shutter Speed Relates to Focal Length

When you shoot a photo on a bright sunny day at the beach, your camera automatically increases the shutter speed to some very high setting, such as 1/1000 of a second. At a high speed like this, you can take a photo while riding a mechanical bull and not get a blurred photo. (Of course, people may wonder why you were riding a mechanical bull at the beach.) The point is, at high shutter speeds, the lens is open for such a short period of time that a little hand movement doesn't hurt the image.

When you zoom out with your digital camera, you increase the focal length of your lens. It is important that you understand that *greater focal length amplifies any camera movement*. Have you ever noticed the photographers along the sidelines of a football game? Most of them have cameras with telephoto lenses that are actually larger than their cameras. Most professional sports photographers use a monopod (a one-legged tripod) that is connected to their lens—not the camera. They need a steady platform because they are shooting at such high magnifications that even tiny movements are greatly magnified by the heavy lens. And they ensure quality shots under many conditions, including low light (see Figure 5-16).

A general rule in photography states that for hand-held shots, the shutter speed should be the reciprocal of the lens length (in millimeters). That means that if you shoot a photo using a 400mm lens, you shouldn't shoot at a shutter speed less than 1/400 of a second. Since your digital camera uses a zoom lens that doesn't have readouts in millimeters, let's rephrase the rule and just say that if your camera is zoomed out to the maximum and your shutter speed is set to a relatively slow speed (less than 1/125 of a second), you should consider stabilizing the camera.

When to Use a Steady Platform

You should consider using a steady platform for the following types of photography:

- Low-light photography
- Macro photography
- Still life
- Panoramas

What is a steady platform? It's anything that is steadier than your hand—and that could include almost any inanimate object. The most obvious steady platform associated with photography is the tripod.

FIGURE 5-16 A tripod helps ensure the best possible shot when photographing under low-light conditions.

Tip

Tripods are limiting. They take time to set up and position. Just because you own a tripod doesn't mean you have to use the tripod every time, but as you get used to shooting, you'll learn when to use and not use your tripod to get the best shots.

Benefits of a Good Tripod

Tripods come in all shapes and sizes, from large professional tripods that are sold in parts (tripods and heads) to little tripods that fit into your pocket. If you are thinking about getting a tripod, remember that the big expensive tripods are heavy. The one I use weighs about eight pounds.

That might not sound like much, but after I've lugged it around for about four hours, it feels like it weighs closer to 80 pounds. If you've never owned a tripod, start with an inexpensive, light plastic tripod that you can find at large discount stores. If after using it for a while you think that it is inadequate, try upgrading to a better one.

Alternatives to a Tripod

You don't have to use a tripod to stabilize your camera. You can also use a monopod (which is much lighter and can be used as a walking stick), a beanbag, and even your hat to steady your camera.

Here are some alternative ways to stabilize your camera:

- Brace one side of your camera against a vertical or horizontal object. If your are near or inside a building, a door jamb works great. Outside, fence rails and benches are my favorites.

- If your camera has a neck strap, you can loop it around something (a post or your foot) and pull it tight to keep tension on it. This isn't the most stable platform, but it is better than nothing.

- Some cameras have a feature that takes a fixed number of photos in rapid succession, and then the camera saves the one photo of the set that has the best detail. In my Nikon Coolpix, this is called Best Shot. How does the camera know which one is the best shot? By the size of the JPEG file—JPEG files increase in size as a direct function of the detail in the photo. Lots of sharp detail means a larger file.

Summary

I hope this clears up some of the fuzzy details about getting sharp photos. Now that you know how to make photos that look sharp, in the next chapter you'll learn how to get the colors correct.

Chapter 6

Get the Right Color

How to...

- Understand the difference between colors produced by film and digital cameras
- Understand how color temperature affects color in an image
- Choose the optimum white balance settings
- Work with different white balance solutions
- Know the advantages and disadvantages of raw files

Digital Photography Myth Number 6: Digital cameras always get the color right because they automatically compensate for the type of light in which I'm shooting.

Fact: That is true—about 20 percent of the time. This chapter covers the all-important topic of the different ways of ensuring that the color in your digital photos is the color that you want.

In making the transition from film to digital photography, you may notice that some photos, especially those that were taken on bright sunny days, don't seem to have the vivid colors that you experienced with film (such as in the photo shown in Figure 6-1A). You might assume that this is a limitation of digital cameras—as you may have done back in the 1960s when we all accepted that the weak

A.

FIGURE 6-1 The colors in digital photos can appear washed out (A), but if the color is correctly balanced the resulting photos look much better (B).

B.

colors of a Polaroid print was the price paid for instant photos.

In this chapter, you will discover that your digital camera can produce exceptional color if it is properly set up. Even though the subject of color is complex and the subject of many heated debates, you will learn some basic stuff that will help you get the colors in your photos to look the way that you want (such as in the photo shown in Figure 6-1B).

6

Why Film and Digital Cameras See Colors Differently

For photographers, one area of digital photography that is uniquely different from film is how color *temperature* is controlled. In conventional photography, color adjustment is accomplished using either color-correction filters or color-balanced film. With the exception of professional films, all films sold are balanced for daylight. The film boxes shown here display two different ways (daylight and outdoor) to indicate film that is color balanced for daylight. Daylight-balanced film is so common that many film boxes no longer indicate that the film is color balanced for daylight.

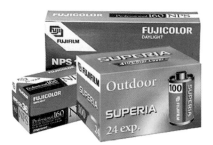

For the digital photographer, color temperature correction is accomplished by the camera. Called white balance (WB), it is a new concept for most conventional photographers, although videographers have always worked with it. Without getting too technical, WB controls what a digital camera perceives as a neutral color. Without WB correction, white objects tend to

Did you know?

What Is White Balance?

The color of light reflected off any object is determined by the color of the light source. Your eyes, in combination with your brain, automatically adapt to the changing colors of the light source and as a result, white objects appear white regardless of whether they are in the shade, in bright sunlight, or under a florescent lamp. Digital cameras attempt to operate in much the same manner, by determining the color of the light source and processing the information from the camera's sensor to correct the color information. The feature of your camera that adjusts the image captured by the camera's sensor to compensate for the different colored light sources is called white balance.

appear reddish-white under incandescent lights, slightly green under fluorescent lights, or bluish on an overcast day, just like daylight-balanced film under the same lighting conditions.

Figure 6-2 shows three photos taken of the U.S. Capitol building using three different WB settings. You can see the effect that the WB settings have on the colors in the finished image.

FIGURE 6-2 These photos were taken at the same time using different WB settings.

Understand Color Temperature

Every light source has a color temperature that effects how colors appear. Table 6-1 shows a brief summary of light temperatures and their respective effects on subjects illuminated by these sources. You don't need to memorize the information in the table; it is provided so you can see the effect that different color temperatures have on how colors appear.

An easy way to remember how the color temperature scale works is that it operates in an opposite fashion of a regular thermometer. For example, high temperatures produce cooler colors and low temperatures produce warmer colors.

Temperature in degrees Kelvin (K)	Source	Color Cast
1000 K	Candles; oil lamps	Deep red
2000 K	Very early sunrise	Red
2500 K	Household light bulbs	Orange
5000 K	Typical daylight; electronic flash	Bluish—cool
5500 K	Sun at high noon	Bluish—cool
6000 K	Bright sunshine on a clear day	Blue
7000 K	Slightly overcast sky	
8000 K	Hazy sky	Heavy blue color cast
9000 K	Shade on a clear day	
10,000 K	Heavy overcast	Blue

TABLE 6-1 Color Temperatures and Their Effects on Objects

How Your Digital Camera Corrects White Balance

Three ways are used to correct the WB on a digital camera. Note that all three may not be available on your camera.

- **Automatic White Balance** Automatically sets the WB
- **White Balance Presets** Presets for different light sources provided by the manufacturer
- **White Balance Calibration** Calibrates the WB to a known color

Automatic White Balance

Your digital camera has a feature called *Automatic White Balance* (AWB) that attempts to adjust the color balance settings automatically for the color temperature of the scene being photographed. In most cases, using the AWB is your best choice. However, in some situations, AWB doesn't correctly read the color in the scene. For example, when you are shooting a photo of someone lit by an incandescent lamp, like the little girl in Figure 6-3, the AWB cannot accurately determine the color temperature, which results in a photo with reddish hues.

White Balance Presets

When you review the photo you just took in the LCD screen and see that the color is incorrect, you can select one of the WB presets and shoot the photo again. Each digital camera manufacturer offers an assortment of WB presets with names like cloudy, incandescent, and fluorescent. With the WB set to tungsten (another name for incandescent lighting), for example, the colors on the photo of the young girl no longer have a reddish hue, as shown in Figure 6-4. While using presets won't guarantee that the colors in your photo will be accurate, it usually reduces the amount of color cast.

White Balance Calibration

Some of the high-end digital cameras offer the ability to calibrate the WB of the camera using a known reference. This is accomplished by selecting the calibrate feature from the camera menu and then photographing either a white or an 18 percent gray target. The camera uses the information to evaluate the color temperature of the light at that moment and calibrate the WB accurately.

While this is great for studio shots, it isn't the best solution for outdoor shooting since the color temperature of outdoor lighting changes pretty rapidly. This is especially true on a partly cloudy day, as the sun plays hide-and-seek behind the clouds.

How Color Temperature Affects Colors

If you know how color temperature affects colors and how the WB settings of your camera work, you can use this to your advantage when taking pictures. Table 6-1 shows you that light sources such as candles, incandescent lamps, and sun near sunset produce warmer colors. The unaltered photograph shown in Figure 6-5 was taken of some stacked rusty steel rails just as the sun was setting. The color temperature made of fading sun made the rust brown steel appear to be bright orange.

FIGURE 6-3 Incandescent light produces a reddish hue on the subject.

FIGURE 6-4 Using a preset WB setting corrects the color shift produced by the incandescent lighting.

Did you know?

What Is Kelvin?

Most of us are used to temperature being measured in degrees Fahrenheit or Celsius, and Kelvin may be new to you. The Kelvin scale is basically the same as Celsius, except that 0 on the Celsius scale is the freezing point of water and temperatures below that are expressed as negative numbers. The Kelvin scale has no negative numbers, because 0 degrees K is absolute zero (−273 C). So, why do are color temperatures expressed in Kelvin? Because the measurement of color temperature is done by physicists and not photographers. Enough said?

6

FIGURE 6-5 Rusty railroad steel appears very orange a few minutes before sunset.

FIGURE 6-6 Fluorescent lamps can make people look green.

The effect of fluorescent lamps creates a green color cast. The photo shown in Figure 6-6 was taken with HP's first digital camera. No megapixels here—we're talking an image that is 640×480 pixels. The couple was standing in a room that was brightly lit by fluorescent lights, and they ended up looking quite green.

Just because your subject is illuminated with fluorescent lamps doesn't mean you need to use a fluorescent lamp WB preset if you are using a flash. My coworker, Glenn, shown in Figure 6-7, was standing under bright fluorescent lighting when I took this shot, but since I was standing close to him, my flash was closer and brighter than the ceiling fluorescent lamps; therefore, he's not green.

Reflected Colors Also Create Problems

Another source of a color cast in a photo has less to do with the color temperature of the light source than the color of the walls near the subject. Figure 6-8A is a photo of a friend's baby, Cooper, in his yellow nursery sitting on his yellow sheets in his crib. The flash reflecting off all that yellow makes little Coop look a little jaundiced. To show just how much he needed improvement, I have used photo-editing software to correct the color (see Figure 6-8B).

Since a digital camera doesn't have a preset for yellow walls, how can you prevent light reflected off the walls from causing an unwanted color cast? That's easy: you can't! Light reflected off walls isn't limited to when you're using flash. It can also happen when someone stands outdoors next to a brightly colored wall. The solution? If you can, change the location. If you can't change the location (let's face it, color cast or not, a mother is going to want to see what the nursery crib looked like), you can either live with it or remove the color using your favorite photo editor.

FIGURE 6-7 Even though he was lit by fluorescent lighting, the flash was close enough to prevent a greenish tint.

Available Light vs. Flash

A more dramatic example of the effect of color temperature from a setting sun and a flash unit is shown in Figure 6-9. Photo A is a close-up of some organ pipes taken using the built-in flash on the camera. Photo B is the same photo taken a few seconds later, except the only available light was the sun about 20 minutes before sunset.

The pipe organ photos show how dramatically the light source can alter the final photo, but they also bring up another

FIGURE 6-8 The color of the walls adds a color cast to the photo (A). The color in in this photo has been corrected to remove the yellow cast (B).

A.

B.

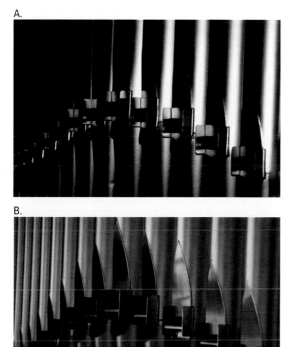

A.

B.

FIGURE 6-9 Close-up photo of organ pipes taken with a flash (A), and illuminated with late afternoon sun (B).

aspect to consider when shooting photos. Which of the two photos looks better? Most studies tell us that people prefer warmer colors over cooler colors. Photos taken in the last hour before sunset (assuming it is not overcast) usually look better, especially people shots.

When to Use WB Presets

In most cases, you should use your camera's automatic WB settings. Here are some exceptions to that rule:

- **Bright sunny days**   If your camera has a setting for sunny days, consider using it to prevent a slight blue cast, like the one shown in Figure 6-10A.

- **Bright overcast days**   Light on these days has an even higher color temperature than a sunny day. Use the cloudy or overcast setting to reduce the amount of blue color cast in the photos. If your camera doesn't have a cloudy WB preset, in most cases you can use the flash preset since bright overcast days have a color temperature close to that of a flash.

- **Early morning seacoasts**   In that first hour after the sun comes up, the coastal beaches tend to produce bluish images. The original photo of the surfer (see Figure 6-10A) was taken with the WB set to Auto; the second photo (Figure 6-10B) used the cloudy WB setting.

- **Subject in the shade**   On a sunny day, if the subject is in the shade, use the shady setting if your camera has one, or use the overcast setting.

- **Subject is lit by incandescent light**   This is a personal choice. I like the reddish-orange hues this kind of lighting creates, but I will sometimes use the preset if the amount of red color is excessive. The photo shown

Did you know?

What Makes Outdoor Color Temperatures Change?

What makes the color temperature of outdoor light vary from the cool colors of a bright sunny day to the reddish-orange of a sunset? Most of the change in color temperature is attributed to the angle of the sun as it passes through the earth's atmosphere. In the early and late parts of the day, the sun is at an acute angle and is filtered by the greatest amount of the earth's atmosphere, while when it is straight overhead, the rays of light pass through the least amount of atmosphere and have a higher color temperature.

The other question that is often asked is "Why are sunsets a burnt-orange color?" Physicists and meteorologists will tell you it has to do with day heating of the atmosphere and the amount of pollution in the lower atmosphere. As a Texan who lives in Austin, I can state that sunsets are burnt-orange because the creator loves the University of Texas Longhorns.

in Figure 6-11 is an interior shot of mission style hotel in Los Angeles shot with WB set to auto. Even with light coming in through the windows, the incandescent light from the chandelier bathes the area with warm colors.

FIGURE 6-10 Coastal early morning shooting can also create photos with bluish photos. The A image was shot with the WB on Auto while the B image was set to cloudy.

A.

B.

6

■ **Color effects**   The WB presets can be used to add color to a photo to produce a color effect. The photo of a bare tree (Figure 6-12) taken last winter was made to look even more stark by using the incandescent/ tungsten WB preset when it was taken. Because the preset assumes that the photo will have a lot of red, it removes the red, making the image very blue (blue is the opposite of red on the color scale).

FIGURE 6-11 The combination of lighting produces warm color cast—much more appealing.

When you use one of the WB presets, make a habit of returning the setting to Automatic after you have finished shooting. If you don't, you may ruin some later photos with the wrong preset.

FIGURE 6-12 WB presets can be used to create color effects, such as using the incandescent WB preset to make this outdoor photo look blue.

Photograph what you love. That's why I have 7963 pictures of my grandchildren!

Carol Bloom, librarian, Los Angeles

Adjusting WB and Auto-bracketing

More and more digital cameras are now offering the ability to increase or decrease the WB preset settings in small amounts (by several hundred degrees K). This is really helpful if you are shooting on an overcast day, but these WB settings are not quite on the money. While every camera is different, most use a system that allows the user to dial in adjustments over a range of +3, +2, and +1 through –1, –2, and –3. Each step represents an increase or decrease of 100 degrees Kelvin. For example, if the WB is set to –2, the WB settings will be –200 degrees from its preset level. A decrease in color temperature means the resulting image will be a little warmer.

Some cameras also offer WB auto-bracketing, which automatically processes the image you just took at multiple WB settings and saves each one as a separate image. This should not be confused with exposure auto-bracketing which required taking multiple photos. WB auto-bracketing does all of the processing from a single exposure. From a menu function, you select how many different WB settings to apply to the image when it is shot. This allows you to select the best photo with the optimum WB setting from the many that were taken after you have loaded it into your photo editor. The major disadvantage to this approach is the extra room that is taken on your memory card and the extra processing time to create the range of images at the different WB settings.

Alternatives to WB Presets

Another way to achieve correct color balance, if your camera supports it, is to save your photos in *raw* format. *Raw* format applies no WB settings when the image is saved so that you can adjust it later. We'll learn more about using a raw format in the next section. The other choice is to calibrate your camera's WB for the light source being used.

Tip

In virtually all digital cameras offering the feature, WB bracketing cannot be used in the raw mode.

Fix WB Later Using Raw Format

To understand the advantage of the raw file format, it is first necessary to understand a little more about how a digital camera processes an image before saving it to the memory card.

When the image is captured by the camera sensor in any mode other than raw, the computer in the camera processes the sensor data before saving it to the memory card. White balance, exposure, tonal corrections, sharpening, and other adjustment are applied to the image before it is saved. If the camera saves images in raw format, the data from the unprocessed charge-coupled device (CCD) or complimentary metal-oxide semiconductor (CMOS) sensor data is saved using a proprietary format that is maker/models specific, such as Nikon's NEF, Canon's CRW, and Kodak's DCR.

These formats are loosely based on the TIFF format, except the resulting image file size is smaller than an uncompressed TIFF image. Figure 6-13 shows the Nikon version of the software that works with raw files. Called NikonCapture, this software gives you the ability to change almost every tonal and color setting of your photo. Only two problems cannot be corrected in an image saved in raw format: if the photo is out of focus or grossly overexposed.

The real advantage offered by saving in raw format is the amount of creative freedom it allows. Using either the manufacturer's proprietary raw processing software or other software, you can change almost anything in an image because you are using your computer to do the processing of the sensor data that is normally done by the camera. You can change the exposure and WB, and with the new Nikon software (Capture 4), you can even automatically remove any dust or debris that may have accumulated on your camera sensor (this is a problem with DSLR cameras with detachable lenses).

Working with Raw Files

The raw image format is composed of either three 12-bit channels or three 14-bit channels (depending on who makes the camera). Traditional RGB files in photo-editing software are made of three 8-bit channels (24-bit color). When the raw

6

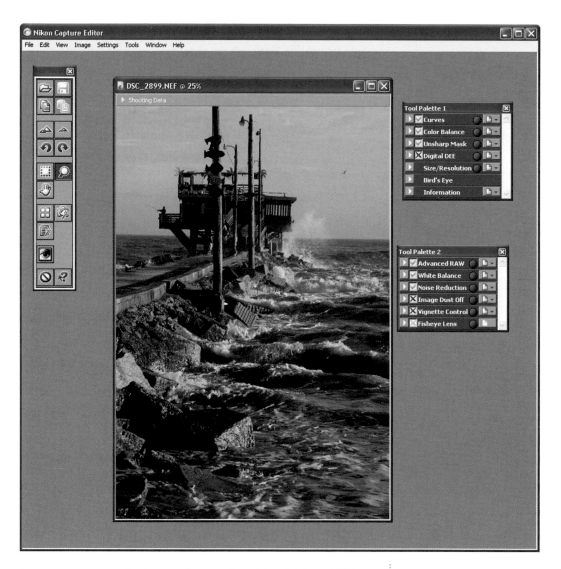

images are converted, they can be saved as either 8-bit or 16-bit files. The disadvantage of a file composed of three 16-bit channels it that is it huge, and many photo-editing software applications offer no or only limited support for such files. The advantage to these files is that they offer greater dynamic range (typically more detail in the shadow regions), and they are great if you are going to blow up the image on a wide-format printer.

FIGURE 6-13 NikonCapture software allows you to adjust and correct your photos to a much greater degree than possible with other formats.

When a raw image is opened using one of the applications that provide raw file processing, you can use your computer to do the processing that is normally done by the camera at the time of the shooting. This means that when you take a photo with the camera set to raw, the unprocessed data from the camera sensor is saved on the memory card. When the raw file is opened on your computer, you can change the WB setting, exposure, and many more settings on your computer just as if you were back at the scene shooting the photo and changing the camera settings.

The major difference is that you are viewing the photo on a large monitor and your computer is several hundred times more powerful than the dedicated processor in your digital camera. The only two factors of a photo saved in raw format that cannot be corrected are focus and shutter speed. For example, if the photo is out of focus or blurred because of incorrect shutter speed, it cannot be saved in this format.

The disadvantage of using raw files is that they are unique, and none of the photo places where you get your photos printed can process them. In addition to the proprietary software provided with the camera (that supports raw format) about six different software packages allow you to open and modify raw image files. Before Adobe added support for raw format in Photoshop Elements and Photoshop CS, these files could be opened only using proprietary software from the camera manufacturer—usually at extra cost or by purchasing Adobe's Photoshop Camera Raw plug-in.

Putting Your Knowledge to Use

While you have learned a lot about WB and the effects of color temperature, it doesn't do any good if you don't put it into practice. Don't let all of the WB settings paralyze you when you shoot photos. When in doubt, keep your WB setting at Auto. As you start evaluating the photos that you have taken, begin to move outside of your comfort zone and experiment with different WB presets.

The key to being able to change your WB settings is to know your camera. If you don't know where the settings are located before you go out shooting, the odds are against you being able to find them in the field. This leads us into the next chapter, where you'll discover all that your camera can do.

6

Part III

Do More Than You Can Imagine

Chapter 7

Discover All Your Camera Can Do

How to...

- Study the manual that came with your camera
- Learn the essential features of your camera
- Identify buttons, dials, and menus
- Find alternatives to the user's manual

Digital Photography Myth Number 7:   The features in your digital camera are identical to those found in film cameras.

Fact: False. Your digital camera has several unique features that don't exist on film cameras.

Even though many digital camera features use the same names as those in film cameras, such as *shutter speed* and *ISO*, several characteristics are unique to digital cameras. These features let you do a lot of cool things with your digital camera that are impossible to do with film cameras. Some digital features are not readily apparent because their names or descriptions don't tell you exactly what they're used for. In this chapter you will learn about your digital camera's unique characteristics and what kinds of things you can do with them. Armed with this information, you will be able to read and understand the camera manual, no matter how technical the manual appears. This chapter will also introduce you to some of the essential parts of your digital camera.

How to Read Your Digital Camera Manual

Most digital camera users I meet have never read the user manual that comes with their camera, and there's a good reason why they don't. The manual that comes with a digital camera is usually

- A small, thick booklet printed in small type (usually in multiple languages).
- Filled with diagrams (identifying the parts) that are so complicated they look like the disassembly instructions for a nuclear weapon. A partial sample is shown in Figure 7-1.

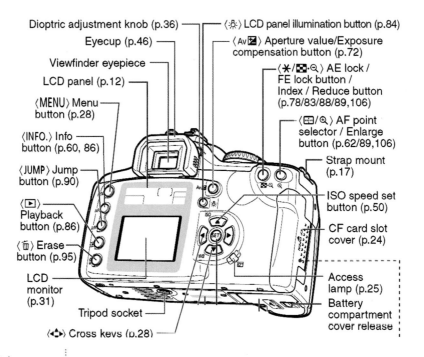

Dioptric adjustment knob (p.36) ⎯⎯⎯⎯ ⟨☀⟩ LCD panel illumination button (p.84)

Eyecup (p.46) ⎯⎯ ⟨Av⊠⟩ Aperture value/Exposure
compensation button (p.72)

Viewfinder eyepiece ⎯ ⟨✻/⊡·�ℚ⟩ AE lock /
FE lock button /
Index / Reduce button
(p.78/83/88/89,106)

LCD panel (p.12) ⎯⎯

⟨MENU⟩ Menu⎯
button (p.28)

⟨🖽/ℚ⟩ AF point
selector / Enlarge
button (p.62/89,106)

⟨INFO.⟩ Info⎯
button (p.60, 86)

Strap mount
(p.17)

⟨JUMP⟩ Jump⎯
button (p.90)

ISO speed set
button (p.50)

⟨▶⟩⎯
Playback
button (p.86)

CF card slot
cover (p.24)

⟨🗑⟩ Erase⎯
button (p.95)

LCD⎯
monitor
(p.31)

Access
lamp (p.25)

Battery
compartment
cover release

Tripod socket ⎯

⟨✛⟩ Cross keys (p.28) ⎯

FIGURE 7-1 Digital camera user
manuals can appear intimidating.

▪ Heavily cross-referenced, making reading difficult.
Here's an example: "The flash mode (page 65) can
be changed using the command dial (pages 12, 23)
in combination with the mode button (page 42)."

▪ Loaded with photographic terminology. Most manuals
assume that the reader has a working knowledge of
photography and explain how the features work using
photographic terminology. For example, here is a quote
from a manual, explaining the AWB setting: "Normally
the AWB sets optimum white balance automatically.
If natural colors cannot be obtained using the default
AWB settings, set the white balance manually to suit
the respective light source." This makes sense to me,
but I have been working in the field for a long time.

In fairness, some manuals are more user-friendly than
others. The manual that came with my Nikon D-100 correctly
assumes that if you are buying a digital single-lens reflex (SLR)
camera that costs as much as your first car, you are probably a
photographer, and the user manual is a 160-page collection of

facts. On the other hand, some camera manuals are written with beginners in mind. An example of this is found in Figure 7-2, which is from a manual for a late model digital camera made by Kodak. Regardless of how good or bad the manual for your camera is, you need to spend some time reading it and learning how the camera works.

Read Your Quick Start Guide

Camera manufacturers want you to like using the camera you just bought, so they usually include some sort of quick start guide to help get you going. Amazingly, many digital camera users have not even gone through these basics. At the very least, you should read this thoroughly and understand how to use your camera to take basic photos. In some cases, the quick start guide will be a separate document, or it may be the first chapter of the manual, entitled something like "Taking Your First Photo."

The quick start guide or the first part of the user guide usually covers only the most basic automatic operation of the camera. Most manuals use the same organization, so if the quick start guide is in the book you will probably need to wade through the following sections before you get to the important parts:

- **Safety Warnings**   Usually a dozen or more warnings are included. (My favorite warning told the user "Do not submerge the battery charger while charging.")

- **Controls, Buttons, and Dials**   This is the typically cluttered map, similar to the one shown in Figure 7-1, that shows the names and locations of all of the buttons and dials on the camera.

- **Shooting Your First Photo**   This is the part that you'll want to review (if you have already read it). This section will take you through a basic camera setup that will help you take a fully automatic photo—with no frills or extras. If you follow the step-by-step procedure outlined in this section, you should get the best possible photos, assuming that the lighting is adequate.

Chapter 2

Taking a Burst Series of Pictures

Burst lets you to take up to 4 pictures in quick succession (approximately 1.4 frames per second). Burst is ideal for capturing sporting events or objects in motion. When you use the Burst feature, the Flash and the Self Timer are disabled.

Turn On Burst

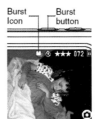

Burst Icon   Burst button

In any Still mode, press the Self Timer button **twice**.

The Burst icon appears in the status area. The setting remains until you change it or turn off the camera.

Take the Pictures

1 Press the Shutter button *half-way and hold* to set the auto-focus and exposure for all the pictures in the sequence.

2 Press the Shutter button *the rest of the way down* and hold it to take the pictures.

   The camera takes up to 4 pictures in quick succession. It stops taking pictures when the Shutter button is released, when 4 pictures are taken, or when there is no more storage space.

   Exposure, focus, white balance, and orientation that are set for the first picture are applied to all 4 pictures.

FIGURE 7-2   Some manuals are more user friendly than others.

Identify the Basic Controls and Features

When I teach a digital camera workshop in the field, the most often asked question will be someone handing me a camera asking, "Where is the [feature name] on my camera?" Because each camera manufacturer makes its cameras and the related features in its own unique way, I often don't know where the feature is located on the camera model. The best way to find all the features is to—you guessed it—read the manual.

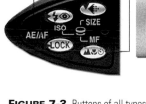

Shutter button

MENU

INFO.

JUMP

Multi-function

Single function   Multi-function

Digital cameras have a lot of functionality jammed into a small package. As a result, the manufacturer has to design buttons and other controls to maximize the number of features that each button or dial controls to keep the actual number of buttons to a minimum. This means that only a few buttons on a digital camera do only one thing. For example, on my Nikon, a single button can be used either to zoom in on the image in the LCD screen or to delete the image—what it does depends on what mode of operation the camera is in.

Basically, three kinds of controls are included on your camera: buttons, dials, and menu selectable items.

All Kinds of Buttons

These are usually multi-function buttons for selecting features that are often used or that need to be changed quickly (such as the shutter button), as opposed to items you select from a menu that take time and some effort to change (such as a compression setting). Buttons are used either to turn a function on or off (like menu or power), perform a single function (like the shutter button) or it can be used to toggle through several choices (like flash modes). Figure 7-3 shows examples of the many different types and styles of buttons found on digital cameras.

FIGURE 7-3 Buttons of all types are found on digital cameras.

Dials

Like buttons, dials allow a quick selection from a series of choices of often-used items or features. An example of how many choices can fit into a dial is shown in Figure 7-4. This dial allows the selection of nine different modes, controls or features.

Menu Selectable Items

Everything on your camera that is not controlled by either buttons or dials is probably found buried in the camera's menu system. Depending on the complexity of the camera, the menu system may be a simple series of just a few choices of settings, or it may be a complex of multi-level controls like the type found in a professional digital SLR (D-SLR). Menu selections may appear superimposed over an image in the LCD screen on a multiple choice screen like the one shown in Figure 7-5. Most user manuals contain a section or chart that illustrates each menu and gives directions to navigate to a specific menu item.

A Sensible Approach to Learning About Your Camera

If you attempt to learn all of the buttons, dials, and menu controls in a single sitting, you will probably forget about more than half of them by the time you use your camera. Most humans learn best by physical association. To learn the locations and uses of your camera's features, try the following approach:

- Hold the camera in your hand (as shown in Figure 7-6) as you read through the manual; don't just look at the diagrams in the user guide. Studies show that your retention rate increases by more than 70 percent if you physically perform the task rather than just read about it.

- Practice locating and changing the essential settings described later in this chapter—learn especially how to review and delete images from the camera.

- Learn how to reset the camera to its factory default settings. This is important to know, and I will repeat it several times in this chapter. There will probably come a time when you'll inadvertently change some setting, and all of your images will look bad or weird. Knowing how to reset the

FIGURE 7-4 An example of a single dial allowing selection of nine different choices

FIGURE 7-5 Menu selection provides a great number of choices from the LCD screen.

FIGURE 7-6 You won't master your camera unless you apply what you learn with the camera in your hand.

camera to the factory settings will get you back to the correct basic settings, and this will help you figure out what went wrong.

After you understand the basics of your camera, you'll probably find that many more advanced features still need to be figured out. The best way to master these features is to learn about them as you need them. For example, if your camera has a noise reduction feature, you don't really need to learn about it until you begin working on low-light or night photography.

How to ... Select and Work with Multiple Images

If your camera supports it, you can select multiple images for deletion instead of deleting them one at a time. This feature becomes most important when, after taking 10 or 20 photos, you realize that the memory card in your camera is still storing photos that you've already downloaded to your computer and that should have been erased. To reformat the card at this point means you would lose those photos you just took, but to delete the 50 photos you already downloaded one at a time would take forever. If you know your camera allows it, you can select several images at once and delete them with a single command.

Conversely, many cameras can protect multiple images by locking them, so they can't be erased. Once you have identified a *keeper* image, it's a good idea to protect it from accidental erasure. Protected images can be deleted only by formatting the flash card.

A Scavenger Hunt for Essential Camera Features

Because digital cameras have so many features, it can be a formidable task to try and learn them all. The following list of digital camera essentials narrows down the features to those that you should be able to locate and use on your camera. I call this a "scavenger hunt" because you will find yourself digging through your manual, looking for the answers. (I could have called it an "open book test," but that doesn't sound like fun.) You should be able to locate and use all of the following features/ functions of your camera. Explanatory text and examples are included where applicable.

Reset Camera Settings

Though already mentioned, this feature is so important that it is worth repeating. This setting, usually found as a menu item, resets all of the camera settings back to the way they were set when the camera left the factory. Called *master reset* or *restore factory defaults*, this is the command that you need to use when you've exhausted other options and the camera still isn't working properly.

Tip *After you reset your camera, make sure that you immediately turn off the digital zoom as it is the one feature that has the potential to degrade your pictures. This tip will be repeated throughout the book, because it's an important one.*

Changing Light Meter Settings

On most consumer cameras, the light meter setting is controlled by a menu setting. On semiprofessional and professional cameras, it is usually a dial setting, similar to the one shown in Figure 7-7, so it can be easily changed as the lighting changes. On a typical shoot, I change my light metering a dozen times as the light and my relationship to the position of the light source change.

FIGURE 7-7 The light meter settings of this camera can be quickly changed as the lighting changes.

Use Quality Settings for More Room

The quality settings control the amount of compression applied to the saved images, and in some cameras you can select from several file formats, such as JPEG, TIFF, and raw formats. In most cases, you'll find a quality setting that suits you and will rarely change it. However, once in a while, you'll discover that you are running out of room on your media card and you don't have another card to use. To take additional photos, you must either remove some existing images on the card or decrease the quality setting (increased compression) of the remaining photos to make more room. For example, suppose my camera is set at the highest quality setting, and it indicates that it has space for only four more images. If I change the quality setting from the highest quality setting to a medium setting, the indicator will show that there is now room for 16 more images.

The quality settings used on a media card can be changed at any time. Ultimately, you must decide to accept the tradeoff between making room for the photos and the decrease in quality caused by increasing the compression. In practice, however, the quality difference between JPEG compression levels is very small at the highest and next levels. For instance, on my Nikon, I can barely tell the difference between JPEG images shot in the Fine and Normal modes. And by moving down to Normal, I get twice as many images per card.

 Because the file size of a compressed size can only be approximated by the camera, it may indicate that space for only one image remains. However, after that last photo is taken, you may find that there's space for yet one more shot.

White Balance Settings

FIGURE 7-8 Many digital cameras set white balance settings through menu selections on the LCD screen.

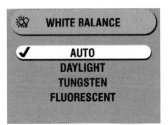

White balance (WB) settings are unique to digital cameras. The WB setting determines the color accuracy of your camera. By default, the white balance setting of your digital camera is set to Automatic. Some cameras use a dial and others use a menu setting to change from Automatic White Balance (AWB) to one of a myriad of presets, such as Incandescent, Cloudy, Daylight, Fireworks, and so on. An example of the white balance selection menu found on a Kodak camera is shown in Figure 7-8.

Control the Focus Distance

Although the auto-focus feature is great, your camera has two other focus modes that you need to be familiar with: macro mode (also called close-up on some cameras) and landscape (infinity lock) mode. Most cameras use a button you push to change to the macro mode. Every camera I have ever seen shows a tulip-shaped icon next to the button you press to put the camera in macro mode. The same icon appears in the LCD status screen to indicate that the camera is in macro mode. If your camera has a landscape focus setting, it will probably show an icon with little mountains next to the macro mode icon, as shown here.

Note *When most digital cameras are set in landscape mode, the flash will not operate.*

Flash Mode Settings

Your camera has several flash modes that are selected by pushing a button on the camera body or by using a dial. The most common flash modes that you will select are auto, red-eye reduction, manual (also called fill flash), and off. Unlike macro and landscape modes, manufacturers use many different icons for flash modes, except most of them are some variation of the bent arrow icon shown here. For information on using your flash (either built-in or external), see Chapter 9.

Finding the Diopter Adjustment

A few digital cameras offer a *diopter* adjustment near the optical viewfinder, like the one shown in Figure 7-9. This optical correction is a godsend for those of us who wear glasses. You can use the diopter adjustment so that what you see through the optical viewfinder appears in focus when you are looking through it while not wearing your glasses.

What if your camera doesn't have a diopter adjustment? You might be able to find a diopter accessory from an optometrist. Even if you have a diopter adjustment but your eye correction is greater than the diopter can handle, you can usually buy an accessory that will increase the correction of the viewfinder even more than the diopter slider can handle.

FIGURE 7-9 Diopter adjustments correct the viewfinder optics for your eyesight.

Diopter adjustment slider

 If you wear glasses, I recommend getting an eyeglasses strap so that you can take your glasses off and let them hang from your neck while taking photos. Don't use a short strap made for sports. You want to get a thin one that lets the glasses dangle out of the way.

Control Your Time-Date Stamp

Film camera manufacturers came up with a cute doodad some years back—a feature that imprints a time-date stamp in a corner of the negative so that when you are looking at the print a few years later, you'll be able to tell when the photo was taken. Some digital cameras have also included this feature and put the date stamp in the lower part of the photo, like the one shown in Figure 7-10. Adding the stamp on your film photos may have

merit, but adding one to a digital photo just clutters up the photo and isn't necessary. If you need to figure out when the photo was taken, you need only to open the file and read the EXIF information that is stored in the original image file. There you'll find the photo date and other information.

This feature is turned on or off through your camera's menus. I strongly recommend that you turn it off.

FIGURE 7-10 On a digital camera, the feature that puts the date stamp in the corner of the photo should be turned off.

Learn to Decipher Your Camera Icons

There isn't enough room on the body of your camera to write out the entire names of button and dial labels, so icons are used to indicate the camera status and to label controls. When you are learning how to use the features of your camera, get familiar with the icons associated with each feature or mode; this way, when you're wondering why the camera isn't working as expected, you can look at the LCD status screen like the one shown in Figure 7-11 (not the LCD viewing screen) and see what features are turned on or turned off.

FIGURE 7-11 The status screen gives a quick summary of important settings on your camera.

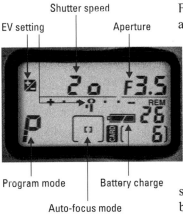

Discover Shortcuts for Your Camera Settings

Some digital cameras have shortcuts included to help you quickly change settings. For example, on my Nikon, if I press two particular buttons at the same time, the camera will prepare to format the memory card without my having to open the menu and select the option there. Most of these shortcuts involve pressing buttons in combination, and they can be real time-savers. Discussions of most of the shortcuts are cleverly hidden in the manual. As you find and learn each feature of your camera, make a note of any feature shortcuts.

In my manual, I use a yellow highlighter to highlight the shortcut or feature I may need to find in a hurry some day. (Yeah, my memory isn't what it used to be.)

Other shortcuts in your camera may be accessed via programmable buttons or dials. On professional digital cameras, many features are used only in certain photographic situations, such as changing the sensor size. For a photographer who needs a particular set of features to be handy, buttons and dials can be programmed so that you can quickly change the settings that they are programmed to control. Programming a dial or button sounds complicated, but it isn't. Usually it is accomplished through menu selection and the procedure is often found in the advanced section of the user manual. Just because it is in the advanced part of the manual doesn't mean you should not be using it.

Alternatives to the User Manual

Some books have been written specifically for a particular model of digital camera. These books are typically found in camera stores or via web sites. A newer, more popular form of this type of book is the e-book, which can be purchased and downloaded from the Web, or the author/publisher will send you a CD. If you haven't reviewed the book, before you buy it online you should check online forums, chat rooms, and reviews to see what others think of the book. I once bought a book by an author (who shall remain nameless) about a digital camera that I was using. I was disappointed (ticked off) when I discovered that the majority of the book was a rehash of a film photography book he had written a few years earlier, to which a few chapters about the camera had been added. Had I read reviews of the book before I bought it, I may have saved myself a few bucks.

Online Digital Camera Forums

Before you buy a camera, you should do a little research to find the unit that offers the best features for you. Online digital camera forums are a great resource to learn about what a particular digital camera can and cannot do. I highly recommend Phil Askey's excellent web site, "Digital Photography Review" (http://www.dpreview.com). In addition to detailed reviews and news, Phil's site offers online forums that are manufacturer-specific.

On more than one occasion, I needed some information that even the manufacturer's technical support couldn't (or wouldn't) provide. I posted the question on the forum and within an hour I had the answer.

Learn What You Can

If you apply yourself and make the effort to learn everything you can about your camera, you'll find that your photography improves; following this advice is better than just buying any accessory you can find. Make the investment of time to learn the ins and outs of your camera, and you will be rewarded for the effort.

A last piece of advice: Even if you do read your user manual as I've advised, don't put it away. Mine is a constant travel companion that I consult often to remember some vital feature I've forgotten (see Figure 7-12).

FIGURE 7-12 Always keep your user manual handy and write your camera's serial number on it.

Nikon

S/N 118716

NIKON CORPORATION
Fuji Bldg., 2-3 Marunouchi 3-chome,
Chiyoda-ku, Tokyo 100-8331, Japan

Printed in Japan
S2I05000301(11)
6MBA0111-03

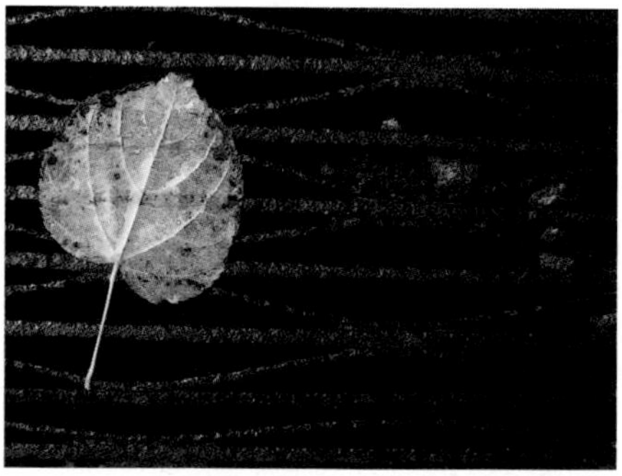

Chapter 8

Get Ready to Share Your Photos

How to...

- Move photos from your camera to your computer
- Print stunning color photos
- Know the difference between inkjet and dye-sub printers
- Select the best color printer
- Attach photos to your e-mail

Digital Photography Myth Number 8: The problem with digital cameras is that they don't take real photos.

Fact: Photos taken by a digital camera are just as "real" as photos taken by a film camera.

After taking digital photos, you can produce conventional, high-quality printed images, but you can also use an astounding number of methods to produce other photo paraphernalia. Did you know that you can have your photo printed onto a cookie? This chapter covers many of the options you have at your disposal when it comes time to print and share your digital masterpieces.

Moving Photos to Your Computer

FIGURE 8-1 This camera dock serves as a battery charger and a connection to the computer.

The first digital cameras used serial connections to transfer photos from the camera into the computer, which was complicated to set up and unbelievably slow. Now most digital cameras offer a USB (Universal Serial Bus) connection to transfer the photos either using a USB cable or, lately, the combination of USB and charging cradle like the one shown in Figure 8-1. Some professional cameras offer a FireWire (IEEE-1394) interface that is about 40 times faster than USB 1.1.

Voices
from the
Community

Digital cameras and photo printers are a godsend to us scrapbookers. It used to take a lot of work to get extra copies of photos I wanted to include in my scrapbook pages. Now I can print as many copies as I want, at whatever size I need.

Denise, single mom and the queen of scrapbooks

On the Windows platform (Me, XP, and 2000), the first time you attach your camera to the computer, the operating system reads data from the camera and then opens a dialog box that allows you to choose the action of importing the images.

Using Card Readers to Import Photos

An increasingly popular method for bringing photos from a digital camera into Photoshop or other photo manipulation software is to use a card reader. These devices, like the one shown in Figure 8-2, are inexpensive and come in many different sizes and configurations. Because card readers do not use the internal processor of the camera, this method is noticeably faster than using a USB-connected camera to transfer the photos, and it doesn't drain your camera's batteries.

FIGURE 8-2 A card reader is an inexpensive accessory that speeds up the transfer of photos into your computer.

Costing around $25 or less, card readers interface with the computer using its USB interface or PCMCIA slots (a great choice for notebook users). You can purchase a reader designed for your specific type of memory card or purchase one of the six-way card readers that can read any of the following memory card formats (listed in the order of their popularity):

- **CompactFlash (CF)**   Currently the most popular memory device for digital cameras.

- **MultiMedia Card (MMC)**   About the size of a postage stamp, it is gaining in popularity because it can also be used in Personal Digital Assistants (PDAs) and MP3 players.

- **SecureDigital card (SD)**   A variation of the MMC offering similar capacities and connectivity, plus it has security features that can be used by PDAs and similar devices to protect sensitive information.

- **Memory Stick (MS)**   Primarily used on Sony equipment, it's about the size of a stick of gum. The Memory Stick supports up to 128MB of data while the Memory Stick Pro supports capacities beyond 128MB.

- **SmartMedia (SM)**   The "BetaMax of memory devices." When consumer digital cameras first appeared, camera manufacturers offered either CompactFlash or SmartMedia. Today, few, if any, new cameras support SmartMedia.

- **xD Picture Card**   This proprietary card is used by Olympus and Fuji cameras. It has yet to see any popular support from other camera or memory manufacturers.

- **Microdrives**   In the early days of digital photography, CompactFlash was expensive and didn't have a large capacity. IBM invented a tiny disk drive called a Microdrive that could fit into the CompactFlash slot of a digital camera if the camera supported it. Microdrives can hold up to 4GB. They are noticeably slower than CompactFlash memory but on very high capacities much more cost effective. The only caveat is that Microdrives are electro-mechanical devices that can fail, and with such large capacities, that represents a lot of eggs in a very small basket.

   Card readers using faster FireWire can transfer images four times faster than the original USB (1.0) readers for a slightly higher price.

Printing Photos with Your Printer

Several years ago your only choice for printing the photos you took with a digital camera was using a computer and a printer. The inkjet printers of the time made photos that looked quite similar to the photos produced by professional photo developers.

Today, photo printers make outstanding prints, and the quality is good enough for any use. With the increasing popularity of digital cameras, several choices are available for making photos from your digital cameras.

Inkjet and Dye-Sub Printers

You can use two types of photo printers to print your photos: inkjet and dye-sublimation (dye-sub) printers. Inkjet printers, the most popular, produce photo-quality images in almost any size you desire. Dye-sub printers print photos in dedicated sizes, with the most popular being 4×6 inches. The quality of dye-sub prints is outstanding, but the cost of each dye-sub print is almost three times that of the same size print made on an inkjet printer. Sony makes an excellent dye-sublimation printer, as does Hewlett-Packard. The Sony photo printer is shown in Figure 8-3.

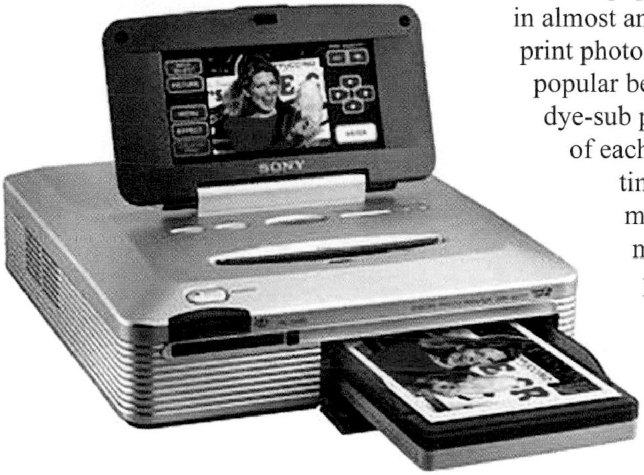

FIGURE 8-3 The Sony photo printer produces high quality photos.

The Difference Between Inkjets

The difference between a regular inkjet printer and a photo inkjet printer is a matter of ink: the photo inkjet uses either six or seven inks, while a standard inkjet uses only four inks. Some potential buyers get confused when they look for a printer because the photo print samples produced by the inkjet printers look remarkably similar to prints produced by the photo printers. Knowing that, should you get a dedicated photo printer or a standard inkjet? The answer depends on what and how much you print. Here are some scenarios and the recommended solutions:

- **Photos only**   You want the printer to print photos and you do very little document printing. Get a photo printer.

- **Mostly documents and some photos**   If the majority of your printing is producing documents and you occasionally want to print photos, you shouldn't get a photo printer because a photo printer is slower and the cost per copy is higher.

- **An even mix of both photos and documents**   If you print a lot of documents and photos, and your budget can handle it, you should get separate printers. However, some manufacturers now offer inkjet printers that use one set of inks just for photos, and a different (less expensive) black ink for text. (The Canon 860i and 960i models provide this functionality.)

8

Printing Photos Without Your Computer

Most photo printers (both inkjet and dye-sub) offer the ability to read the media card from you camera and print without involving your computer. Some of these printers offer limited cropping and photo enhancement ability. The printer shown in Figure 8-4 has the ability to preview and print photos without the use of a computer.

Photo courtesy of Hewlett-Packard

Advantages and Disadvantages of Printing Your Photos

There are many services that will print your digital photos. Why print at home? Here are some of the advantages to using a home printer:

FIGURE 8-4 The self-contained photo printer allows you to preview and select photos before printing them.

- ▨ You can print photos in sizes greater than 4×6 or 5×7. Depending on the printer you use, most inkjet photo printers can print sizes up to 8×10. Some can print 11×17 and panorama images. Enlargements of photos at photo developers are much more expensive than printing at home.

- ▨ You can choose from a wide variety of photo papers and print each shot on a different type of paper if you want.

- ▨ You can adjust the color of the photos using your computer. The photo developer processes the digital image as is. When you print the photos at home, you can adjust the colors before you make a print.

- ▨ You can print multiple photos, even different sized photos, on the same sheet of photo paper. Most photo editors offer this ability.

The disadvantages of the printing with your own printer include these:

- ▨ You incur the expense of buying the printer and the sustaining cost of buying supplies for it.

■ The time and bother it takes to make prints as opposed to taking a media card to a developer or uploading it to an online photo site may make home printing not worth your while.

Photo Papers

One of the best options with an inkjet printer (both photo and standard inkjet) is the ability to print on a variety of photo papers. Papers come in standard printer sizes in a variety of custom configurations, such as gift bags, greeting cards, stickers, double-sided brochure blanks—and the list goes on.

In addition to the standard mix of photo papers, glossy and matte finish, some companies offer museum quality media such as watercolor paper and even canvas. Some of the specialty papers offer increased print longevity by reducing the natural susceptibility of inkjet prints to fade over time—which brings up the next topic: making prints that last.

Making Prints That Last: Dye-Based vs. Pigment-Based Inks

Almost every inkjet printer that is sold today uses dye-based inks. These inks are brighter and more vivid than the pigment-based inks that are used by commercial printers. The problem with dye-based inks is that they are less resistant to fading over time. The issue of print fading has really gotten blown out of proportion over the past few years, so it's important that you understand the truth and the practical workarounds.

Everything fades. Dye-based prints fade over time. That is a fact. Color photos made from film fade over time. That is a fact as well. Color photos made using a pigment-based inkjet printer also fade in about 100 years. The only images that have not faded significantly over the years are the frescos that were buried in Pompeii and the hieroglyphics deep inside the Egyptian tombs. With everything else, it's just a matter of how long it takes for the colors to decrease in intensity.

Tip   *To slow down the fading of photos, regardless of how they are produced, keep them out of direct sunlight and limit exposure to air. Short-term studies have shown that images behind glass and away from direct sunlight will last six times longer than unprotected images. Most faded images are the result of continual exposure to daylight.*

Did you know?

The Difference Between Dye-Based and Pigment-Based Printers

The colors produced by dye-based inks are bright and vivid, while the colors produced by a printer using pigment-based inks typically look a little dull by comparison. The advantage of the pigment-based inks is longevity. A typical pigment-based color print is expected to last 100 years, while a dye-based photo may begin to fade in less than 20 years. Epson is the sole manufacturer of pigment-based ink printers. Their original pigment-based printer is the Photo Stylus 2000.

Although the colors may last, they didn't compare well with the prints from a dye-based photo, so Epson went to work to improve the printer. After making serious improvements to this printer, Epson released a new version, the Photo Stylus 2200, that offers the print longevity of pigment-based inks and the vivid colors of dye-based inks. So, why aren't all of the inkjet printers pigment-based? Cost. The 2200 costs four times as much as a typical dye-based inkjet printer.

To put the fading color issue into perspective, here's a scenario: Let's assume that you used your dye-based printer to make a print of a photo you took with your digital camera. Fifteen years later, you decide that the print isn't looking as vivid as it once did. You take the CD containing the digital photo, and using the new photo printer that you bought a few years ago (which is vastly superior to the one you originally printed the photo with 15 years ago), make another print that looks even better than the first one you printed.

Other Ways to Print Your Digital Photos

It is no longer necessary to use a printer to print images from your digital camera. Two alternatives to printing your own photos are available: local film developers and online developers.

Local Photo Developers

Most local film developers can accept images from your digital camera and print color photos just as they do with film. Many developers use a kiosk setup, like the one shown in Figure 8-5, that allows you to insert the media containing your photos and

FIGURE 8-5 Kiosks like this one offer an easy way to print images.

select the images that you want to print. Just like film, you can usually get one-hour service as well as the normal turnaround times. Some of the kiosks even let you make minor photo enhancements at the same time that you select the images.

Most of these photo developers accept media other than film media, such as a CD-ROM disc, and a kiosk I work with even accepts a Zip disk. The most commonly asked question concerns the type of photos that are produced. The photos are the same as those that are created from film negatives—same paper, same colors.

Online Photo Developers

In addition to printing and using a local photo developer, some great online photo sharing sites also serve as photo developers. You simply upload your photos to an Internet site like the one shown in Figure 8-6. You can order prints, and they can be mailed to you. A real advantage to this approach is that you can e-mail the web site information to others and they can view the photos online. The even better part is that they can also order prints from the same site (which means that they will be paying for the prints, and not you).

Most online sites offer much more than just photos. You can get your photos printed on just about anything, including

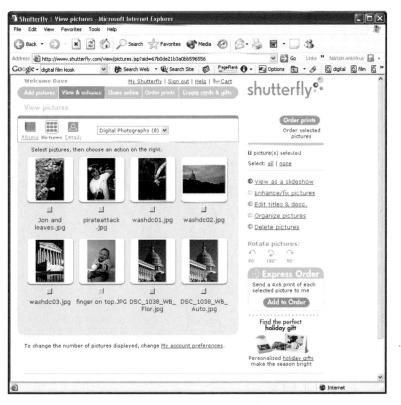

FIGURE 8-6 Online photo sites like this one are a good way to share and print photos.

coffee cups, t-shirts, and even cookies. Here are two of the more popular photo sites (of many) on the Internet:

- **Ofoto, http://www.ofoto.com** Owned by Kodak; need I say more?

- **Shutterfly, http://www.shutterfly.com** Another major online photo service offering a wide selection of services.

Advantages (and Cost) of a Professional Finisher

On some occasions, when you have taken a fantastic or important photo and you want to get the best possible print, you can usually find camera stores that offer custom digital photo printing. You can also find digital printing services online that are often used by professionals. This usually involves enhancement and correction of any problems in the photos by one of their staff before printing. These services cost a premium price, but for really important photos, it's worth it.

Share Photos Using E-mail

In addition to posting photos on a photo-sharing site, another popular way to share your favorite photos is to send them to people with e-mail. You can add photos to e-mail in two ways:

- **Attach photos to e-mails** Photo image files, like any other kind of file, can be attached to an e-mail.

- **Embed photos in e-mails** Photos can be embedded in e-mails, so that when the e-mail is opened the photo appears.

Image Size, ISPs, and Connection Speed

When sending photos to people via e-mail, be aware that different e-mail services have built-in size limitations. Your Internet Service Provider (ISP) or your recipient's ISP may not allow attaching an image that is larger than a few megabytes (MB). While these numbers are always subject to change, Hotmail and AOL currently don't allow file attachments greater than 1MB in size. Going over the limit will usually result in the e-mail never arriving at its destination.

You should also be aware that sending someone a big file in an e-mail may be inconsiderate. Unless you know the person receiving the e-mail has a broadband connection (DSL or cable modem), sending a 1MB download to someone with a slow dial-up connection can take anywhere from 1 to 10 minutes to load onto their computer. When your recipient checks e-mail, he or she will have to wait until the entire image is downloaded—there's no way to tell the software to quit downloading a specific e-mail.

Another factor regarding the file size of your photo is how the figure will display on the recipient's screen. If your high-resolution 21-inch monitor is running at a resolution of 1280×1024, a photo that fits neatly on your screen will appear many times too large to someone running 800×600 on a 14-inch display. To accommodate this problem, your best bet is to resize your photo before you send it.

How to ...   Resize Your Photo to Fit

Most photo editors now offer an e-mail feature that will automatically resize your photo to a smaller size and attach it to an e-mail for you. The only problem with this approach is that you have no control over what size the final image will be or the quality setting of the compression. Since it is the job of the application to make the image as small as reasonable for attachment to an e-mail, the photos can at times suffer in the conversion.

The best way to resize the image, then, is to use your photo editor's resizing feature, and after it's resized, apply a little sharpening to the final image to compensate for the softness that results from making the photo smaller. For simple display on your recipient's screen or printing to a snapshot size from e-mail, an image resolution of 640×480 at 72 pixels per inch (ppi) is ideal and won't cause your recipients' computers to bog down.

Attach a Photo to an E-mail

Attaching a photo (or any other file, for that matter) to an e-mail is easy. Follow these steps to attach a photo to an e-mail using Outlook Express.

1. Create a new e-mail, similar to the one shown in Figure 8-7.

FIGURE 8-7 Begin the process of attaching a photo to an e-mail.

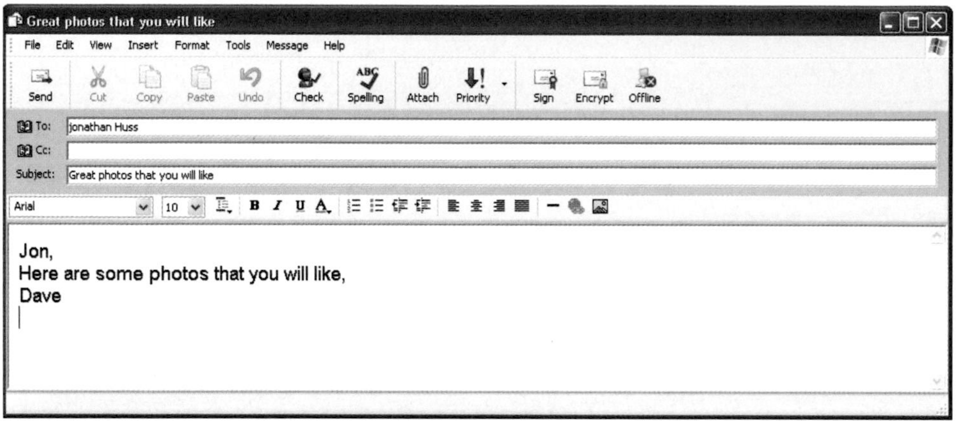

2. Click the paperclip icon, and when the Insert Attachment dialog box opens, select the file that you want to attach to the e-mail (see Figure 8-8) and click

FIGURE 8-8 Select the photo file to attach.

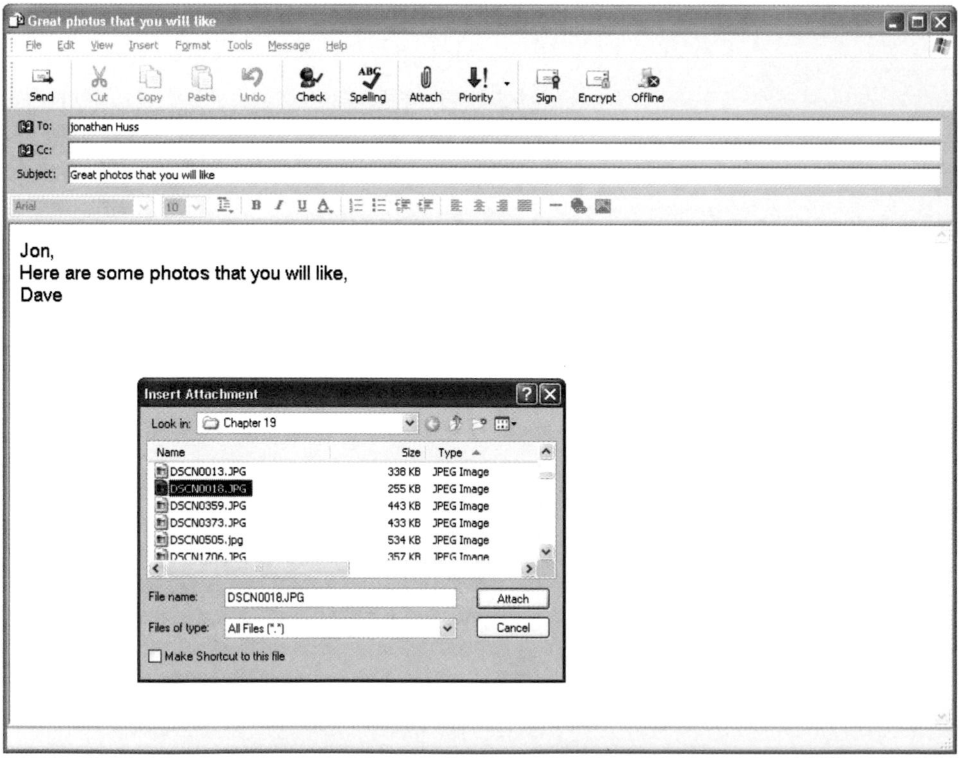

OK. You may have to navigate to the appropriate file or folder.

3. Click the Send button and the e-mail is sent with the photo attached.

How the photo appears to the recipient of the e-mail depends on the operating system and e-mail software he or she is using. The photos may appear as an attachment or they may actually be displayed in the e-mail.

Embedding a Photo in an E-mail

If you want to make the photo appear in the actual e-mail message, you need to embed the photo in the e-mail. You should be aware that some restrictions and limitations may affect this approach. First, the mail must be in HTML format; if the e-mail is formatted in plain text, no option is available for embedding a picture into the mail. One major restriction of embedding a picture in an e-mail is that some of your recipients may not be able to open it or in some cases see the photo.

Here is how to embed a photo to an e-mail using Outlook Express:

1. Create a new e-mail.

2. Choose Format | Rich Text (HTML) or Send Pictures With Message.

3. Choose Insert | Picture.

4. When the Picture dialog box opens, choose the photo you want to embed in the e-mail. You may have to click the Browse button to navigate to the folder that contains the image. The e-mail will display the photo in the message area, like the one shown in Figure 8-9.

5. Click the Send button and the e-mail will be sent.

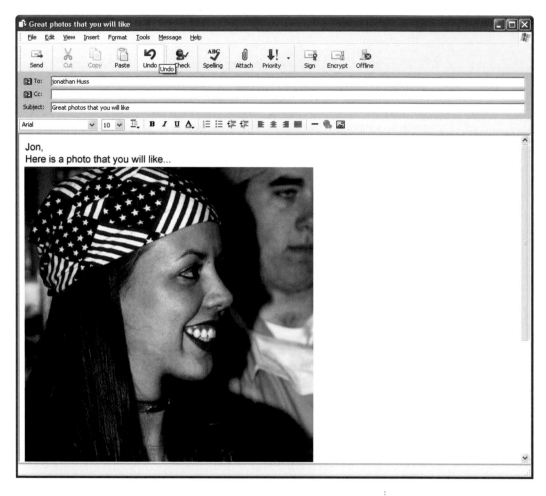

Now that we have covered the basics of sharing your digital photos, in the next chapter you will learn some tips and tricks to help you take perfect flash photographs.

FIGURE 8-9 Embedding a photo in an e-mail

Chapter 9

Use Flash Photography to Your Advantage

How to...

- Understand basic flash operation
- Know the various types of flash units
- Use your flash effectively
- Identify and avoid flash problems
- Use your flash creatively

Digital Photography Myth Number 9:   Using the red-eye reduction flash setting on your digital camera prevents red-eye.

Fact: It's been known to happen—but don't count on it.

Because you can do so much with the built-in flash on your camera or with an optional external flash, this chapter is dedicated to the subject. You will discover how to get the most out of using a flash, including some tricks to get rid of red-eye when the red-eye reduction feature doesn't work (which is most of the time). You will also learn about the types of flash devices that are available, some professional but easy ways to use the flash to reduce or remove shadows on outdoor shoots, and other photo-saving flash tricks.

FIGURE 9-1 If not properly used, the flash on your camera can ruin a photo.

What Your Flash Can Do

All digital cameras have built-in flash units that automatically fire when insufficient light is available to get a proper exposure (or at least an automatic flash is *supposed* to happen). Your camera's flash is a marvelous tool that can be used in many different shooting situations with mixed results. The problem most people experience when using their flash is that it can make the subject appear washed out, as in the photo shown in Figure 9-1. In this case, because the flash provided too much light, most of the detail in the photo is unrecoverable.

Another terrible thing that a flash can do is reveal and exaggerate all of the imperfections in a subject's face and make him or her look grotesque.

Nevertheless, flash is a valuable tool for taking photos in darkened or ill-lit rooms or outside at night, shooting backlit

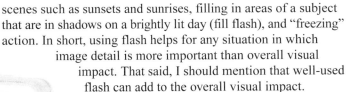

Flash

Flash sensor

FIGURE 9-2 The integral flash that's flush with the camera body is unobtrusive.

FIGURE 9-3 The pop-up style built-in flash is more effective at reducing red-eye.

scenes such as sunsets and sunrises, filling in areas of a subject that are in shadows on a brightly lit day (fill flash), and "freezing" action. In short, using flash helps for any situation in which image detail is more important than overall visual impact. That said, I should mention that well-used flash can add to the overall visual impact.

The Need for Flash

Given a long enough exposure, digital cameras can capture images with almost any amount of light, even from sources as dim as candlelight or moonlight. Even in low-light conditions, the amount of time it takes to expose an image today requires only a fraction of a second; still, if you want a sharp image in low-light situations, you will need to provide some extra light to get a proper exposure.

Camera manufacturers recognize that a built-in flash is a required feature. Nearly all digital cameras, including advanced SLRs, have a built-in flash that is integrated with the camera body, as shown in Figure 9-2, or that has a pop-up flash, like the one shown in Figure 9-3. As you will learn later in this chapter, a pop-up flash is the preferred type, because having the flash further off the axis of the lens reduces (but does not eliminate) the phenomenon of red-eye.

How Your Flash Works

The operation of your flash is remarkably simple. Most digital cameras feature a flash sensor, similar to the one shown in Figure 9-2, that reads the amount of light available to the subject; when the illumination from the flash is correct for a proper exposure, it turns off the flash automatically. If the subject is far away, the flash will output maximum power, and if the subject is close, the flash will fire for a shorter period of time. Since all of this measuring and controlling the flash output occurs in less than a second, you (and the subject you are blinding with your flash) are unaware that it is happening.

If you're shooting using the automatic settings, most digital cameras make the decision of whether or not to fire the flash for you. Having the camera activate its flash automatically is a real convenience—in most cases. Often, when you're busy composing a photo, you aren't thinking about whether enough light is available for a good exposure, so it's a good thing that the camera is looking out for you. Having said that, this automatic wonder can sometimes fire when you don't want it to, which is why it is so important to learn what flash modes your camera offers and how to control them.

 *Some digital cameras have a built-in flash unit that slides up from the top deck of the camera. If you're shooting with automatic flash and holding the camera incorrectly, your left hand may keep the flash from sliding up and prevent the camera from taking a picture.*

Working with Pop-up Flash Units

Digital cameras with pop-up style flash units can require the user to press a button to make the strobe unit pop up, or the unit can automatically pop up whenever the flash is needed.

Did you know? Flash Has Been Around a Long Time

During the American Civil War (1861–1865), a photographer by the name of Mathew Brady became famous for his war photos. His early cameras required long exposure times, usually measured in minutes, which was why you never see actual photos of famous battles—only the battlefield after the fighting was over.

Back then, the exposure times were so long, even in daylight, that it was necessary for the subject to be very still or the photo might be blurred. Capturing a subject in motion was impossible.

The 1880s saw the introduction of flash powder. It was spread on a metal dish and then set off by *percussion*—sparks from a flint wheel or an electrical fuse, or it was lit with a candle. Early flash photography was not *synchronized*. The photographer had to mount the camera on a tripod, open the shutter, trigger the flash, and close the shutter again—a technique known as *open flash*.

Flash powder was dangerous stuff, but it allowed the camera to capture subjects in motion and was used until the invention of the flashbulb in the late 1920s. While the first electronic flash tube was invented in 1931, flashbulbs remained the popular choice for flash photography through the 1960s, when inexpensive electronic flash units became available; they have been improving ever since.

Most professionals and advanced amateurs don't like the flash popping up whenever it feels like it—it can be a minor annoyance, especially for those who use an external flash unit. They usually turn off the auto-flash feature through a menu selection.

Flash Photography and Batteries

Whether you are using the internal flash in your digital camera or an external flash, you will quickly discover that they need lots of power to operate. If you use only the internal flash in your digital camera, you should be aware that it will quickly drain your camera's batteries. If you know that you will be shooting an indoor event (such as a school pageant or wedding), you should come prepared with an extra set of batteries.

If you are using an external flash, you will also need an extra set of batteries, and you will need to be alert for signs that your flash battery level is getting low. As the battery charge decreases, it will take longer and longer between shots before the flash is ready to fire. When you begin to notice that it is taking a long time for the flash ready indicator to come on, it's time to replace the batteries.

FIGURE 9-4 Two examples of external flash units that can be used with digital cameras.

Choosing the Best Flash

Two basic types of flash units are available for digital cameras: built-in units and external units. You have no choice about the flash that is built into your camera; you can't change it, but that doesn't mean it's the only flash you can use. If you decide to add an external flash, several choices are available.

External Flash Considerations

Many types of external flashes are available for your camera, and photo magazines are full of ads for them. Two examples of external flash units are shown in Figure 9-4.

The external flash that I use has an adjustable head and is shown in Figure 9-5. This type allows me to use a *bounce* flash. (You will learn more about the advantages of bounce flash later in this chapter in the section "How to… Use Bounce Flash.")

FIGURE 9-5 An adjustable head gives your flash greater flexibility.

External flash units usually attach to a camera's synchronized hot shoe or they attach via a cable connection. Figure 9-6 shows an example of a typical hot shoe on a digital camera.

Many digital cameras do not offer a hot shoe connection. This is especially true of the consumer digital cameras at the low end of the price range. Camera manufacturers assume that most buyers of these relatively inexpensive cameras are not interested in the additional expense or hassle involved in attaching an external flash unit. In addition, digital cameras can be very small as many consumers favor size over complexity. Plus, sometimes the difference in size between the camera and the external flash can be downright silly, such as the digital camera with an external flash shown in Figure 9-7.

External flashes can cost from $50 for a basic model to thousands of dollars for a radio-controlled studio kit. The first and most important consideration when you're looking for an external flash is its compatibility with your camera. While all hot shoes look alike, if you try to mount an incompatible external flash on your camera, the hot shoe can damage either the camera or the external flash unit—or, in rare cases, both.

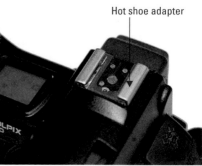

Hot shoe adapter

FIGURE 9-6 If your camera has a hot shoe like this, you can attach an external flash.

FIGURE 9-7 Some digital cameras can actually be smaller than an external flash unit.

 *If you try to mount the incorrect flash on your digital camera, you can damage the camera, the flash unit, or both.*

Choosing a Smart External Flash Some external flash units are sophisticated devices. Some flashes in the market today are so smart that you almost can't take a poor flash photo. Although some of these feature-laden flashes are expensive (costing several hundred or thousands of dollars), they're definitely worth it for some users.

Before buying one of these marvelous wonder flashes, however, you first need to check which of the flash's cool features can actually be used by your digital camera. I use a Nikon Speedlight with a lot of features—for example, it knows when and how much the camera is zoomed in or out to provide more accurate control of the flash, and it can also analyze the different parts of an area being illuminated and make adjustments to get the best possible exposure without blowouts. While the flash is listed as being compatible with my Nikon Coolpix camera, most of the sophisticated features don't work on the Coolpix because the camera wasn't designed to control them. This is because the flash unit was originally designed for a film camera.

Newer cameras and the latest external flash units are very digital-camera aware and work together seamlessly. It's a good idea to double-check to make sure which flash features will and will not work with your camera before buying it.

Internal Flash Considerations

Internal flash units are built into the camera body, either as a small window adjacent to the lens or a pop-up unit. When working with a built-in flash, you must make sure that you are aware of the location of the flash sensor. It is usually located on the camera body near the lens. Some camera designs make it too easy to cover this sensor with your fingers while holding the camera. When this happens, the sensor can't read the flash reflected off of the subject and results in a photo that is grossly overexposed.

FIGURE 9-8 Most red-eye reduction flash settings don't work as advertised.

Before you begin shooting with a built-in flash, you should be aware what the maximum distance is for your camera and try to keep your subject within that distance.

The closer the flash is to the lens, the greater the probability of a phenomenon known as red-eye, demonstrated in Figure 9-8.

Preventing Red-Eye in Your Photos

You can use the red-eye reduction feature that is available on some cameras and flashes to reduce, but rarely prevent, red-eye. How red-eye reduction works on your digital camera is particular to your camera, and some of the descriptions here may sound familiar. Some cameras use a pre-flash, which occasionally causes the subject to blink; then, when the actual flash goes off,

9

What Causes Red-Eye?

Red-eye occurs in photos when flash lighting is used to shoot people or animals. It never happens in natural lighting, such as the sun. When the angle between the flash and camera lens is too narrow, the ambient lighting is too dim, or your subject has had a few drinks, red-eye can occur.

Red-eye occurs when the subject is in the dark and the subject's pupils have dilated to adjust to the darker environment (alcohol also dilates the pupils); when you take a flash photo, the light from the flash reflects off of the retina in the back of the eye. The reflected light is picked up by the camera. What you actually see is the reflection of the blood in the eye.

the subject's eyes are closed. Other units shine a bright light into your subject's eyes, moments before the actual flash, which can have the same effect.

Most cameras fire several fast pre-flash bursts before the shutter releases. Regardless of how it is done, the objective is to reduce the size of the pupils and thereby reduce the effect of red-eye. The success of this feature is dependent on your subject, as some people's pupils react slower than others—this is especially the case at parties when people have been drinking, as alcohol slows the reaction of the pupils.

Photos of animals experience similar problems, except that animal pupils typically show up yellow in flash photos, like the dog shown in Figure 9-9.

FIGURE 9-9 Even dogs and cats can experience problems with red-eye—though the color is rarely red.

Other Ways to Reduce Red-Eye

In addition to using the red-eye reduction feature of your camera, you can try a few other techniques to reduce or prevent red-eye from occurring. Here are a few suggestions:

■ **Increase the ambient lighting** This reduces the size of your subject's pupils—the brighter the better.

Increasing the amount ambient lighting won't influence your flash exposure, as the flash is much brighter than any interior light source.

- **Increase the angle between the camera lens and the flash** This can be done either by getting closer to your subject or by moving the flash away from the lens. The second method requires that you have an external flash with a synchronizing cord. Using an external flash located further from the lens axis is a sure-fire way to eliminate red-eye. Off-camera flashes are either connected to the camera by an extension cord or are activated by the light from the on-camera flash. Using one or more off-camera slave flashes is an effective way to eliminate red-eye and improve the lighting of your human subjects.

- **Use bounce flash** Bounce the flash off a nearby white surface (such as a ceiling) or use a pocket bouncer, such as LumiQuest's Pocket Bouncer (http://www.lumiquest .com), which is attached to your flash with Velcro.

After doing all of this, you may still end up with red-eye in your shot, so now let's cover electronic darkroom methods of correcting and repairing red-eye.

A.

B.

FIGURE 9-10 Sometimes you cannot prevent red-eye (A) and must use red-eye reduction tools to remove it (B).

Use the Electronic Darkroom to Fix Red-Eye

Using the camera's red-eye reduction mode *may* eliminate the devilish looking red pupils from your subject, but it doesn't always work. If red-eye still appears in a print, you'll need to use a photo editor to correct the problem. Jasc's Paint Shop Pro (http: //www.jasc.com) offers one of the best red-eye removal features available. With this application, you can select eye color from a large selection of colors, and the tool even has an option to remove red-eye from animals.

I used the Paint Shop Pro 8 tool to the image shown in Figure 9-10 (A) and was able to remove all traces of the red-eye (B).

9

If you are accustomed to using your flash indoors and not outdoors, start thinking backwards. You'll get warmer and richer photos using indoor's natural light and you'll eliminate dark shadows from a sunny day by using fill-in flash. Flashless indoor photos that look dark can usually be corrected using your photo-editor in minutes.

Rick Altman, host of the PowerPoint Live User Conference

Asking Too Much from Your Flash

Built-in flash units are remarkable devices so far as they are designed. One of the biggest problems is when the photographer asks too much of a unit that is designed to cover no more area than a dozen feet from the camera. I call this the "half-time show syndrome," when someone attempts to take a photo of a dimly lit stadium full of people and the resulting photo looks like a lightning bug mating ritual. In fact, most of the lights that you see in such a photo are probably caused by other people using the flashes on their cameras to take similar photos.

These photos appear dark because your camera doesn't know that the subject is too far away for the flash and sets the shutter speed for proper exposure at the flash's maximum distance. Since the subject is too far away, not enough light is available to expose the image. The result of all those flash pictures in the stadium is, of course, the well-exposed backs of heads three rows down, and a dark patch where the subject should be. Even if you are not in a stadium, if you are too far away from your subject (12 or more feet), the photo will appear dark, like the one shown in Figure 9-11.

FIGURE 9-11 If the subject is too far from the camera, the flash cannot illuminate it properly.

Typical On-Camera Flash Controls

Most digital cameras offer several flash modes that can be used for different lighting situations. These are shown as icons in either the camera's menu or on its LED control panel. The typical flash modes are shown in the following list—but keep in mind is that not every digital camera has every flash mode described here, and the icons on your camera may differ from those shown here.

- **Auto**   The flash is always in shooting mode and is fired when the camera determines it is needed.

- **Auto Red-Eye Reduction**   The flash fires automatically as in auto mode, but pre-flash red-eye reduction is implemented before the actual flash occurs.

- **Always On**   Also called fill flash, the flash fires with every exposure. This is good for fill lighting for backlit subjects.

- **Always Off**   The flash is turned off for every exposure. This is useful for available light fanatics and in places (such as museums) where flash photography is prohibited.

FIGURE 9-12 Photo taken without flash (A); same photo taken with a slow sync flash mode helps the tree stand out (B).

Many consumer digital cameras also have unique user modes that incorporate flash. Typical of these is the "night scene," in which a slow shutter speed and wide aperture are incorporated with a flash to light the foreground subject and provide a natural looking background. If you use the night scene mode with your camera, be sure that you are close enough for the flash to light the foreground subject properly.

The photo in Figure 9-12A was taken without a flash, while the photo in Figure 9-12B was taken using the slow sync mode. In this mode, the shutter opens at a slow speed to allow the dimly lit background to be exposed before firing the flash to illuminate the tree.

A.   B.

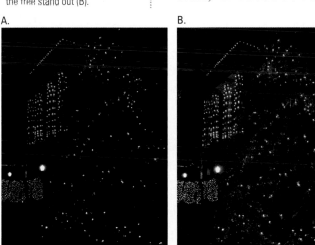

Because the camera is using a slow shutter speed in dim light to capture the background, the camera must be mounted on a solid platform, such as a tripod, to prevent blurring.

You can also use this delayed flash mode for such effects as capturing a sense of motion in a scene. The photo shown in Figure 9-13 was taken in the famous Pantry Café in Los Angeles during a typical weekend breakfast rush. By using slow synch mode on my camera, the motion of the people was slightly blurred and all of the patrons could be seen. The resulting photograph has a Norman Rockwell painting feel to it.

FIGURE 9-13 Using delayed flash can be used to create effects like this.

Preventing Flash Problems

The most common flash problems can be avoided with a little effort before you shoot the photo. Here are some typical flash problems and how to prevent them.

Overexposing Shots

Overexposed or too light images (like the image shown in Figure 9-1) are most often the result of using the flash when you're shooting too close to the subject. Many digital cameras have a control that reduces the amount of light available to the camera by fractions of f-stops. The recommend solution is to move farther away from the subject and use the zoom lens to frame the image. In addition, a piece of translucent tape or exposed film can be attached over the flash head to reduce the output of the flash.

Another cause of washouts when using your built-in flash occurs when you inadvertently place your finger over the flash sensor. On some cameras, this is easy to do. Covering the flash sensor prevents the camera from accurately reading the light produced by the flash, and the camera increases the flash output to its maximum, trying to provide enough light.

Shooting from Too Far Away

If you use your built-in flash beyond its useful range (usually beyond 12 feet), your image will be underexposed—dark to

black, like the photo of a late night basketball game taken with a telephoto lens shown in Figure 9-14. Notice the white rectangle on the right side of the photo. It is a sign that is painted with reflective material which reflected the flash and as a result was brightly lit. The only sure-fire method of improving this situation is to move closer to the subject or to add more light by using an auxiliary flash.

FIGURE 9-14 A flash has a limited effective distance, and the subjects in this photo were about 10 feet too far way.

9

How to ...   **Use Bounce Flash**

Many external flash units can be mounted on top of the camera via a synchronization cable or hot shoe, and the flash head can be aimed at the ceiling to incorporate what is known as *bounce flash.* Bounce flash is useful when ceilings are relatively low and painted white; this would provide a bright white flash color that projects on the image subject. On the other hand, a beige or yellow ceiling, for instance, can result in a yellowish light cast on the image.

You can also bounce flash off a side wall to create a dramatic side-lighting effect; again, the color of the wall will affect the final image color.

Many news photographers use a combination of bounce and direct flash by aiming the flash head at a 45-degree angle and taping a 3×5-inch card to the back of the flash so it reflects a small portion of the light directly toward the subject.

Several manufacturers offer bounce attachments for external flashes. One of the best and most extensive is LumiQuest (http://www.lumiquest.com).

Shooting Shadows

When shooting a backlit subject (because the sun or another strong light source is located behind the subject), you'll probably get a dark silhouette. If you compensate for exposure, the background may become too light. Using fill flash to compensate for the backlighting is a useful technique.

Simply turn your on-camera flash to the Always On setting and take your photo, making sure the distance from the camera to the subject is within the flash's range. Your camera will set its exposure for the overall lighting and the flash will illuminate the subject, which would have otherwise been in deep shadow.

You can also use fill flash to take a photo on a bright, sunny day. The photo of Mr. Marx, shown in Figure 9-15, was taken during a lunch break. The sun was so bright that most of his face was in the shadow of his hat. All that was necessary to get the photo was too turn the flash to manual mode (Always On) and compose the photo as normal; the camera and flash did the rest.

FIGURE 9-15 Using fill flash prevents the hat from making a shadow on Mr. Marx's face.

Chapter 10

Gain a New Perspective

How to...

- Use contrasting colors and textures for stunning photos
- Use your camera as a journal
- Identify locations in your photos
- Capture more than a single view
- Find and capture humor with your camera

Digital Photography Myth Number 10:   Digital cameras do not have the great versatility found in film cameras.

Fact: False. Digital cameras and film cameras have many features and controls in common. In fact, because some digital cameras have an adjustable LCD screen that can be rotated away from the camera, the digital camera photographer can frame a photo even with the camera positioned over the photographer's head.

This chapter is a visual cookbook of ideas and suggestions of views that are not in any way the usual family pictures. It is my hope that by seeing the possibilities that can be achieved using a digital camera, you will be inspired to go a little beyond the ordinary and experiment with the wondrous tool that is your digital camera.

FIGURE 10-1 Lit only by the light of the moon, the solitude of a winter evening is captured by the camera.

Go Beyond the Common and Mundane

We live in a world that is riotous with colors and textures, whether it is a bare tree illuminated only by moonlight in winter (see Figure 10-1) or a leaf resting on some denim cloth (see Figure 10-2). The challenge is to see and capture just some of the wonder that is around you every day or night.

Because the nearest town was almost 50 miles away, the tree in the

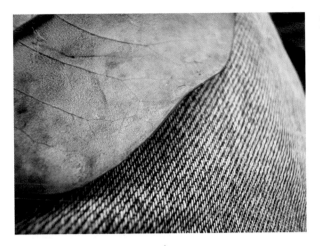

FIGURE 10-2 A combination of colors and textures makes up this still life photo.

photo in Figure 10-1 was illuminated solely by the light of a full moon. The digital camera I was using held the shutter open for almost 30 seconds to achieve the exposure. You can learn more about low-light photography in Chapter 17.

The photo in Figure 10-2 was unplanned. I was sitting in the driver's seat of my car, brushing off the leaves that had gathered in my open car during an afternoon shoot, and I noticed one of the leaves had fallen on my pant leg. Setting the camera for macro photography, I made a composition of the leaf (which looks like leather) and the denim cloth. This leads us to the first topic—combining contrasting colors and textures.

Look for Contrasts

10

I enjoy shooting photos just for the beauty of the contrasts. Even though some may think such photos don't "tell a story," I think they do. Consider the photo of the patio umbrellas in Figure 10-3. I took the photo to capture the point of intersection, where the bright colors came together. From a technical standpoint, the umbrellas were illuminated by the sun shining down into the patio, so it took several attempts to find the best metering system selection and exposure value (EV) setting.

FIGURE 10-3 A timeless photo of brightly colored umbrellas

If bright colors create a problem while you're shooting, you can make a slight adjustment to the Hue setting in your photo-editing software to adjust the colors, as shown in Figure 10-4. The important part of becoming an observer of the world

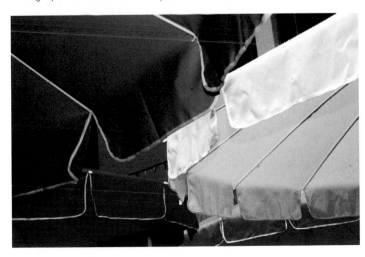

around you is to discipline yourself to look at what surrounds you.

Look at Figure 10-5, where the yellow flower appears to be growing right out of the gray bark of the tree. In fact, it had grown under the tree to get at the light. I took the photo to capture the contrast of the bright yellow and gray.

While taking photos of the fall foliage, I came upon

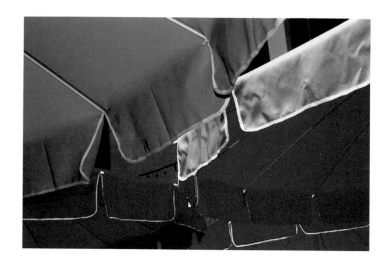

 When photographing brightly colored flowers, use spot metering on the brightest part of the flowers to prevent them from being overexposed.

FIGURE 10-4 By shifting the Hue setting in your photo-editor, you can change all of the colors in the photo.

a single red leaf lying in a creek made uniformly gray by the clay that had washed off the local outcroppings. I took the photo shown in Figure 10-6 to capture the red of the leaf contrasted with the nearly perfect gray background. Fall foliage is wonderful to view and a little difficult to capture with your camera, but sometimes you can find a single example that coveys the fall colors and the winter that necessarily follows. I'll talk more about photographing fall colors in the next section.

FIGURE 10-5 Is the yellow flower growing out of an old gray tree trunk?

Using Contrast for Better Fall Photos

I find it ironic that someone who enjoys the change of colors associated with fall as much as I do constantly finds himself living in either an arid or a tropical climate. Still, with a little effort, I can find great fall colors, even in Texas.

FIGURE 10-6 Sometimes the most beautiful fall colors are expressed in a single leaf.

Fall colors can be a tricky to capture with any camera, especially with a digital camera. If you have ever taken photographs of fall foliage, you may have experienced that sense of disappointment when you looked at the photos and all of those brilliant reds, yellows, and oranges you expected to see seemed flat in the photo.

This failure of the camera to capture what you saw when you took the photo could be caused by several reasons. First and foremost, your eyes are vastly superior to your camera. So what you see is definitely far and beyond what you camera can capture. (See the following Did You Know box, "How Your Eyes Maximize Color," for more on this topic.)

10

Did you know?

How Your Eyes Maximize Color

Look at a scene rich with thousands of leaves comprising hundreds of hues of red. Take a photo of that scene, and when you look at it later, all of the vivid red colors now seem flat. The fall landscape in the shot looks a dark reddish burned color. So what did the camera do wrong? The color is not the camera's fault. As I learned a few years ago from my optometrist, your eye automatically increases your sensitivity to reds while you are staring at the color. Unlike our eyes, your poor camera cannot dynamically adjust its sensitivity to a particular color.

Your eye sees color similarly to how your camera does—as combinations of red, green, and blue (RGB). When you view a scene that has lots of dominant colors in a single range, such as red, the eye automatically increases its ability to sense the red, while decreasing its sensitivity to the lesser colors in the scene. So while your eyes and mind are enjoying the super colors of fall, your camera can capture only a small portion of the color spectrum that you have been enjoying. It's not that your camera isn't doing its job, it's that your eyes are too good.

You can use several workarounds to get better fall photos. The first workaround involves technique. Look at the photo in Figure 10-7. The colors in this tree are really bright. When I was shooting, the shiny surface on the leaves produced a glare that even a polarizer filter could not remove. I took the photo by positioning myself "inside" the tree, getting the sun behind the leaves. The sunlight lit up the entire tree like a lantern, and I got a great photo of the leaves without any reflections.

To make fall and similar bright colors stand out, you need to ensure that you have contrasting colors in the photo. For example, the leaves in the photo in Figure 10-8 are backlit by the afternoon sun. The complimentary colors of the leaves, reddish-orange against the green background, and areas of hard contrast between, really make the colors stand out.

FIGURE 10-7 Backlighting the leaves shows off their color without the glare of shiny reflections.

FIGURE 10-8 The backlit leaves with the contrasting hues makes the colors in this photo appear vivid.

Use Your Camera as a Journal

In many places that you photograph, either on vacation or just while shooting photos for fun, you can use your camera as a

FIGURE 10-9 Signs like this provide a wealth of information and are easy to record with your digital camera.

journal to mark where you've been and what shots you've taken. You can shoot historical markers or signs that tell you something about the subject of your photo.

With a film camera, it's difficult to justify taking these shots, since developing these photos can be expensive and they're usually not as interesting to look at as more creative shots. But with a digital camera, you can capture a lot of information about a subject by taking a single photo, like the one shown in Figure 10-9. This helps you remember where you've been and the importance of an area where you shot.

This "note-taking" ability is not just limited to factual historical markers. For example, while in Athens a few years ago, I read the inscription shown in Figure 10-10. I found it profoundly moving and was also struck by the fact that it was written more than 2500 years ago. I took a photo of it because I knew that if I wrote it down on a piece of paper, it would get lost in short order.

10

FIGURE 10-10 Capturing writings like this transcription ensures that they are preserved.

Ampharete and her Grandchild.

„I am holding here the child of my daughter, the beloved, whom I held on my lap, when alive we beheld the light of the sun; and now I am holding it dead, being dead myself."

Tombstone. End of 5th century B. C. from the Sacred Way. Inv. I 221 / P 695.

While taking such photos, it is useful to set the quality setting of your camera lower. This gives you more images per card and doesn't waste storage space on an image that will never get printed.

Another valuable use of your digital camera is to make a visual inventory of the items of value in your home for insurance purposes.

Record Works of Great Art

Have you ever noticed that when teachers have their young charges create artwork, it is often the size of a football field? The art projects are too large to

- Scan without a lot of effort
- Fit into any known size of file folder
- Protect from the silverfish that seem to love newsprint

FIGURE 10-11 Sometimes the entire work of art will fit in a single frame.

One way to forever enshrine these masterpieces is to photograph them with your digital camera.

To capture a child's work of art, first hang it up on a wall and then take a photo of it, like the one shown in Figure 10-11. Sometimes the only way to get the entire image into a single frame requires shooting so far from the picture the details become too small to see. In such cases, after you take the full-frame photo, you should then photograph detail areas.

Change Your Camera's Viewpoint

FIGURE 10-12 Bamboo coming at you!

Often, the most ordinary things look completely different when you photograph them at an unusual angle. You can make the most of your digital camera's ability to shoot some creative and abstract-looking photographs.

In Figure 10-12, I photographed the junction at which several bamboo poles were lashed together. Because I chose to use a limited depth of field, only the ends of the bamboo are in focus, while all of the remaining poles appear as blurred lines.

What is in the photo shown in Figure 10-13? It is a stone column that is part of an office complex's garden in Los Angeles. Even though the pillar is the same diameter at the top and bottom, it appears to taper. Using the techniques you will learn in Chapter 20, I replaced the original overcast sky with the Texas sunrise to give this photo even more punch.

In San Antonio, just across the street from the Alamo, is a pathway to the famous River Walk. Tucked in under a stairway is the fountain shown in Figure 10-14. If you look at it from the front, it doesn't look like much, but if you put your camera right up against the edge of it, looking down across all of the water paths you get a completely different view. This is because when you face the fountain, each of the grooves through which the water flows is about a foot apart. When viewed from the side, the distance between them is compressed and they appear much closer together.

In the photo shown in Figure 10-15, I photographed the old gas pump from underneath, so that the price per gallon would dominate the photo. I'm an old guy, and the best I can remember is 25 cents a gallon.

If you are willing to get down on the ground, you can play with some fun angles. Setting the camera in macro mode, I took the photo of the mushroom shown in Figure 10-16 with the office building slightly out of focus in the background. It offered a cool way to make visual size comparisons.

10

FIGURE 10-15 Photographing from underneath emphasizes the sign showing the price of gas on this old pump.

FIGURE 10-16 With the camera at grass level, I captured the mushroom and the office building in the same frame.

 Tip *If you're lucky enough to own a digital camera with a tilting/rotating LCD, obtaining extreme angles of view is easy. Try placing the camera in a grassy yard and shooting with a macro setting, so that the blades of grass look like a forest. Or gain two to three extra feet of height by holding the camera above your head and shoot aiming down.*

Adding a Point of Reference to a Photo

When you look at a photo like the one shown in Figure 10-17, it is difficult to imagine its actual size. Is the mushroom two inches tall or two centimeters tall?

FIGURE 10-17 Digital cameras with macro mode can make things appear larger than life.

When taking shots like this—if you care about reality—it is a good idea to include a reference shot that includes some object of known size. You can include a small ruler in such photos, but you can use anything familiar. So, how big are those mushrooms? Look at the photo in Figure 10-18; I have added an AA battery to the photo. The mushrooms shown in Figure 10-17 are near the upper-left edge of the shot.

FIGURE 10-18 Adding a familiar object to one of the photos provides a good reference for the viewer.

Establishing Where You Are

Whenever I am shooting in a different city, I always try and find something unique that visually declares where I am shooting. Figure 10-19 was taken in Chicago.

FIGURE 10-19 The marquee of the Chicago theater says it all in a single photo.

10

Capturing Names, Numbers, or Letters for Impact

If you like to make composite images, you can find several good sources for text, letters, and numbers that can be easily captured with your digital camera. I made a quick (10-minute) montage in Figure 10-20 using the following: the public library sign in Chicago, letters from Chicago's Navy Pier, *TRIOT* from a brass sign in Texas, *Q* from St. Louis, the front sign at a museum in Houston, a Stone Park sign in New York, and the lone star from Texas, of course. (This piece was just thrown together, so don't study it looking for some hidden symbolic meaning!)

FIGURE 10-20 It's fun to combine parts and pieces from names, numbers, or letters to create a montage.

The digital camera has opened up a whole new world of creative possibilities for me. I am able to photograph, review, and make adjustments to produce results that would have been impractical with my film camera.

Pat Gibson, CorelDRAW trainer

Getting More than a Single View

When I was in Los Angles a few years ago, a number of angels appeared throughout the downtown area. Not real ones—actually, each angel was sponsored and painted by the sponsoring organization, with all of the proceeds of sale of the angels going to charity. Photographing the angels was a challenge, since they often had wonderful decorative work on both sides. I finally decided to take a documentary approach and photograph each angel front and back, as shown in Figure 10-21.

FIGURE 10-21 It is often necessary to take multiple photographs of a subject to capture its essence.

(In case you are wondering why I didn't wait for the bus to leave before taking the rear photo…. It seems when Los Angeles bus drivers take lunch, they park their buses at this bus stop.) Some angels had such great detailed work that I had to take four or more photographs of each one to capture the breadth of all the art they contained.

Looking for Patterns

Patterns occur all around us in both nature and architecture. Figure 10-22 shows examples of patterns.

 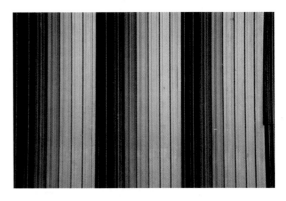

FIGURE 10-22 Two examples of repeating patterns

Photos of patterns can make great backgrounds for title pages and reports, like the one shown in Figure 10-23.

FIGURE 10-23 Patterns make great background for titles and posters.

Modify Photo Color for a Cool Effect

I took the photo shown in Figure 10-24 at a farmer's market. It's a photo of cactus pads (*nopales* in Spanish)—not an uncommon sight at a Texas produce stand. Here is a simple way to modify the photos for a cool effect. Use the Hue adjustment in your photo editor to change the colors in the photos, as shown in the other two photos.

FIGURE 10-24 Cactus patterns and color variations

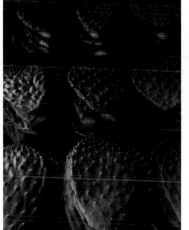

Don't Miss the Humor

Just as patterns appear everywhere, funny stuff also appears everywhere. Keep your camera handy at all times and you will be able to capture some of the insanity that passes by every day.

When I returned from shooting a sunrise, I stopped for gas next to the car shown in Figure 10-25.

FIGURE 10-25 Who would have thought that a car could make a great cactus planter?

The only problem with the photo is that the background (a tattoo parlor) is so busy it is difficult to see the car. I used the selection techniques described in Chapter 20 to isolate the car (using a photo editor) and to replace the background, as shown in Figure 10-26.

Summary

That wraps up this chapter on some of the unusual things you can and should try with your digital camera. Next, you will discover how to take some great action photos.

FIGURE 10-26 Replacing the background with a different one makes the car stand out.

Part IV

Special Opportunities for Stunning Photographs

Chapter 11

Capture the Action

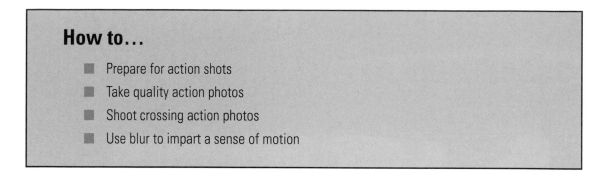

How to...

- Prepare for action shots
- Take quality action photos
- Shoot crossing action photos
- Use blur to impart a sense of motion

Digital Photography Myth Number 11:   You cannot take action photos with digital cameras.

Fact: False. Taking action photos with a digital camera can be done—if you know how to go about it.

In this chapter, we will discover why it can be difficult to take action photos using digital cameras; however, once you have learned the cause of the problem, you will know how to work around it and take great sporting action shots of the kids.

Action photos like the one shown in Figure 11-1 are great. As much as parents like to have school photos of their children with neatly combed hair in a nice outfit, you find the boys (this includes dads) and some of the girls would much rather have an action photo of them dunking a basketball, leaping on a skateboard, or sliding home in a plume of dust. Taking good action photos involves two parts: setting up the camera properly and positioning yourself in reference to the action that is happening.

FIGURE 11-1 Action photos like this are cool, but they can be a challenge to capture using your digital camera.

The Reality of Shutter Delay

The first time you try to take action photos with your digital camera, you may be unpleasantly surprised. While you may press the shutter button at the right moment, by the time the camera finally takes the photograph the event is finished or the subject is no longer in the frame. While I normally don't let anyone see my failures, I thought some photos I took at a team roping event will let you see that all of us have problems at one time or another while taking action photos.

The four photos shown in Figure 11-2 represent attempts to capture both the calves and the riders as they came out of the chute. This was my first experience taking action photos with this camera. Even though I could hear when the calf was released and had set up the camera for action photos, it seemed that every time I pressed the shutter button and looked at the resulting photo in the LCD screen, the photo was either out of focus, the riders or calf were partially out of the frame, or both.

The frustratingly long waiting period from the time you push the shutter button until the photo is taken is called *shutter delay* or *shutter lag* and it is unique to digital cameras.

FIGURE 11-2 Four examples of what can go wrong when taking action photos with a digital camera.

11

Did you know?

What Is Shutter Delay?

Using a film camera, you do not experience shutter delay. When the shutter button is pressed all the way down a photo is made—no delay. With most digital cameras, when you press the shutter button, the camera doesn't immediately take a picture. This is because the shutter button doesn't actually control a shutter (except with digital SLR cameras), but instead begins a long sequence of events inside your camera. With your camera powered up, the image sensor begins a series of technical housekeeping tasks to prepare it to take a photo.

Depending on the camera settings, your camera may try to focus (which can take a long time, especially with a moving subject). The resulting shutter delay can be anything from a barely noticeable lag up to a full second or more between the moment that you press the shutter and the point at which the camera actually captures the image. A second may not seem like much time, but when you're trying to photograph a moving subject, that second may make a lifetime of difference between taking a good action photo or an empty frame.

Compensating for Shutter Delay

If your camera has a long shutter delay, or if you are not satisfied with your action photos, here are some things that you can do to get better pictures.

Use the Continuous Feature

Many digital cameras today offer a burst or continuous shooting mode that will take several pictures a second until the camera's temporary storage (called a *buffer*) is full. In most digital cameras, selecting this mode is a menu option. This feature allows you to shoot a series of photos as long as the shutter button is held down. The number of photos that your camera can take in a single burst is limited to the size of the camera's buffer. The continuous feature is different from the camera's video feature, in that it takes multiple exposures like those shown in Figure 11-3 and saves them as individual photos, while the camera's movie mode saves the images as a single video stream.

 You can't use your flash when using the burst/continuous mode.

FIGURE 11-3 The continuous feature of a digital camera grabs several frames in a few seconds.

11

Once you have taken a series of photos, you can go back and pick out the single frame that you want to keep and discard the rest of the photos. Both of the photos shown in Figure 11-4 were taken from a series of photos that I shot one afternoon.

Keep Your Camera Ready

All digital cameras go into a standby mode after a period of inactivity to conserve their batteries. On many digital cameras, you can set how many minutes of inactivity triggers the camera to go into standby. If your camera supports this feature (and not all do), it is usually selected through the menu system on the LCD. If you are taking a lot of action photos, you may want to consider

increasing this setting to prevent the camera from
going to sleep at the worst possible moment.
Remember that increasing the standby delay
discharges the battery more quickly.

When you are ready to take your action photo,
make sure your camera is on and not in standby.
If it has gone into standby, push down the shutter button.
The camera won't take a picture, it will take the camera
out of standby.

FIGURE 11-4 Both photos were
a single photo that was selected
from a series of photos taken using
continuous or burst mode.

Control the Auto-focus

To focus on any subject, the camera zooms its lens in and out
until it thinks it has achieved focus. This operation can take
anywhere from a half second to two seconds. You can reduce
this time in several ways. You can point the camera at a subject
that is roughly the same distance as the action shot you want to
take and prefocus the camera by pressing the shutter halfway,
which will cause the camera to focus and make the exposure
settings. This is called a *focus lock*. Then point the camera at
the moving target, and when you are ready to take the photo,
just squeeze the shutter button the rest of the way.

Another way to prevent auto-focus delay is to disable your
auto-focus either by changing to manual focus and setting it to
infinity or by changing the focus mode to landscape setting.

Tip

Placing the camera in infinity lock disables the flash on most digital cameras.

Landscape mode/Infinity lock

FIGURE 11-5 Setting your camera to landscape mode (infinity lock) disables the auto-focus and the delays it causes.

This setting, which usually features an icon of a mountain on the camera body (as shown in Figure 11-5) turns off the auto-focus and changes the focus setting to infinity. This means that any subject that is about 10 feet or more from the camera will be in focus.

Practice Shots

You should practice taking action shots using your camera on a moving subject—someone on a merry-go-round or on a swing. Your objective will be to capture the person in the center of the photo frame. It may seem easy, but on the average it will take you about 20 minutes before you can consistently capture the subject in the center of the frame every time. After you have done that, you will have developed what is called a *learned response,* and when taking action shots you will be able to push the shutter at the right amount of time before the event so as to catch the action.

Voices from the Community

You can never be too rich, too smart, or have enough memory for your digital camera.

Lynette Kent, author and artist

11

Catch the Action Like a Pro

Until now, we have been focusing on how to overcome the limitations of some digital cameras. Here are suggestions for taking action photos that apply equally to both film and digital cameras. If you use these techniques, your action photos won't appear flat or static.

Set Up Your Camera to Freeze the Action

Every time you shoot a photo using your camera's automatic settings, the camera adjusts the exposure settings using a combination of shutter and aperture settings. The camera doesn't know when you are shooting a subject that is moving fast, requiring a higher shutter speed. If you take a photo outdoors on a bright sunny day, the shutter speed will be sufficiently high to freeze the action.

The problem with using the fast shutter speeds is that the resulting photos can sometimes appear just that: frozen. The photo shown in Figure 11-6 was taken during a soccer practice, and the goalie had just stopped a shot. At the time the photo was taken, both the ball and the goalie were moving very fast. With the high shutter speed, though, it appears that the ball is attached to his body.

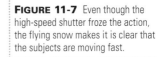
FIGURE 11-6 High shutter speeds froze the action in this photo, making the subjects look like statues.

In some cases, freezing the action using high shutter speeds works really well because the composition of the photo, like the one shown in Figure 11-7, makes it clear that the subject was frozen in time.

Sometimes the pose of the subject implies action, like the runners shown in Figure 11-8, which shows another way to give a sense of movement to a photo.

Pan the Camera with the Action

Viewers associate blurring with movement. If the action is moving across your field of vision, such as in a bike race or while watching a running dog, try panning your body so that the camera sweeps with the action. This results in the camera moving with the subject. This is called *panning* a shot, and

FIGURE 11-7 Even though the high-speed shutter froze the action, the flying snow makes it is clear that the subjects are moving fast.

because the camera is moving at roughly the same speed as the subject, the subject remains in focus while the background is blurred. Using a relatively slow shutter speed, the subject remains sharp while the background is blurred. To take this kind of photo, you'll need a shutter speed that is fast enough to capture the subject with minimal blurring while slow enough for the panning action to blur the background.

FIGURE 11-8 Sometimes the pose of the subjects and the composition of the frame imply the action.

 Shutter speed is controlled by using shutter priority (if your camera has this feature).

Position yourself so that the action is coming at you from a 3/4 angle relative to the subject, allowing you to freeze the action with a slower shutter speed than panning. If the action is coming directly at you, an even slower shutter speed can be effective.

11

 **Pan Your Camera**

Here's how to pan your camera for action shots:

1. Set the camera to single, continuous or burst mode and shutter priority.

2. Change the shutter speed to 1/60 of a second. This setting is a starting point. If the ambient lighting is really bright, reduce the shutter speed to 1/40.

3. As the subject approaches, point the camera at it (them) and focus. As it moves across in front of you, rotate your body, and as smoothly as possible keep the camera centered on the subject while shooting the pictures.

4. Review the photos. If the subject is too blurry, like the one shown in Figure 11-9, you need to increase the shutter speed. If the background is not blurred, try decreasing the shutter speed.

Panned action shots should be made with the camera set in landscape rather than portrait orientation. The wider field of view in landscape makes it easier to keep the subject in the frame while you're panning.

The digital camera is valuable for this type of action photography, because the instant feedback allows you to review and make adjustments that would be impossible with film. The photo shown in Figure 11-10 is a panned shot that resulted in the rider being in focus and the background blurred.

FIGURE 11-9 If the shutter speed is too slow, both the subject and background can become blurred.

Tips for Better Action Shots

Here are some tips that may help you improve your action photos.

- **Zoom out to catch more action** Use as wide a lens setting with your zoom as reasonable. The more you zoom in the lens, the narrower the field of view, which makes it all the more difficult to capture the subject. Better to have extra to crop off than to have an empty or partially empty frame.

FIGURE 11-10 Panning the camera gives the viewer a real sense of motion.

- **Move around** Experiment with different shooting positions in relation to the action you are trying to capture. Some positions are better than others; this is something that is difficult to figure out just by thinking it through. You will be amazed how much difference changing your shooting location can make until you have tried several different ones. To demonstrate the importance of your position relative to the action, look at the runners in Figure 11-8. They are running across the frame. Now look at the runner in Figure 11-11, and

11

Did you know?

How Shutter Priory Works

Many digital cameras offer a setting called *shutter priority*. If your camera offers this option, when you set it, you set the shutter speed of the camera and the camera automatically adjusts the aperture setting for the selected shutter speed.

Generally, shutter priority is selected through the menu. Be aware that while the camera will select an aperture setting to compensate for the higher shutter speed, it is possible for you to select a shutter speed that is either too high or too low for the camera to compensate through aperture settings. In most cases, when the shutter settings are too fast or too slow for the camera to compensate with aperture settings, the camera will blink one of the indicators to let you know that you need to adjust your shutter settings.

Conversely, by using aperture-preferred settings and establishing a wide-open aperture (a small number such as f:2.8), you can force the shutter to its highest setting to achieve a good exposure.

FIGURE 11-11 Because of the camera position, he appears to be standing still even though he is running.

you'll notice that several things are wrong with this photo. He is running almost straight toward the camera, so there is no sense of motion. The background enforces the sense of non-movement by the fact that he is perfectly aligned with the concrete bridge pillars. This imparts a visual sense that he is not moving.

Blurring for Effect

Because high shutter speeds can freeze action of even high-speed subjects, the resulting photo may look static. Earlier you learned that you can blur the background by panning the camera. Another way to impart a sense of motion in an action photo is to blur the subject and keep the background in sharp focus, like the photo shown in Figure 11-12. While this subject is covered in Chapter 12, the effect is achieved using a tripod and a slow shutter speed.

FIGURE 11-12 The speed of a passing train is created by using slow shutter speeds and a tripod.

One way to give a sense of motion is to blur everything in the photo. The result is a blurry photo, like the ones shown in Figures 11-13 and 11-14. Although the blurring diminishes details in the photo, more importantly it imparts the sense of the action. With the biker photo everything is blurred but recognizable; parts of the photo of the running horses are in focus, but the foreground horses are out of focus, imparting the sense of speed.

FIGURE 11-13 Lower shutter speed blurs the subject, giving a sense of the action.

Capture Action Coming Toward You

One of the more difficult action photos to capture with your digital camera is when the subject is moving toward you. When the subject is moving toward you, the auto-focus

FIGURE 11-14 Some of the horses in this photo are blurred to give a sense of speed.

FIGURE 11-15 The auto-focus feature of digital cameras may not be fast enough to keep in focus subjects moving toward you.

of the digital camera may or may not attempt to keep the subject in focus. For traditional film SLR cameras, the auto-focus feature of the camera is very fast, while the focusing system in the typical digital camera is comparatively slow.

The photo shown in Figure 11-15 was taken of a young lady on a bicycle who was coming toward me quite fast. The camera was focused on her before she started moving, but as she moved toward me, the camera didn't change focus fast enough (she was really fast).

Changing Auto-Focus Modes

Some cameras offer a choice in how your auto-focus operates. Some cameras continuously attempt to focus on the subject—which sounds great, but when taking a photo you may experience delays with this setting since the camera may be in the process of refocusing when you attempt to take the photo. The other choice is to use single mode that will focus on the subject when you press the shutter button halfway down. The disadvantage of this mode of focus is that most cameras that use it will not allow the photo to be taken if the camera thinks the photo is not in focus (even if it is).

How to ... Blur the Subject for Effect

1. To achieve a blurred effect, mount your camera on a tripod.

2. Choose a position that has a static background in front of which the subject will pass.

3. Choose a slow shutter speed.

4. As the subject moves in front of the camera, shoot the photo.

Of course, setting your focus to manual and infinity (the mountain icon again) will give you an excellent chance of stopping action to within 10 feet.

Summary

You now know enough to take good action photos, including how to use blurring to impart the sense of motion. In the next chapter, you will discover how to use your camera to get some great blurred photos to create interesting photographic effects.

Chapter 12

Make Blurred Photos on Purpose

How to...

- Take advantage of slow-shutter speed photography
- Set up your camera to take slow-shutter photos
- Understand how to use shutter priority
- Set proper exposures for blurred photos
- Blur photos for effects

Digital Photography Myth Number 12: Digital cameras do not have the necessary advanced features found in film cameras for slow-shutter photography.

Fact: Some low-end digital cameras have limited features and controls, but most have sufficient controls to take blurred photos.

In this chapter, you will learn how to create photos in which part of the image is in clear focus and part is blurred. Called *slow-shutter* or *still-motion photos*, they make great images, especially when photographing moving water, such as waterfalls, creek, or fountains.

Photographing Creeks and Waterfalls

FIGURE 12-1 This speeding wave was frozen in time using a fast shutter speed on my camera.

A camera shooting at a shutter speed of 1/125 of a second or faster can freeze the motion of water in a creek, waterfall, or a rushing wave like the one shown in Figure 12-1. You will learn later in this chapter that the key to successful still-motion photos is a steady tripod. When I came upon the waterfall in Figure 12-2, I didn't have my tripod on me so I placed the camera on a wooden railing.

If you use a slower shutter speed, the area surrounding the creek or waterfall remains in focus, but the water becomes blurred and takes on a moody, ethereal quality. In the photo of a small waterfall in Minnesota, shown in Figure 12-2, I wanted the water to appear moving, and the blurred water conveys the sense of a tranquil mood.

Wide angle lenses are probably more useful for shooting waterfalls, although a telephoto may sometimes be useful. Generally, though, you'll probably use 35, 28, and 24mm lenses most often. Later on, you'll learn that slow shutter speeds are essential for creating the sense of water in motion. This means that you *must* use a tripod when shooting waterfalls. A solid tripod and cable or remote shutter release will make the difference between success and failure in your waterfall pictures.

FIGURE 12-2 Blurring the water using a slow shutter speed evokes a sense of tranquility.

Capture the Motion Slowly

The concept behind this style of photography is simple. The following points summarize how it is achieved:

1. Mount the camera on a stable platform, such as a tripod.

2. Compose the image you want to capture.

3. Change the camera settings so that the shutter speed is no faster than 1/4 of a second.

4. Take the photo, review, adjust, and shoot again if necessary (it is always necessary).

The following sections cover each step in greater detail.

Use Still Motion Camera Equipment

In almost all cases, shooting water requires a good tripod. The object is to have the camera body mounted so it doesn't move during the slow exposures. The beefier the tripod, the more stable it is and the steadier the camera is during exposure. A lot of inexpensive tripods are very light (which is a good thing when you have to carry it any sort of distance), but if you extend the legs out to their maximum extension, the tripod is wobbly.

12

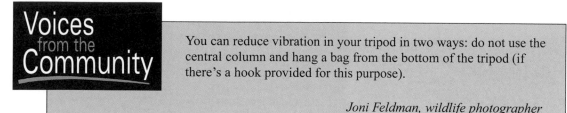

Voices from the **Community**

You can reduce vibration in your tripod in two ways: do not use the central column and hang a bag from the bottom of the tripod (if there's a hook provided for this purpose).

Joni Feldman, wildlife photographer

Other than your camera and a tripod, little else in the area of equipment is really necessary to take these photos. If you intend to shoot photos of subjects in the bright sun, it may be necessary to use a filter that will reduce the amount of light coming into the camera. Either a neutral density (ND) filter, a polarizer filter, or both will dramatically reduce the amount of light that enters the camera, allowing you to shoot at a slower shutter speed than would otherwise be possible on a sunny day. You will learn more about these filters later in the chapter in the section "Circular Polarizer (CP) Filter."

Also, if you're going to be taking pictures around water, it's important to protect your photo equipment. It's a good idea to have a sealable, thick plastic freezer bag in which you can put your digital camera, especially in areas where there's a lot of spray. Also, carry plenty of lens-cleaning tissue or a lens-cleaning cloth to wipe any moisture that gets on your camera lens, and to dry your camera if it gets wet.

Finally, if you must shoot in manual mode to get blurred effects, you'll need a hand-held light meter to make sure your camera's settings are correct.

Position the Camera

Before you settle on a shooting position, study the scene you are attempting to capture from several viewpoints. Don't just choose the one closest to the trail. When I took the photo of Walnut Creek falls, shown in Figure 12-3, the tripod and I were in the middle of the creek. I wasn't swimming, as the water was only ankle deep, but I did have to take off my hiking boots and put on a pair of flip-flops that I keep in my camera bag for such occasions. I looked at this waterfall from about four different viewpoints before deciding on this one.

FIGURE 12-3 Position the camera to get the best view for the blurred effect—even if it means standing in the middle of the creek.

Adjust Your Camera Settings

Two factors control how much light strikes your camera's sensor: the amount of time that the shutter is open (shutter speed) and how large the opening is (aperture). These two factors are interactive, in that if the shutter is open longer (a slower shutter speed), the opening must be made smaller (increase the aperture) so that less light enters the camera. If it's in total automatic mode, the camera, like a diplomat, will always try to find the middle ground. It attempts to set the shutter speed fast enough for most types of photos (usually 1/125 of a second) and an aperture setting that lets in the correct amount of light for the selected speed. So, what happens when you need the camera's shutter speed to be slower to take a blurred photo? You have two options: manual settings or shutter priority.

When you change your camera settings to manual, you override all of the camera's automatic features. This means using a hand-held light meter to measure the light and then manually changing the shutter and aperture settings on the camera—just as I did with my first Kodak back in 1959. The preferred method for taking blurred photos is using shutter priority. If your camera doesn't have this feature, you will need to use the manual settings.

When your camera is in the shutter priority mode, you select a shutter speed and the camera chooses an appropriate aperture. Shutter priority mode can be used for a faster shutter speed to freeze the action of fast-moving subjects or for a slower shutter speed to blur moving subjects and create a sense of motion.

The opposite of shutter priority is *aperture priority*, in which you set the desired aperture and the camera selects the necessary shutter speed for a proper exposure. Not all digital cameras offer shutter priority. However, if your camera has aperture priority, it can be used to force a slow shutter speed. Set your aperture to its smallest setting (highest number, f:16 or f:22). The smaller the aperture, the longer the shutter must stay open.

12

After you set your camera in shutter priority mode, change the shutter speed to 1/4 second for starters (the slower the exposure, the more blurred the water). Adjust the exposure to try several different shutter speeds to see which you like best. As the shutter speed slows down, the camera increases the aperture to prevent overexposure.

As a general rule of thumb, pictures taken at shutter speeds below 1/60 of a second will begin to blur water that's moving fast. I recommend that you avoid taking pictures faster than 1/8 of a second, to ensure that the water is fully blurred. Best results are usually had when dealing with exposures of between 1/4 of a second up to 2 seconds; however, taller waterfalls may require longer exposures. The most important thing you need to remember when attempting to take slow shutter photos is to use as high an aperture setting as possible, ensuring a slow shutter speed and the greatest depth of field.

If too much ambient lighting is available, it is possible the camera cannot make the aperture small enough to prevent overexposure. Most digital cameras I have worked with blink the speed setting in the LCD status screen, but the camera will still take the photo. (See the Did You Know box entitled "About Light Reducing Filters.")

FIGURE 12-4 Because matrix metering was used, the bright areas of the waterfall are blown out.

If you don't have light reducing filters, you can increase the maximum aperture of your camera lens by zooming out to its maximum setting.

Note *When setting exposure for photographing moving water, you need to use either center-weighted or spot metering. See Chapter 4 for more on metering.*

The photograph shown in Figure 12-4 was taken using an average (also called matrix) metering system setting. As a result, the brightest part of the photo (the water in the falls) is blown out.

FIGURE 12-5 Using spot metering to measure the light on the waterfall prevents blowouts.

FIGURE 12-6 Reflections without a polarizer filter

FIGURE 12-7 A CP filter attached to your camera's lens prevents reflections, allowing you to see under the water.

The photo taken in Figure 12-5 was taken using spot metering on the waterfall, and brightest parts of the water aren't blown out.

Circular Polarizer (CP) Filter

When photographing water, you may need to attach a Circular Polarizer (CP) filter to reduce or remove unwanted glare from rocks or reflections in still water (or glass). You need to use a CP (not a linear polarizer) with an auto-focus camera. A CP filter may also saturate some colors, remove unwanted over-saturation of others, and may darken the scene. A CP filter reduces the light entering the camera by the equivalent of two f-stops. The photo of the river shown in Figure 12-6 was taken without a CP filter, resulting in a bright reflection.

The same photo taken with a CP filter (see Figure 12-7) reveals the rocks under the water.

Weather Considerations

It's not a big secret that weather here in Texas is anything but predictable. In fact, my Texas mom's favorite expression was "only a fool or a Yankee would try to predict weather in Texas." Almost always, clear, bright days are not good for still-motion water photography, because too much sunshine limits how slow you can make your shutter speed. Overcast days are the best times to photograph waterfalls, because the clouds filter out direct sunlight and disperse it evenly over the ground.

12

Did you know?

About Light Reducing Filters

Light reducing filters for most digital cameras either screw or are pushed onto the camera lens. Neutral Density (ND) filters reduce the amount of light passing through the lens without changing the colors in the photo. ND filters are available in different values; their labels identify how much light is reduced in f-stops.

For example, an ND3 filter reduces the light entering the camera by the equivalent of three f-stops. Some of the newer digital cameras have built-in digital ND filters (such as the Canon G3), which act the same as an actual ND filter. ND is an important accessory for a digital camera, especially for cameras whose aperture settings are limited to f:8 or f:11.

After You Take the Photo

If your camera supports the raw file format (discussed in Chapter 6), here is a trick that you can use with your waterfall photos to prevent the white part of the falls from blowing out.

Use the spot meter setting and read the brightest part of the falls. Use exposure lock to hold the setting while you compose your shot. The resulting image will properly expose the falls, but the surrounding area will be too dark. When you process the raw file format, make two images: one with the water properly exposed, and another with the surrounding area correctly exposed. In Photoshop or another photo editor, use a layer mask and combine the two images.

If your camera doesn't support raw format, using a solid tripod take your reading using center weighting and lock the exposure. Compose the shot and immediately press the shutter button a second time. The second photo will be properly exposed for the surrounding area. Take the two images in Photoshop and selectively combine them.

Blurring Other Subjects

The most popular form of stop motion photography involves water, but that doesn't mean you are limited only to shooting blurry water.

FIGURE 12-8 Slow shutter settings cause traffic lights to blur together.

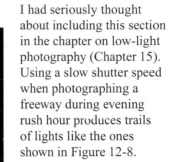

Photographing Blurred Traffic Lights

I had seriously thought about including this section in the chapter on low-light photography (Chapter 15). Using a slow shutter speed when photographing a freeway during evening rush hour produces trails of lights like the ones shown in Figure 12-8.

Taking photographs like this is simple but requires a little practice. As with photographing water, photographing moving lights requires use of a tripod. It isn't necessary to use shutter priority, however, because such a photo is usually taken under low light condition. You can use automatic exposure settings and the camera will still select a slow shutter speed. To increase the amount of blurring, use shutter priority to decrease the shutter speed.

FIGURE 12-9 Slow shutter speeds give the blades a sense of motion.

Using Blurring for Effect

In the previous chapter we learned that blurring impacts a sense of motion. Using a tripod and shutter priority, you can achieve some great blurring effects. The windmill in Figure 12-9 was shot using shutter priority. Had this been taken at normal shutter speed on a bright, sunny day (1/250), the blades of the windmill would appear to be stopped. By using a slow shutter speed of 1/30, the blades are blurred while the rest of the windmill remains in sharp focus. For the record, I did not use a tripod for the shot; instead, I chose to steady the camera up against the doorjamb of my truck.

Slow shutter speeds and panning can also be used with running people or animals. With luck—and this technique does require some—the subject's legs will

12

be a blur while the body is in relatively sharp focus for a dramatic picture of speed.

Creative Blurring

Sometimes I like to blur photos of lights just for the fun of it. The photo shown in Figure 12-10 was taken of some holiday lights at a slow shutter speed as I deliberately moved the camera. The result is pop art that makes nice backgrounds for presentations and web sites.

FIGURE 12-10 Moving a camera set to a slow shutter speed produces pop art.

Summary

Now that we have covered all of the creative photo stuff, in the next chapter you will discover how to take better photos of friends and family.

Chapter 13

Take Great Photos of People

How to…

- Respect your subject's wishes
- Adhere to basic rules for photographing people
- Photograph couples and groups
- Take a great bio picture
- Take better vacation photos

Digital Photography Myth Number 13   Digital cameras are good for taking landscape photos, but they aren't good for taking photos of people.

Fact   False. The digital camera and film camera take equally good photos of people. In fact, when shooting people pictures, the digital camera has an advantage over the film camera because you can review the photos immediately after they are taken. If you don't like what you see, it's convenient to set up the shot and take more photos immediately. This instant feedback helps make the digital camera the optimum choice for people pictures.

When you take a picture of someone you are entering into an unspoken understanding between you, as the photographer, and the subject of your photograph. Your goal is to capture a meaningful image of the person or persons with your camera. When you take photos of family and friends, the usual intention is to capture a moment in time—be it a vacation, a family gathering, a graduation, or a wedding. In most cases, the subject's primary concern is how he or she is going to look in the photo; fears that he or she will appear fat, too skinny, old, balding, or worse, can crop up during a shoot.

This chapter is all about what it takes to make great people photos. It involves a little technical savvy but lots of people skills. You will discover where and how to photograph one of the most difficult subjects on the planet: people.

The Basics of People Pictures

FIGURE 13-1 Composition, lacking here, is the first step in taking good photographs.

Since your camera is taking care of many of the technical details of the shot, such as exposure and focus, you can concentrate on the part that the camera cannot do: compose the photo. Look at the photo that appears in Figure 13-1 and ask yourself these questions:

- What is the main subject of this photo?

- What does the photo tell you?

The photo shown in Figure 13-1 was taken at a community college luncheon, and the person taking the photo, my wife, was attempting to show people eating—or she may have been focusing her attention on the two ladies in the upper-left corner of the shot. The main problem with the photo, obviously, is that the center of the frame is filled with the sides and backs of the people eating lunch. This is a common mistake many people make when they are taking photos. They may see a person in the camera's viewfinder, but they don't compose their shot before they click the shutter.

 If possible, avoid taking pictures of people while they are eating. The act of eating isn't very flattering in photos.

13

The Most Important Rule for Photographing People

Photographing people can be challenging, because unlike photographing a mountain, your pet, or the Sleeping Beauty castle at Disneyland, people tend to be self-conscious. Some people believe that they aren't photogenic, some believe that taking their picture will in some way capture their soul, and others are just plain shy. How do you deal with such subjects? That's easy. Always respect their wishes. If someone indicates he doesn't want you to take his picture, don't do it.

Here's one technique a lot of portrait photographers use to make flash pictures appear warmer. Rather than set the digital white balance on their camera to FLASH when they are in the studio using flash strobes, they set to SHADE or CLOUDY to give the subject a warmer lighting appearance. Shoot the same subject with the same lighting but run a test shot with each WB and then determine on your computer monitor (not the camera LCD) which one gives them the skin tones they like best.

—*Mike, Mike Hickey Photography*

Taking a good photo is all about composing the scene in the camera frame before you shoot. The goal is to select a viewpoint that organizes the elements and individual details of the scene into a balanced arrangement. That said, composition is largely a matter of personal taste: what one person finds pleasing, another will not appreciate.

Rules of Composition

If you follow some basic rules of composition in photography, your photos are guaranteed to look better. Even so, you should never treat a rule of composition as a hard-and-fast rule that must be observed. In fact, some of the most famous photographers violate all the rules of composition and the photos are applauded

 In photography, there is no definitive right or wrong way to compose a shot. A composition that conveys a photographer's intended meaning is an effective one. A composition that doesn't do this, or that confuses the viewer, is not effective.

excellent pictures. This doesn't mean that the rules are without value, however. They are time-proven, and a few rules provide great guidelines for photographers at any level.

The Rule of Thirds

As mentioned in Chapter 3, one of the most popular rules of composition—the Rule of Thirds—says that you divide each shot into three sections as you compose the frame. Imagine the viewfinder is divided into thirds, both horizontally and vertically. This grid creates four intersection points. Place your

FIGURE 13-2 The composition of this photo obeys the Rule of Thirds

subject at a point where the lines intersect, instead of in the center of the frame. The photo shown in Figure 13-2 is a good example. Many digital cameras now have features that place frame lines in the viewfinder to help you compose using the Rule of Thirds as you shoot.

What happens if you don't obey the rules? Figure 13-3 shows a rodeo rider enjoying a cup of coffee and the subject is dead center in the photo. Is it a bad photo? According to the rules of composition, yes, the composition is poor but I like the expression on the rider's face, and so the rules take a back seat to personal preference. As we go through different types of photo settings in this chapter, you should always be aware of the Rule of Thirds, but don't be a slave to the rules.

FIGURE 13-3 This photo breaks the rules of composition. Does that make it a bad photo?

To Pose or Not to Pose

Photographing someone who is not aware that you are taking her photo is called "candid photography." You don't need to pose the subject, since she isn't aware of you. Some of my best photos were of people who weren't aware that I was taking their pictures. The photo in Figure 13-4 is a good example of a candid shot.

13

FIGURE 13-4 Candid photos can produce some of the best people photos.

Candid photos are most successful when the subject's attention is fixed on some activity.

Some people love to pose for the camera. The photo in Figure 13-5 shows of one of my favorite subjects. Her name is Morgan, and if you point a camera at her, like I did while she and her friends were packing for a trip, she immediately stops what she is doing and poses for the camera. People like Morgan are fun to photograph. Unfortunately, many people are reluctant to be photographed.

Except for professional models, most people that you photograph don't know how to pose for the best-looking shot, so if you ask them to pose just by saying "cheese," for example, chances are you may end up with a worse photo than if you *hadn't* ask them to pose.

FIGURE 13-5 Some people love to pose for the camera.

 Saying "cheese" doesn't really produce a flattering expression on a person's face— usually a display of the subject's teeth in a sort of grimace. Many photographers use "say whiskey" or some ridiculous term that automatically makes people smile. "Say aardvark" is almost always followed by a smile.

You will learn more about specific posing later in this chapter, but after the subject is in position ready to be photographed, I recommend that you use the following guidelines while photographing anyone over the age of three:

- **Prepare them.** Tell them you are going to take more than a single shot, so they don't bolt after they see the flash go off or hear the shutter click.

- **Talk with them while you're shooting.** This means getting *them* to talk—not just preaching at them. While they are talking, you should be shooting. People can be very expressive when they are talking about something important to them. Get them talking about their favorite subject, and you will get a much more open response and a better photo.

■ **Review your photos and make positive comments.** This is an important part of taking anyone's photo with a digital camera. After you take a photo or two, review the images in the LCD screen of your camera, and even if they are out of focus, the flash didn't go off, and the person's eyes were closed, be positive in your comments. For example, say "Wow! That's a good one." Or "You really looked good in the last one." It is a fact of human nature that people will wait longer for more shots if they hear positive feedback from you. (If you've ever sat in a plane on a runway waiting for takeoff because of a problem, you probably appreciated a pilot who made the effort to keep the flyers informed of the problem rather than having to endure long periods of silence. The same is true when you are asking someone to stay still while you take photos.)

FIGURE 13-6 Avoid shooting from a position under the subject. It always produces an unflattering photo.

■ **Shoot fast.**   This is especially important if toddlers are in the photo, because they have limited attention spans and will start wandering soon after you begin shooting. Once their kid starts to wander, parents in the shot will focus on their child and you won't get a good shot of the family.

■ **Focus on the eyes.**   An important rule of thumb for portrait photographers is to make sure the subject's eyes are in sharp focus.

■ **Avoid shooting from a low position up at a subject.** Known as a "nostril shot," these are not flattering—consider the photo shown in Figure 13-6.

Taking Photos of Couples

Taking pictures of couples is probably the most fun for me, offering some of the greatest chances of getting a good shot. When you are photographing only two people who know each other well, you have a better chance of interaction and a great shot.

13

Figure 13-7 was a quick shot I took of a father and his daughter in their home. This photo gives a nod to the rule of thirds, in that the father anchors the left side of the photo. Even though a flash was used, I attached a diffuser over the flash unit, which allowed the subjects to be well exposed without being washed out. I find that her father's hand on her shoulder completes the photo. I didn't ask him to do that; he did it naturally.

FIGURE 13-7 The warm familiarity of a father and daughter makes a good composition.

If your subjects are interacting with each other, they may pay less attention to you and your camera, and you will have a better chance of getting a cool, candid shot. Regardless of the subjects' ages, let them interact and don't try and get them to sit in a special way. You can capture more feeling in a shot when it's not too posed. With candid shots of couples, you can freeze a split second in time that will never occur again. The photo shown in Figure 13-8 was taken on Christmas morning, after he got his new stethoscope. He was really pleased to get it, and he was cutting up a little when I snapped the photo.

Another style you can use when shooting couples is to have the patience to wait until the opportunity arises for a good photo. The two cousins shown in Figure 13-9 are good friends. I caught them talking to each other early one morning in winter and asked if I could

FIGURE 13-8 Candid couple shots can show a lot of expression.

take their photo using the available light from the sunrise—rather than light up the entire front room with a flash. What I like most about this photo is how they are positioned so comfortably with one another. I also like the darker shadows that resulted from using available light.

Figure 13-10 shows my daughter, Grace, and her brother. This was shot in Athens, Greece, and it was taken on the day we were preparing to leave him in Greece to return to school and we were going back to the United States. Grace's love for her brother is evident in her expression and in how she holds him.

FIGURE 13-9 Comfortable available light and great poses were already available when I entered the room to take this shot.

FIGURE 13-10 You can see how close this brother and sister are by their poses in the photo.

I set the metering to center-weighted so that it would correctly expose the pair, even though it meant blowing out the background. Their feelings for each other are expressed by their hug rather than having them stand shoulder-to-shoulder facing the camera, which would result in a less emotion-filled shot.

On the other hand, if you're photographing people who don't get along with each other, don't ask them to pose in any way that makes them feel uncomfortable.

Taking Great Bio Pictures

Truly good publicity photos rarely happen all by themselves. They take a little planning. If you can use a visual prop in the photo to indicate a person's profession or interests, for example, it conveys a lot about the person to the viewer.

The term "publicity photo" is rarely used these days. The current slang of the trade for a photograph that you use for promotion is a "bio pic"—which is short for a biographical photo.

13

Figure 13-11 shows Doc, a renowned local chef, with one of his culinary creations. Even though I was using a flash, I wanted the food to be slightly out of focus so that it wouldn't take away from the shot of him. To take this photo, I chose a wide aperture setting, which reduced my depth of field, resulting in the food being slightly out of focus and Doc's face being sharp.

FIGURE 13-11 Visual props improve the impact of a bio photo.

FIGURE 13-12 The soundboard makes a strong visual prop for this disk jockey.

The photo in Figure 13-12 shows "Stormin' Norman," a local disk jockey in his Bob Marley wig, looking at the camera across his soundboard. I chose to use available light rather than a flash for this image. I liked the contrast of the blue knobs with the colors in his hat.

Photographing Musicians

When photographing musicians, you should include their instruments. I love the expression on the drummer in Figure 13-13; even though you can barely see the drum head, his expression and how he is pointing to the camera makes him someone you want to know and hear play.

The sitar in Figure 13-14 takes up a lot of the frame in the musician shot, but the instrument looks great. Since the musician was concentrating on his playing, I didn't have to worry about a pose for this shot. The hard cast shadow that was produced by the flash I was using could have been improved by using a bounce flash or a large diffuser on the flash unit to reduce the flash effect. Nevertheless, when you look at this photo, you can almost hear the music.

FIGURE 13-13 When photographing musicians, they should look as they do when performing.

Taking Great Photos of Young People

If you want to take terrible photos of youngsters, have them sit perfectly still on a bench with their hands folded in their laps. When photographing kids, it's better to expect them to interact with one another, like the boys shown in Figure 13-15. Expressions like these make this photo one that you'll want to see again a few years from now. Still portraits in front of a backdrop do have a place in a portrait gallery, but this kind of candid group photo has great memories built into it. Did you notice the fingers behind the head of the boy on the left?

FIGURE 13-14 The musician's instrument can take up a substantial portion of the frame.

FIGURE 13-15 The key to a good group photo is to let the subjects be themselves.

Putting boys and girls together in a shot can have unpredictable and often humorous results, like the photo shown in Figure 13-16. (These antics usually subside after 15 to 20 years.) Even if they act up in front of the camera—let them do it, and take the shot. Some day, these photos will come in handy for bantering (or blackmail).

FIGURE 13-16 Sometimes having the boys and girls in the same photo prompts acting out—and fun photos.

13

Taking Good Group Photos

Whether you're photographing three or thirty, the hallmark of taking a good shot of a large group is to take control and leave little to chance. People are sheep—I say that meaning no disrespect. People preparing for a group shot are usually pretty docile, and they can follow clear directions.

FIGURE 13-17 This photo gives the viewer the feeling that these people like each other.

If only a few people are in the group, let them arrange themselves in a comfortable manner, like the photo in Figure 13-17. Technically speaking, several things are wrong with this photo—the middle gal has her eyes closed, and everyone's hair is a little haywire. Is it a good photo? Absolutely! These three massage therapy students were close friends, and it shows in the way they are smiling and holding on to one another.

FIGURE 13-18 Why you must take several photos in a group shot to get everyone looking her best (A) and (B).

More People, More Photos

The more people in a group, the more photos you need to try and take before they get tired of a flash going off in their eyes. When shooting group shoots with a flash, you must keep in mind that the more people in your photo, the greater the odds that someone in the group will close his or her eyes when the flash goes off. In Figure 13-18 A-B, only three people are in the group, yet on the first shot the woman on the left closed her eyes and on the second shot the woman on the right closed

A.

her eyes. Had I taken a third or fourth photo, I might have captured all three with their eyes open.

Arrange the Group

The best way to get good group shots is to arrange the subjects if more than three or four are in the group. Here are some suggestions for arranging people for a group photo:

- Keep the background simple to avoid distracting elements.

- In general, it's easier to take group pictures outdoors; if you have a choice, move everybody outside. If this isn't an option, try to find a place large enough so that you can stand back a reasonable distance from the group before taking the shot.

- Have the group strike varied poses—some looking directly at the camera, others looking to the side; some standing, some holding onto something and leaning. If you're trying to fit a lot of people into the camera frame, have the tallest people stand in the back and ask people to sit in chairs in the front row. The people in back can stand with their shoulders pointing toward the camera and their faces turned toward the camera.

- If small children are included, have them sit up front.

- Position the group so they are no more than two rows deep. Make sure you can see everyone's face in the frame.

- You will need to use a flash for indoor group pictures. Its limited range also limits your creativity. Keep the group inside the maximum flash distance range.

- Try standing on a chair or step ladder when taking the photo.

B.

13

Figure 13-19 shows an example of a farewell luncheon photo of a marketing team taken in the worst possible environment. With little room in the restaurant, everyone was squeezed together. Still, I had my large external flash and I was able to get about eight shots off before individuals began to complain that they hadn't brought their sun block. I eventually had to stand on a chair to get the best photo.

FIGURE 13-19 A good group photo can be a real challenge to assemble.

Taking Great Vacation Photos

Everyone knows how important it is to document important family events, weddings, graduations, and other activities. But it can be just as important to preserve the everyday occurrences that make up your daily life.

When you go on a family vacation, the obvious photos you take are the landmarks and the family standing in front of the landmarks—proving that You Were There. The photo shown in Figure 13-20 was taken by a passing stranger. I'm in the photo, but I didn't take it. The camera needed to be closer (many photographers stand too far away from their

FIGURE 13-20 Classic family vacation photo with all of the classic mistakes

FIGURE 13-21 Taking photos of the little moments in addition to the big ones on a trip serve as a visual reminder of the experience.

subjects). A shadow from my head shows on our daughter's face, and we are blocking the view of the Acropolis.

Whenever you take a trip, make a point of capturing as many of the little moments as you can, remembering that later on, these will serve as visual reminders of your trip. The photo in Figure 13-21 is an example that reminds us of how tired we were while traveling overseas. It was taken in an airport after a 14-hour flight.

Travel Tips

When on vacation, make sure that you bring along everything that you might require for your digital camera. Here is a brief checklist of items you need to have packed:

- **Spare batteries** At least two sets of rechargeable batteries

- **Battery charger** Make sure the battery charger works in the country you will be visiting. Some chargers in the U.S. won't work with 50Hz current, which is the common supply line frequency in Europe. Make sure to bring a receptacle adapter.

- **Enough digital film** Memory for digital cameras is reasonably priced and readily available at home. Make sure that you bring enough memory for the entire vacation, and/or bring a notebook computer or other device to which you can transfer the photos.

- **Camera bag** Don't get a fancy camera bag with the product name on it. When I do a lot of traveling, I use a well-built diaper bag. It has lots of pockets, and no self-respecting thief will steal a diaper bag!

13

Plan on packing your digital camera in your carry-on baggage. I don't recommend packing an expensive digital camera with your checked luggage. It could get stolen or damaged.

Now that you have learned how to take general people photos, it's time to discover how to photograph the subject of more photos than anything else in the world—babies and children.

Chapter 14

Get the Best Pictures of Babies and Small Children

How to...

- Photograph babies
- Shoot at different angles
- Shoot photos of toddlers
- Group toddlers for better photos
- Take photos during a performance

Digital Photography Myth Number 14: It takes a professional photographer to get great photos of your children.

Fact: False. Really, the opposite is true. When you take your infant or toddler to a photographer, you usually dress the child in a new outfit. The photographer and the environment (the studio) are foreign, as well. When you take the photos yourself in a familiar environment, your child feels much more at ease, and a better and more natural looking photo results.

In this chapter you will discover how to photograph babies, toddlers, and small children. You'll learn how to capture their most expressive moments and become part of their world so that they become unaware of you taking their photo—which is when you get the best pictures. You will also learn how to take great photos of them during the most terrifying time of their lives— the school play.

FIGURE 14-1 Cute baby pictures are the result of patience and taking lots of photos.

Photographing Babies

Babies are fun to photograph. They aren't camera shy—in fact, they aren't even camera aware. Posing is not a problem with babies because they have no idea what a camera is. The trick with taking pictures of babies is that they change expressions several times a second. If you want to get good photos, you need to take as many photos as possible. The photo in Figure 14-1 was one of six photos

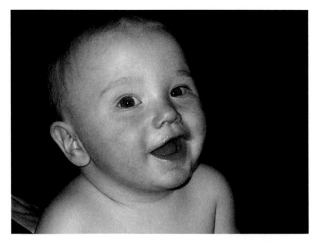

FIGURE 14-2 Even eating food produces a wealth of baby photo opportunities.

that were taken within a two-minute period. As cute as this photo is, the other five taken at the same times weren't nearly as cute.

Because everything is new to a baby, everything they do is fun to capture using a camera. Even eating can be an odyssey of expressions, like the photo shown in Figure 14-2.

Shoot at Their Level When Possible

Whenever possible, you should try to take baby photos at their eye level. In the case of the first two photos, the baby was sitting in a high chair, making it easy.

 When taking photos of your children, take as many photos as you can. When it comes to your children, you cannot take too many pictures. When using a digital camera the photos are virtually free, so there is no excuse for not taking a ton of photos.

You can get down to a baby's level in two ways: The most obvious choice is to get down on the floor with him. You will get better expressions when you do that, because he doesn't

14

 Did you know?

Use Your Continuous Feature

Many consumer cameras have a *continuous,* or burst mode, feature that allows you to take several images in succession. This is especially useful when photographing children, where the first exposure may be followed by many more interesting expressions. (See Chapter 11 for more information on using this feature.) The primary disadvantage of using this feature is that your digital camera disables the flash when this mode is selected because the flash doesn't have sufficient time to recharge between pictures.

have to look up at you. A second choice depends on the type of LCD screen your camera has—if it's a swing-out style LCD, like the one shown in Figure 14-3, you can put the camera at the baby's level and view while standing (or more than likely, you'll be bent over).

I find that I do better if I am down on the floor with the baby, but the advantage of this approach is that you can position the camera away from you, which gives you an opportunity to grab some great photos of the baby while he is staring at you and not the camera.

FIGURE 14-3 The swing-out style of the camera's LCD screen provides a more flexible capability with which to snap great candid photos of children.

Be Creative When Holding the Child

A classic approach is to have someone hold the child. The happy dad shown in Figure 14-4 is an example of how well this kind of pose works.

FIGURE 14-4 This little costumed baby clearly feels secure sitting in dad's arms.

If a baby doesn't feel secure with the person who is holding him, he is quick to make his concerns known in the most visual and vocal way possible. So if the baby seems unhappy, and the pose doesn't seem to be working, don't try and force it to happen.

With dad holding the child, you can capture the size comparison between father and child, which provides a great way to chronicle the baby's growth. These photos will be greatly enjoyed as the child gets too old (or too large) for dad to hold.

The Effect of Clothes

Regardless of how secure a child may feel in the arms of her mother or father, when you put her in an outfit she's not accustomed to wearing, like new clothes or a Halloween or holiday costume, all bets are off. She isn't old enough to understand the concept, and costumes can feel strange to an infant. Still, if you are patient and take a lot of photos, you can end up with a dandy, like the image shown in Figure 14-5. She may have not been terribly happy with the bunny outfit, but the expression is a classic.

FIGURE 14-5 This cherub was having second thoughts about being a bunny.

FIGURE 14-6 I don't think she was ready for the nap.

Shooting at Other Than Eye Level

While the idea of pointing the camera down to photograph a baby isn't my first choice, you have few options when shooting a baby in a crib, unless you are interested in the prison bars motif produced by shooting the child either through crib bars or playpen netting. I took the photo in Figure 14-6 of the little girl who was supposed to be taking a nap. I was making faces at her over the top of the camera; hence her smile.

The LCD screen of a digital camera can be a great advantage in taking photos of small children and babies. If you are looking through the viewfinder, the camera covers your face and the child can't see you, and to the child you may appear like my friend in Figure 14-7.

Now you understand why babies sometimes get a strange look on their face when you go to take a picture. An adult hiding behind a box that flashes can be a little scary. You can position a digital camera away from your face and compose the frame looking at the LCD screen at the back of the camera. This allows the child to continue to have eye contact with you, even as you shoot the photo.

FIGURE 14-7 Here is how you appear to your subject when taking a photo.

14

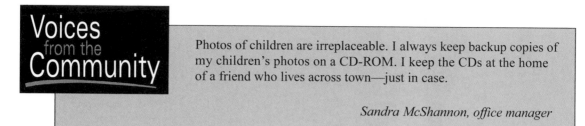

Photos of children are irreplaceable. I always keep backup copies of my children's photos on a CD-ROM. I keep the CDs at the home of a friend who lives across town—just in case.

Sandra McShannon, office manager

Photographing Toddlers

Just about the time children learn to walk, they also become aware of cameras. Most toddlers will pose for you once they have become accustomed to you. If you are fortunate, they can be real hams, like our friend's granddaughter shown in Figure 14-8.

The key to getting a good photo is to talk with the child about what she is doing, while taking photos as fast as you can. Ask her questions. The best questions are those that relate to what she is doing at the moment, such as "Is that your favorite toy?" "How old are you?" or "What's the name of your doll?" If you ask the age of a child under the age of six, you can probably capture some hand movement as she expresses her age by holding up fingers.

If your camera fires the flash, it will distract the child, but the flash quickly becomes part of her experience and she will become accustomed to it. Be patient and keep talking to the child while taking photos. At some point, she will no longer be interested in the camera clicking and the flash firing and she will focus attention on answering your questions, like Byron telling me how much he likes his new sunglasses in Figure 14-9.

FIGURE 14-8 Some children love to mug it up in front of the camera.

Tip *Many parents teach their toddlers to "say cheese" whenever a camera appears, often resulting in a phony and often ludicrous expression.*

Tip *The easiest way to ease the tension in a group of antsy kids is to tell them all to make the goofiest, scariest, silliest, or weirdest face they can make. Let them change their poses a few times, while taking their pictures.*

FIGURE 14-9 Talk with the child about what he is doing or what he likes—a new pair of sunglasses worked in this shot.

Make Photo Taking a Game

Your digital camera has a built-in feature that is a godsend for taking photos of young children—the ability to review photos on the LCD screen. After you take a picture of a child, pop up the photo on the LCD screen and show it to the child. Children love seeing themselves on the screen and they will quickly get excited about you taking more photos. My favorite trick when showing a child the photo is to ask him "Is that you in my camera?" The child generally responds by giggling. I next ask, "How did you get into my camera?" More giggles. This can quickly turn into a game, and while it takes extra time to let the child review your photos, the results are always worth it.

Using Distraction Works— Sometimes

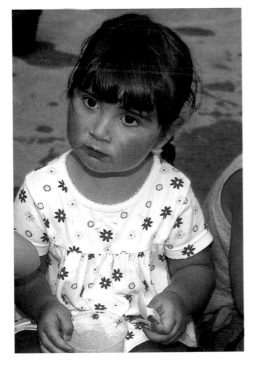

FIGURE 14-10 Sometimes the subject gets a little too distracted.

Distraction works if you can shoot one-handed or you have someone with you to talk to the child as you shoot. Of course, sometimes the distraction can be distracting. In Figure 14-10, the child was puzzled by the hand motion I was making with my non-shooting hand. I ended up with a picture of a real cutie with a really puzzled expression on her face.

If a helper or the parent of the child is nearby, have the person stand behind you to focus the child's eyes toward the camera. In the photo shown in Figure 14-11, can you figure out where grandma and grandpa are standing?

Another way to get a child to focus on the shooting without having her pose is to have a toy

14

nearby. Sometimes the child will want whatever it is that you are holding. In this case, give it to him and photograph him exploring the toy; if you don't let he have it, you might end up photographing a temper tantrum—which might not be a bad photo, actually, because at times later in the child's life, you might want to revisit these photos (at his wedding, for example).

 Tip *As much as possible, chronicle all of the important events in your children's lives. As your children get older, don't expect them to be excited about you taking all of these photos—but these photos are absolutely necessary so you will have great photos to embarrass them with later in their lives!*

FIGURE 14-11 It's a good idea to have someone get the child's attention, but only if they're standing behind you.

Add Friends for Greater Photo Opportunities

Toddlers are very social. Given the chance, they will usually cluster together in little groups. What makes them such good subjects is that because they are so young, they have almost zero verbal communication skills. As a result, they watch each other and don't pay much attention to the photographer. One of the things I enjoy about taking photos of toddlers that are gathered together without being involved in activity is the looks on their little faces. The kids in Figure 14-12 have already made their paper bag projects and they are waiting for the flavored ices. They haven't a clue what to do, so they just sit there and stare.

FIGURE 14-12 The toddler's dilemma: lots of friends but no one to talk to.

I don't remember what was going on when I took the photo shown in Figure 14-13. They both have cups of flavored ice, but the girl on the left looks like she is going to protect her ice cup at all costs.

FIGURE 14-13 Expressions of toddlers when they are together can be priceless.

Using Your Zoom to Get a Priceless Shot

Let a toddler sit by herself without distractions, and she usually enters a world of wonder. I have no idea what—if anything—goes through toddlers' minds at this age, but I do know they sit and stare into nowhere for great lengths of time for a young person.

If your camera has a good zoom feature, you can become an unobtrusive observer of these moments, like the photo shown in Figure 14-14. In both photos, the children were not aware I was taking their pictures.

Whether the photos are good or bad, keep them all. You can lose the black, blown out, and out-of-focus images, but keep the rest. To keep your hard drive from getting too full, you should archive the photos to a CD or DVD.

FIGURE 14-14 A zoom lens allows you to capture the contemplative moments of these young people.

14

Photographing Children on Stage

If you or a friend's child is performing either in a play, concert, or another public event, you should be aware that taking photos of her during the actual performance will rarely result in a good photo. There is a valid psychological reason for this: in most cases, the child is scared, and looks scared. In some cases, she is worried that she is going to miss her cue, or mangle her lines, like the youngster in Figure 14-15— although I think it's a really cute photo.

Some children are just nervous about standing in front of a bunch of adults, and even though adults think it's really cute when a child blows a line or drops a prop, it can be really embarrassing for the child. To make the situation worse, some children are also embarrassed when their parents make a scene during a performance while taking their photos. Sound hopeless? Not at all. There is a simple solution but it involves some additional time and effort on your part. See the How to... box, "Photograph a Performance Like a Pro," for more.

FIGURE 14-15 Nervous children on stage can make poor subjects for close-ups.

How to ... Photograph a Performance Like a Pro

1. Find out when dress rehearsal is scheduled and make arrangements with the person in charge to shoot pictures during the rehearsal.

2. If the person in charge OKs it, announce to the performers (not the stage hands) that you will be taking their photos.

3. If costumes are involved, take those close-ups on the set during breaks—don't shoot individual photos during the rehearsal. The same is true if the person is singing or dancing solo. Get them alone and have them do their thing.

4. During the actual performance, take some photos that show the entire scenes with the audience. When you create the slide show or paste the prints in an album, it will appear that all the photos were taken during the performance.

Alternatives to Dress Rehearsals

If you can't make it to the dress rehearsal, arrive at the actual performance early to get a front row seat. Even if the stage is farther than 12 feet (a realistic distance for the flash built into your camera) from the first row of seats, you can still shoot, since many stage productions are brightly lit.

The photo shown in Figure 14-16 was taken from the front row during a Christmas play and it came out pretty good. Even though these children were performing, they had no lines, which made them more like stage props and therefore much less nervous. (In fact, I think one of the wise men appears to be interested in Mary.)

FIGURE 14-16 A good zoom lens and a powerful flash can capture the heart of the play.

Tip

When your digital camera is zoomed out to its maximum setting, the amount of light entering the camera is decreased. You need to accommodate for this by changing settings on the camera and using a tripod or by using a flash, if it's appropriate and allowed.

If the lighting isn't bright enough or you cannot get close enough, you will need to find somewhere to set up a tripod and try an available light shot. The performers may be blurry if they are moving fast, but the rest of the stage/production won't be moving so it won't be blurry. It might be better than nothing at all. If your camera allows it, increase the ISO setting to a higher number, which allows you to take photos in low-light conditions.

Candid Shots vs. Posed Photos

As mentioned earlier, if you ask a subject to pose or say cheese, especially children, you'll probably be disappointed with the shot. Unless the person is a professional model, if she attempts to smile or pose for the picture she'll usually look like she's in pain or worse. Candid shots, photos that catch the subject unaware while involved in a familiar activity, usually have the highest probability of resulting in a good photo.

14

Use Your Flash Effectively

Children are seemingly boundless sources of energy. They jump, run, and climb on just about everything. On a bright sunny day, this isn't a problem, but the bright outdoor light can cast shadows on their faces. Setting the flash to manual will produce a fill flash that prevents cast shadows.

The subject of fill flash is covered in greater detail in Chapter 9. In early morning, evening, and indoors, there is insufficient light to allow you to capture all of the speed of the children on photos without blurring. When shooting moving subjects in relatively low light conditions, you should set the flash so it always fires rather than depend in the automatic settings to fire the flash. This way, you can be ensured that photos of even the fastest youngster will be sharp.

Tip *Be patient. You shouldn't expect to get the perfect shot immediately. Wait for the right moment, and then shoot quickly.*

The little girl in Figure 14-17 is trying to blow a soap bubble that cannot be seen in the photo, while the girls in Figure 14-18 are dancing for all they are worth. Both of these candid shots were worth the wait.

FIGURE 14-17 Candid photos like this one of a girl blowing a soap bubble are always better than posed pictures.

FIGURE 14-18 Weddings allow children the opportunity to tear up while being dressed up.

FIGURE 14-19 The child was so absorbed by the candlelight that he didn't notice me taking the pictures.

On some occasions, it isn't necessary to use a flash to shoot under low-light conditions. During a candlelight service, the young man shown in Figure 14-19 is completely absorbed by the flame of his candle. Because the room was lit only by candlelight, the camera shutter speed was very slow, so I used a tripod. Since the boy wasn't moving and the entirety of his attention was on the candle, I was able to take several shots without a flash to distract him (and the others).

Make Children Feel Comfortable and Secure

When children feel safe and secure, you will have a much better chance of getting a good photo. When the child feels safe, he will probably forget that you are taking photos (unless you are using a flash). In Figure 14-20, the young boy wasn't too sure what I was doing. I had just met Aaron and his dad on a hot Texas afternoon. When I began shooting, Aaron held tight to his dad's arm.

FIGURE 14-20 When the shooting started, Aaron wasn't too sure about me.

After about two minutes, his attention was focused on getting the blue gumball at the bottom of the cup (see Figure 14-21). He forgot I was shooting and relaxed with his dad.

FIGURE 14-21 After a few minutes, his attention returned to getting the gumball at the bottom of the cup.

Did you know?

Always Let the Kids Play

As a general rule, children do not want to sit really still, smile at the camera, and fold their hands nicely in their lap. Because posing doesn't come naturally for adults it is even worse for toddlers and pre-kindergarteners. So, you should make the experience as non-intrusive as possible by making it much more enjoyable. If you let the children be comfortable and be themselves you and they will have more fun and your photos will be better.

Shoot, Talk, Shoot, Talk

When shooting a picture of a child in which you don't have the luxury of standing a far distance away, you need to talk to the child all the time while you are shooting. Ask questions, shoot, ask more questions. Typically, children two to four years of age are not self-conscious, and they make good subjects if you can keep their attention while taking their picture. Because digital cameras tend to have a very wide lens, you must sometimes get closer than you would wish to fill the frame with the subject.

The young lady in Figure 14-22 was having her face painted and therefore had to keep still while I took her photo. Even though I was using a flash (it was late evening), she eventually started smiling at my stupid jokes.

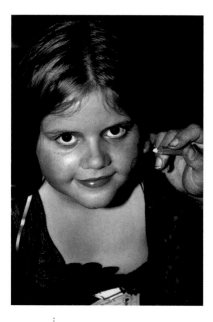

FIGURE 14-22 Even close-up flash photos work if you can keep the subject's attention.

Summary

Now that you know how to photograph people, in the next chapter you will learn how take photos in low light.

Chapter 15

Low-Light Photography: Taking Great Night Photos

How to...

- Take advantage of early morning and evening lighting
- Photograph holiday lights
- Capture great fireworks and lightning photos
- Take photos at night without flash
- Overcome digital noise problems

Digital Photography Myth Number 15: Digital cameras cannot be used for night photos.

Fact: Not true, but because digital cameras tend to produce noisy pictures under low-light conditions, shooting at night requires some technique to achieve the best results.

The world is revealed anew by either the cool stillness near dawn or the fiery warm colors produced within an hour of sunset. You'll discover common scenes take on an entirely different appearance when shot in low light. In a similar manner, night photography exposes a world of shadows cast by streetlights and neon signs, making images that look nothing like their daylight counterparts.

When you have finished this chapter, you will know what equipment is necessary and how to set up your camera to get the best possible photographs with the minimum amount of digital noise (the equivalence of film grain in film photography). You will also discover how to remove or cover up that digital noise, using photo editing software in your computer.

Low-Light Photographic Opportunities

When the sun goes down, everything looks different. To show just how much different day and night can be, consider the next two photos: The daylight photo in Figure 15-1 was taken of a storefront in Georgetown, Texas. The night photo is of the same place, just after the sun went down.

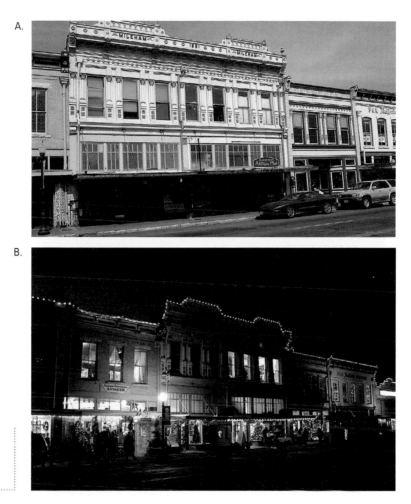

A.

B.

FIGURE 15-1 (A) Daylight photo of an historic Texas town; (B) the same street at night looks very different.

Some subjects actually look better at night. When it comes to Las Vegas, for example, the city was designed for the night. The photograph in Figure 15-2 was shot from a hotel balcony.

15

Low-Light and Night Photography

Although both types of photos are taken without flash, the two types of available light photography, low-light and night photography, require different photographic approaches.

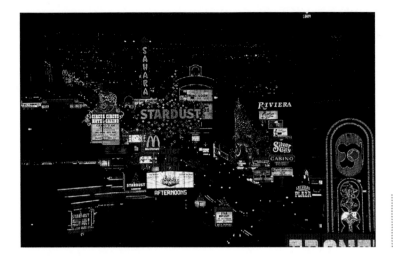

FIGURE 15-2 If there was ever a town that was meant to be photographed at night, it's Las Vegas.

FIGURE 15-3 Low-light photos like this require long exposure times.

Available light photography is generally defined as making photos without the aid of a flash. Low-light photos are usually shot using very low light output sources, such as candles, a setting sun, or by another limited light source.

Figure 15-3 is an example of an available light photo taken of a windowless chapel in a California mission illuminated entirely by candles. Night photography typically uses light from distant light sources, such as the moon, car lights, or neon signs.

The photo shown in Figure 15-3 could have been taken with a flash, but it would have lost the warmth that is produced by using candles as a source of illumination. The key to taking this photo was to stabilize the camera before pressing the shutter. Since I didn't have a tripod, I placed a beanbag on the floor and fit the camera into it so it was level with the scene. To make sure that the camera didn't move when I pressed the shutter button, I used the camera's self-timer to take the photo. I changed the flash mode from auto to off so that the camera didn't try and add its own light to the scene. The camera didn't require any other special settings. Because the light from the candles was so low, when the timer went off the camera held the shutter open for two seconds.

FIGURE 15-4 This room is lit by a combination of daylight and incandescent lights.

FIGURE 15-5 This photo of the moon behind the clouds required a very long exposure time.

The photo shown in Figure 15-4 is also an available-light shot. Even though it was a little after noon on a bright sunny day, the only light that was illuminating the inside of the mission church was some daylight streaming in from four small arched windows near the ceiling. The areas in the photo that are illuminated by daylight have a cool appearance, but the incandescent lamps above the alter flood the area with a much warmer color.

I took a quick light reading with the camera and discovered that it needed a shutter speed of 1/8 of a second, which is way too slow for hand-held photography. I wedged the beanbag and camera on a pew and shot the photograph.

Night photography takes more preparation than low-light photography. In almost all cases, time exposures are necessary. This means using shutter speeds measured in seconds and sometimes even minutes.

The photograph of the moon behind the clouds shown in Figure 15-5 was taken using a four-second exposure. The camera was mounted on a solid tripod so it didn't move, but the shutter was open for so long that the photo of the moon and clouds are slightly blurred because *they* moved during the long exposure.

Advantages of Early Morning and Evening Light

My favorite time to take photographs is during the first few hours after sunrise and a few hours before sunset. The color temperature of the light at these times is distinctly different.

15

When shooting early morning shots, use center-weighted metering if your camera has it. If not, experiment with spot metering. The clouds will usually have a bright area in the middle, and you should try and read that area of the clouds or it may be overexposed.

Mornings Offer Cool Colors and Stillness

Getting up early in the morning isn't fun for most people, but the photographic rewards of doing so make the effort worthwhile. As the earth rotates, the sun catches the clouds and puts on quite a show. I've found that the most magnificent cloud illumination occurs during a 20-minute period before the sun rises. By the time the sun has come up, the show is over. The photo of the U.S. Capitol in Figure 15-6 was taken at 6 A.M.

FIGURE 15-6 The sun rising behind the U.S. Capitol made a grand display.

When the clouds begin to change colors, you can begin shooting photos. As the earth rotates, the clouds will change color and then return to their morning gray. You usually have only a few minutes to catch the scene before it disappears.

Another aspect of shooting in the early morning is that not many others are out wandering around. The photo shown in Figure 15-7 was taken early in the morning near San Diego. It was low tide and the surfer was patiently waiting for the surf to come up.

FIGURE 15-7 A lone surfer waits on a beach at low tide.

If you want to shoot the beaches at low tide, always check the tide tables. Low tides come two or three times a day and not necessarily at dawn.

FIGURE 15-8 Just after the sun goes down, the sky often turns reddish-orange.

Evening Light Makes Colors Appear Warm

If you shoot photos within an hour of sundown, the colors in the photo will appear warm, like those shown in Figure 15-8. Often, the most beautiful effects will take place in a 20-minute period before and after the sun sets.

The Beauty of Night Photography

Night photography is fun. You can rarely predict how the lighting will affect the final photo when the shutter is held open for long periods of time. When I took the photo of the main street of Hutto, Texas, (pop. 200) shown in Figure 15-9, multiple light sources affected the shot: holiday lighting of the building and window displays and the street lighting.

Most street lighting today uses bulbs filled with mixtures of different gases that produce a wide array of colors. I set the white balance on automatic for this shot. The street lamps appeared to be a light whitish pink visually, but the camera recorded them with a definite greenish tint.

FIGURE 15-9 The streetlights produced an unexpected green tint to complete the holiday lighting scene.

15

The best time for night photos is often not in the middle of the night, but at dusk. During the hour before and the hour after sunrise, you will still get the mood and effects of nighttime photography while being able to capture more detail in your subject. And you can use a faster shutter speed.

The photo of the city street in Figure 15-1 was taken 20 minutes after the sun went down. That's the reason there is a lovely blue gradient behind the buildings. The photo in Figure 15-9 was taken several hours after the sun had set, which is why the sky is black.

 With extremely long exposures, you can capture more detail in a scene, but you'll often get a sky that more closely resembles daylight.

Shooting the Moon

Have you seen beautiful crystal clear photos of the moon? They were probably taken either with a telescope or with an SLR camera with a telephoto lens that cost more than a compact car. Shooting photographs of the moon or the stars is a challenge at best. Until now, we have been talking about low-light photography using nearby light sources.

To photograph the night sky requires exposure times measured in minutes. It also requires that you avoid something that's often found in the city—light pollution. The lights from your town flood the night sky, masking all but the brightest stars and planets. Even if you travel a distance from a major city, city lights can still reflect off of the lower atmosphere, diminishing your photo opportunities.

 A good rule of thumb for shooting a full moon is to use manual mode, set your aperture to f:16, and use a shutter speed that approximates your sensitivity (ISO) setting. A shutter speed slower than 1/100 results in a blurring of the moon's features.

Photographing by the Light of the Moon

If you want to take photographs using the moon as your primary light source, time and a little bit of luck are essential. Moonlight is bright enough to use as a lighting source for only a few days a month. Although the night of the full moon is the brightest night, you'll usually have sufficient light for photographing either a few days before or after the full moon. The tricky part is the weather, since while the moon follows a fixed calendar cycle, the weather does not.

Try to do your shooting during the first two to three hours after the moon rises. At this time, the moon will be high enough in the sky to illuminate your subject, without losing shadows. You will find that in some months, it's impossible to shoot at all because the moon rises extremely late—or worse during the daylight hours. Check the weather almanac on the Internet to find out what time the moon rises and sets in your area.

Night Photography and EV Compensation

If you are shooting the stars or a cityscape, try using your EV (Exposure Value) Compensation settings to capture more detail in low-light situations. EV Compensation is usually set on a +2 or –2 scale. Begin with a –2 setting for low-light situations. How much detail you want to capture will vary from one low-light situation to the next, but if these techniques don't provide the results you want, try moving to your manual shutter speed settings.

Most security personnel agree that someone lurking about in the dark, late at night, is probably up to no good. With this preconception in mind, any plans you have about setting up your tripod and camera on corporate or private property, near restricted areas, or in abandoned buildings is usually not a good idea, unless you have obtained written permission.

—Jessica Lofthus, artist and photographer

Photograph Holiday Lights

15

During the holidays, many people and municipalities become quite creative in festooning everything with strings, webs, and other complicated schemes of lighting, like that shown in Figure 15-10.

The important thing to remember when photographing holiday lights is to use a tripod. If you don't use a tripod, you will end up with a photo like the one shown in Figure 15-11. If you don't have a tripod, use a fence post or the hood of your car for a stable platform.

FIGURE 15-10 Holiday lights can be a cinch to photograph.

FIGURE 15-11 Photographing holiday lights requires a tripod to prevent blurring like this.

Here is how to photograph holiday lights to get the best photos:

1. Mount the camera on a tripod.

2. Set your camera's settings to automatic white balance and exposure.

3. Turn off your flash.

4. To be totally sure of a sharp exposure, you can use a remote cable shutter release. An alternative method that

may work best for those without a remote cable is to prepare your shot and then use your camera's timer. This way, your hands won't be touching and potentially shaking the camera during the long exposure.

Digital Noise

Digital noise is the appearance of random pixels throughout a image, giving it a grainy look. Several different types of noise can appear in a digital photo, but they all degrade the photo quality. The noise is particularly noticeable in very dark nighttime photographs. The major cause of noise in digital camera photos is long exposure times and/or increased sensitivity (ISO) settings.

Night Photography and Noise

The source of the noise is the sensor in your camera. Taking photos under low-light conditions requires longer exposure times. Longer exposure times means the sensor is active for longer periods of time. The longer the sensor is on, the more internal heat is generated, creating more noise. Figure 15-12 is a classic example of noise produced by the camera sensor using a long exposure time in a low-light shot.

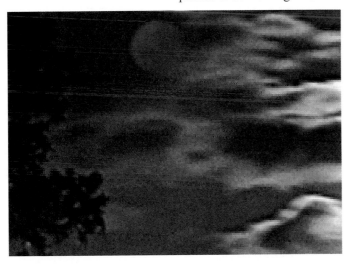

Here are several suggestions to reduce (but not prevent) noise when taking low-light or nighttime photographs.

FIGURE 15-12 Noise is a problem with photos taken under low-light conditions.

15

- **Turn off the auto-ISO feature**   Most digital cameras automatically increase the sensitivity (ISO) setting of the camera under low-light conditions. This is both good and bad. The good part is an increased ISO, meaning the exposure time is reduced; but increasing the ISO setting also greatly increases the noise produced by the sensor. If your camera allows you to do it, set your ISO setting to its lowest value (which produces the least amount of digital noise) and turn off the feature that automatically changes the ISO. If your camera has this ability, it will be a menu function.

■ **Turn on noise reduction**   I see more digital cameras ever day that offer a noise reduction feature. If your camera has one, you should turn it on during night shots. On my camera, the feature works by applying noise reduction to images taken with exposure times of 1/20 second or greater. If you plan on removing the noise later using software (as discussed momentarily), you should follow the recommendations concerning the settings of noise reduction. Most software I have worked with require that you turn off the camera's noise reduction while you shoot.

After you have taken the photos, if you discover that your photos have an excessive amount of noise, you can remove the noise. Even so, if the subject of your photo is more important than the technical quality of the image, it might be better to live with the noise and enjoy the photograph. The singer in Figure 15-13 was taken during a concert. She was out of range of my flash and lit only by the stage lighting. The noise produced by this kind of shot is shown in the insert to Figure 15-13.

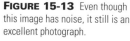
FIGURE 15-13 Even though this image has noise, it still is an excellent photograph.

Remove the Noise Using an Image Editor

Most photo-editing software offers tools for removing noise. In most cases, however, while these tools do remove the noise, they usually also remove all of the sharpness of the image. The question you must ask yourself, then, is this: "Is the cure worse than the disease?"

If most of the noise in the photo is limited to only part of the image, you can select the area in the photo using one of the software's selection tools, such as the Magic Wand, and apply the noise reduction or removal feature only to the selected area. However, if the entire image is noisy and you want to remove it, specialized software is available.

In the past two years, several companies have produced software especially designed to remove digital noise from images produced by digital cameras. The best solution on the market today is Dfine by nik multimedia. This product not only can dramatically reduce the digital noise in a photograph, you can even buy optional camera profiles for the specific noise characteristics of your model of camera, which makes the operation even better. You can find out more by visiting the company's web site at http://www.nikmultimedia.com.

Photographing Fireworks

Whether you use a film or digital camera, photographing fireworks is fun and only a little challenging. Many towns offer impressive fireworks displays for their citizens—if only to help reduce the number of people setting off their own fireworks, which is usually illegal within city limits.

I took the shot in Figure 15-14 using a Sony digital camera that actually had a setting for fireworks. The source of light from fireworks is brilliant but dissipates quickly. That's one reason why photographing fireworks can be a real challenge with digital cameras.

A tripod is absolutely necessary, since your exposures can range from 2 to 30 seconds. This stability ensures smooth, sharp photographs of the shell trails and the fireworks bursts. A monopod won't work because of the side wobble.

FIGURE 15-14 Fireworks displays are difficult to capture with digital cameras.

15

Fireworks explode a great (and safe) distance from you. If you want photos that are something other than colored blurs, you need to either use a digital camera that has a really high optical zoom factor (not very common) or invest in an inexpensive *doubler* or *tripler*. These are screw-on lens modifiers that, like their name says, either double or triple the focal length of your camera's lens. Many professionals look upon these devices with contempt because they slightly degrade the lens quality, but for most consumer photography, it is $30 to $40 well spent.

The best setting for shooting fireworks is infinity. This means that any subject that is 30 feet away or greater will be in focus. If the fireworks are exploding at distances closer than 30 feet, you should review the burns chapter in your first aid book. On some cameras, infinity lock is called Landscape mode.

How long you hold the shutter open depends on the effect you are trying to achieve. Do you want to capture a single burst or capture multiple bursts in the same frame? There is no fixed formula for this; it involves a lot of trial and error.

How to ...   Capture a Single Burst of Fireworks

If your camera has a Bulb setting, when using Bulb, the shutter closes when you release the cable release. By releasing it in mid-burst you'll get a different effect. The fireworks explosion is literally painting itself on the unexposed image. Bulb works best when used with a cable release.

1. Set your camera's exposure setting to Bulb.
2. Wait until you hear the sound of the fireworks being launched—a dull thump sound.
3. Open your shutter and wait for the fire to explode.
4. Keep waiting until the burst has completely finished and all the twinkling is done. Then release the shutter.

How to ...   Capture Several Bursts of Fireworks

1. Wait for the sound of the shell being launched.

2. Open your shutter.

3. Wait for the burst to disappear, and then carefully cover your lens and wait for the sound of the next shell being launched.

4. Uncover your lens, and wait until it's over. Then cover your lens again. There are numerous ways you can cover your lens between bursts without moving the camera. A classic technique is to put a black baseball cap over the digital camera, or you can use a piece of non-reflective black velvet or black felt cloth to cover the camera.

Tips for Getting Great Fireworks Shots

Here are some tips to help you capture the best shots:

- **Keep upwind**   Try to be upwind of the fireworks show. As the show progresses and the smoke builds up, you'll find that it obscures the fireworks.

- **Include landmarks**   Try to include landmarks to give the fireworks display a sense of location. Photographing fireworks as they're fired out over a lake or a harbor will enhance your fireworks photographs since you can also capture the reflection of the fireworks in the water.

- **Beware of street lamps**   If you want to *diminish* the quality of your photos, after you have found the ideal location, make sure that a big, bright street lamp is either in the frame or close by.

Photographing Lightning

Getting a photo of lightning is similar to photographing fireworks, except you haven't got a warning thump to let you know the lightning is about to strike. This type of photography

15

is perfect for a digital camera. With a film camera, you must hold the shutter open to wait for the strike; if the lightning doesn't strike, the exposure is lost. The same situation with a digital camera requires only pressing a delete button and the image is ready to be reshot.

Figure 15-15 shows an example of a lightning photo.

Be Safe

First and foremost, don't be stupid. In the U.S. last year, more than 600 people were killed by lightning strikes. Don't add yourself to that number. When shooting lightning during a thunderstorm, make sure that you stay away from the heart of the storm and out of lightning range.

Set Up and Wait

Frame the picture in your camera's LCD screen where it appears that most of the lightning is occurring, or where the most spectacular clouds are. Thunderstorms are very mobile, and you may need to reframe often to keep the camera centered on the eye of the activity.

Observe the Lightning

Before you begin shooting, watch the lightning for a few minutes. This will help you determine how to set up to shoot. Several different types of lightning can occur. Cloud to ground (called CG) lightning strikes fast (in a fraction of a second, it has flashed and disappeared). Other CG bolts can strobe or pulse for up to two seconds. Sheet lightning generally lasts longer, usually more than a fraction of a second.

Set Your Exposure

If the storm is moving toward you, exposure times should not exceed 10 seconds—preferably less than 5 seconds. Anything greater than 10 seconds will blur the clouds (especially if more than one lightning bolt occurs during the exposure). If the storm is a fair way away, or you cannot see it developing or moving, exposures can be set between 20 seconds and 2 minutes.

Use Manual Exposure mode, and set the aperture at a relatively small stop (f:11 or f:16). The lightning strikes will still be bright enough to expose themselves on your image.

Summary

Now that we have shed some light on the topic of low-light photography, in the next chapter you will discover all of the cool things that are possible when you get really close to the subject.

15

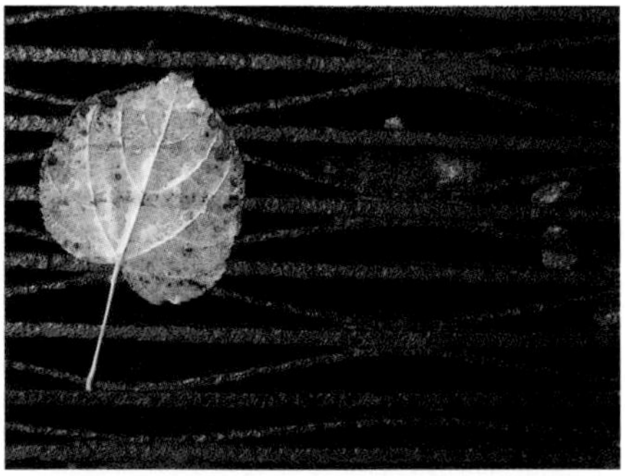

Chapter 16

Create Great Close-up Photos

How to...

- Understand macro photography
- Determine your camera's macro capability
- Set up your camera in macro mode
- Find creative macro subjects
- Master low-light macro photography

Digital Photography Myth Number 16:   It takes a lot of special (and expensive) equipment to do close-up (macro) photography.

Fact: Poppycock! (U.K.) No way, dude. (U.S.)

Macro photography is something that most digital cameras do really well. In fact, many current consumer cameras can focus on an object from one to four inches in front of the lens, which is far better than most SLR cameras can do without special equipment.

A common misconception about macro photography in general is that it's all about photographing tiny things in nature, such as butterflies, flowers, and bugs. But you'll find many uses for macro photography—from taking detailed photographs of mechanical parts to capturing details in small collectable objects. Here you'll discover how to capture the incredible world of shapes and colors that exist at the smaller end of the size spectrum.

When shooting outdoors in the snow or at the beach, always lower the EV (exposure value) by half a step, at least, to prevent a mild overexposure that can wash out colors.

Daniel Samson, sports photographer

Mastering Macro Photography

FIGURE 16-1 A camera with macro capability makes small subjects like this butterfly larger than life.

FIGURE 16-2 Gears of a printing press appear like huge industrial components when viewed close up.

Many digital cameras offer a macro mode. In short, the macro mode of your camera is designed to focus at very short distances with up to life-size magnification of the image. The butterfly shown in Figure 16-1 was shot in macro mode.

The macro mode of your camera gives you the power to focus the attention of the viewer on the extraordinary colors, textures, and shapes that surround us, such as the close-up of the gears of an old printing press shown in Figure 16-2 or the contrast of something as simple as a leaf that had fallen on my leg (see Figure 16-3). While such tiny items seem to flood our visually cluttered days, by taking a photograph and making the Lilliputian object appear larger than life, you show the viewers aspects of the object that they have never seen before—you transform the ordinary into the extraordinary.

Does Your Camera Have Macro Capability?

Most digital cameras offer some sort of macro mode. Here is the best way to determine whether your camera has a macro mode: *read the manual*. Even if your manual is nowhere to be found, rest assured, because every digital camera with macro capability that I have worked with uses the same icon, either on an external button or in the LCD screen, to indicate macro. It is the little tulip shaped icon shown here.

16

Decipher the Technical Descriptions of Your Macro Settings

Even in macro mode, your camera still has a minimum focus distance, which is different in every camera. There may also be a maximum distance that the camera can focus when in macro mode, meaning that you will not be able to bring distant subjects into focus. Here is a sampling of macro focus ranges for several popular digital cameras

FIGURE 16-3 The macro mode of your camera lets you capture the color and texture of a small leaf on denim.

Brand	Model	Macro Focus Range
Sony	DSC-F828	0.8–19.7 in (2–50 cm)
Nikon	Coolpix 3100	1.6 in (4 cm)–Infinity
Canon	PowerShot A70	Macro (W): 2.0–18.1 in (5–46 cm) Macro (T): 10.2–18.1 in (26–46 cm)
Kodak	EasyShare DX4900	2.7–27.5 in (7–70 cm)

Note that most digital cameras have a minimum focus range of around 2 inches. The exception is usually found in the more expensive "prosumer" cameras, like the Sony DSC-F828. (The Nikon Coolpix 5700 that I used to take the photo in Figure 16-1 also falls into this category.) These cameras let you get your lens closer than an inch to your subject.

Note *The Nikon Coolpix line features macro to infinity settings in most of its models, allowing you to leave the camera set in macro mode for all photos.*

The second item to note in the table is how the focus range changes on the Canon PowerShot camera and how the minimum distance increases as the lens is zoomed in (T) and zoomed out (W). The phenomenon of a lens's zoom factor affecting the minimum focusing distance has existed since the first zoom lens was invented. This model was one of the few digital cameras I found that exhibited this property. If you own a camera whose minimum focus distance varies with the zoom setting, it is important that you be aware of it. *Read your manual.*

Did you know?

You Can Add Greater Magnification to Your Digital Camera

You can buy filters to increase the magnification of your digital camera to make the subjects appear even larger. These filters screw on to the existing threads on your lens and they are simple magnification lenses. They are identified by their powers of magnification: 1+, 2+, and 3+.

You can use one or any combination of filters, as they screw together. More lenses mean more power. Just stack them all together for maximum magnification. Be aware that adding a magnifier lens to the front end of your camera may degrade the resulting photo slightly, especially if you stack multiple lenses. Nevertheless, magnification lenses are relatively inexpensive, thereby providing increased magnification with little negative impact either financially or optically.

 Always remember to return your camera to its normal focusing mode after you have finished your macro photography, or a photo opportunity may be missed as you discover, too late, why you cannot focus on the distant subject—like a rare appearance of the Loch Ness monster.

How to Set Up Macro Mode on Your Camera

On most digital cameras, there is a button like the one shown in Figure 16-4; on a few, it is selected from a menu.

Macro and Auto-Focus

If you are having trouble with your auto-focus when shooting in macro mode, check and see whether your camera's zoom setting must be within a specific range to work. For example, the icon displayed in the LCD screen of a Nikon Coolpix 5000/5700 changes from yellow to green when the zoom setting is within the required range. If it isn't, the auto-focus almost never focuses.

I spent a frustrating morning attempting to shoot close-ups of wildflowers (see Figure 16-5) when I first got my Coolpix.

Macro button

FIGURE 16-4 Some cameras have a button to enable macro mode.

16

Sometimes it would work, but not always. I was quite angry at the camera for not working properly, when in fact it was an operator error. During lunch—somewhere between the barbeque brisket and the apple pie—as I *read the macro section of the manual,* I discovered what I was doing wrong. It discovered that I had to zoom in until the icon on the LCD screen changed color.

FIGURE 16-5 Not knowing the ins and outs of your macro feature can result in an out-of-focus macro photo.

Position Your Camera for a Better View

Macro photography subjects tend not to be at eye-level— perhaps another example of Murphy's Law of Photography. Consider the basket flower that I photographed in Figure 16-6. The first shot (A) shows a photo that I took looking down at the plant. Despite its name, it doesn't look anything like a basket. So I placed the camera underneath the flower, looking up (B); now you get the strong contrast of the blue sky and you can see the intricate detail that makes up the flower. It looks like a basket, doesn't it?

This plant is less than a foot tall, so you might wonder how I got under it to take the photo. The camera I was using had an LCD screen that rotated away from the camera, allowing me to place the camera on the ground and still see what I was focusing on.

FIGURE 16-6 Shooting down on the flower (A) doesn't show the detail discovered by getting the camera underneath (B).

A.

B.

How to ...   **Shoot Low Subjects**

Here is how to shoot the underside of a low subject:

1. Place something on the ground, like a cloth or even an empty potato chip bag, to protect the camera. I often use my felt hat.

2. Check your settings. Set the camera to macro mode, and the metering mode should probably be spot.

3. Place the camera on the ground cover with the lens pointed at your subject. If the subject you are photographing allows, you can get directly behind it and align the axis of the lens with the subject.

4. If your camera has a self-timer, this is a good time to use it. If not, gently squeeze the shutter button and take the photo.

5. Flip the camera over far enough to see the LCD screen, changing the camera's overall position as little as possible. Using the image in the LCD screen as a reference, change the camera position and repeat steps 3 and 4 until you have captured a good photo. It may take some time, but the results are worth it.

Since most digital cameras have their LCD screens built into the back of the camera, getting a photo like this involves a little trial and error.

Sometimes you must be willing to be uncomfortable to get a good photograph. While out shooting in the nippy early morning, I found a field of Texas bluebonnets covered with dew. I tried and tried to get a shot that showed the dew and realized the only way was to lie on my stomach in the wet field and take the photo (see Figure 16-7). Was it worth getting wet (and I did get wet)? Absolutely.

At times discomfort isn't the problem; sometimes, it's a feeling of embarrassment. Once I was shooting a small flower on a bright day and couldn't see the resulting image due to the bright sunlight. I grabbed my jacket and placed it over my head while I was lying in the field in the Texas hill country. In the short space of time it took to get the photo I wanted, two different people stopped to make sure I wasn't dead. (That's Texas for you. Had it been Manhattan, I'm sure no one would have looked twice.)

16

A.

B.

The point is, when you are trying to take a picture you can't be self-conscious. Focus on your subject and if someone walking by thinks you are a raving lunatic, just remember you don't know him, he doesn't know you, and your paths will probably never cross again.

FIGURE 16-7 (A) The bluebonnets were wet with dew when I shot this photo (B). Afterward, I was wetter than the flowers!

Find Subjects Everywhere

Thanks to all those wonderful nature programs, most people tend to think the primary use of macro photography is to photograph natural subjects, like close-ups of flowers, butterflies, and other tiny creatures—like a favorite of mine, shown in Figure 16-8.

FIGURE 16-8 Macro photography gets you up close and personal with a variety of tiny wildlife creatures.

The most creative use of your camera's macro mode is to take a photo that makes the viewer look at common objects from a perspective he probably has never seen. For example, one afternoon while I was getting the oil on my car changed, rather than sit and smell old coffee in their waiting room, I went around back and took the photos shown in Figure 16-9.

A.

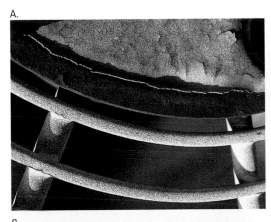

B.

C.

Figure 16-9A is a partial view of the grill over an air conditioning compressor. I liked the symmetry of the grill and the texture of the weathered materials. In Figure 16-9B, you are looking at the rim of an oil drum that used to be painted blue. Most of the paint has been replaced with rust. The rim is in sharp focus but, because of the narrow depth of field, the focus on the other parts of the drum is soft. Did you figure out what was photgraphed in the last shot (Figure 16-9C)? It's a barrel used to store (red) transmission fluid. I choose the shot because I liked the two colors together.

FIGURE 16-9 (A) Close-up of an AC compressor grid; (B) macro photo of a oil barrel rim; (C) what is that thing?

Take Low-Light Macro Photos

The challenge of taking photos under low-light conditions is that in most cases, you cannot use your camera's built-in flash. Why? Because the whole idea behind macro photography is that the camera is very close to the subject. So if the subject is one inch from the lens, the image would be completely washed out if the flash fired.

Several specialty light sources are available for macro work. Most of these devices are composed of a lamp in the shape of a ring that attaches to the end of a lens and an external power source.

Several possible light sources can be used to illuminate a macro subject if you take a moment to be creative. For example, early one morning I was trying to get a photo of a huge garden

16

Did you know?

Micro vs. Macro Photography

Macro photography is often confused with another form of high-magnification photography. In the scientific world, a further subdivision of macro photography is the photography done with the aid of microscopes, called *photomicrography* or *micro* photography. This technique requires a microscope and an adapter to attach a camera to the microscope, and it is used to achieve very high magnification shots (such as 40× and higher). This very specialized field requires special equipment to accomplish (and usually a degree in biology or some other science), but there's nothing like it when you want to get a highly magnified, romantic photo of pond water microbes.

spider in the center of an almost perfect web, glistening with dew. The problem was that it still wasn't light enough to shoot the photo without using my flash. I solved the problem by repositioning my car and using the headlights to illuminate the spider and its web. It took several attempts to get the headlights in the best position, but it worked. If you are shooting indoors, lots of light sources can be used—just remember to change the color balance for the type of light you are using.

Capture Macro Photos of Shy (Moving) Subjects

If your subject isn't moving, make sure that the camera is on a stable platform. This is especially true if you are taking a photo at an unusual angle, because if you are trying to hold a camera underneath a ledge, for example, you usually have only a few moments of steadiness before your arms begin to shake.

As mentioned earlier in the book, you can stabilize your camera in a number of ways. You can wedge your camera against a solid object, use a pocket tripod, or place the camera strap around your neck and pull it tight. It isn't the best solution but it works better than just holding the camera without any other support.

The photo in Figure 16-10 was taken at a shutter speed of 1/60 of a second, which is about as slow a shutter speed as

FIGURE 16-10 This tiny flower grows in the shade and is smaller than a dime.

FIGURE 16-11 The low-light features of the camera allowed a sharp photo of the aphids at a low shutter speed.

you should use for hand-held. The light was low enough that a tripod could have improved the sharpness but I was standing hip-deep in a creek while taking this one, so I had few (if any) options to stabilize the camera.

If the subject is moving, and if you cannot use a flash because the subject is too close, your choices are limited. Here are a few suggestions to help your get a good shot:

- **Take lots of photos**   When shooting at low shutter speeds, the more photos you take, the better.

- **Use your camera's low-light features**   Some cameras have features to accommodate low-light photography.

- **Have patience**   The photo of the aphids hiding in the shade of a leaf (Figure 16-11) was taken using the Best Picture setting of a Coolpix camera. This feature takes up to 10 photos, one after another, and then saves the one with the sharpest detail. So why did I take a photo of aphids? Because they were beautiful— a transparent red, lit from behind on a green plant.

It was early in the morning when I saw a large blue dragonfly on the hood of my car. The light was low, but I carefully approached the dragonfly, hoping not to make it fly away. A small tripod would have placed the camera too high above the subject so I used the hood of the car as a platform by setting the camera on my ball cap.

Since I didn't see any movement, I thought the dragonfly was dead, so I took a lot of shots from several angles. I thought I was getting some good

16

pictures (see Figure 16-12). The dragonfly must not have thought so. Much to my surprise, it flew away.

FIGURE 16-12 The power of a macro shows all of the intricate details of a dragonfly.

Chapter 17

Photograph Your Stuff Like a Pro

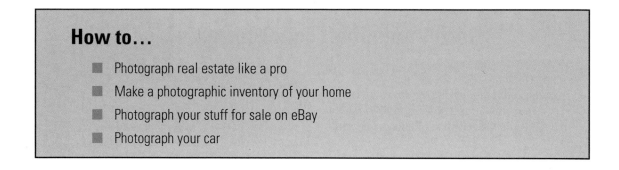

Digital Photography Myth Number 17: Digital cameras are designed to photograph people and landscapes but cannot be used to photograph houses, cars, and products for sale because they do not have the color or tonal latitude of film.

Fact: That was true about 10 years ago, but not anymore! When it comes time to take a photo of a house you're selling, a product, or a project (be it for a science fair or something you want sell on eBay), you want the photos to look good—especially if you want to get a good price. You can get great shots of any of these using a digital camera.

In this chapter you will learn how to photograph all of the things you want to record and document, such as homes for sale, home inventories, information for science projects, and shots of products to sell. You will learn how to set up a mini studio with some basic materials from your local super-discount store and make professional-looking photographs.

Before you begin taking pictures, keep in mind that digital cameras can capture images at different resolutions; choose the resolution that best meets your intended end use. For instance, images that are intended exclusively for web pages (like eBay) use can be made at 640×480 pixels (standard monitor size) and a resolution of no more than 100 pixels per inch (ppi). On the other hand, if your intention is to make beautiful prints for people to view, shoot at the highest resolution and then resize your images; perform a *save as* for use on the web or on a monitor.

Real Estate Photography

In the past few years, digital photography has become an essential tool for anyone working in the real estate market. With so many advantages to using your digital camera when it comes to selling or showing off your home, you would almost think that the camera was made specifically to address the needs of this market.

Professional Ideas for Digital Photography

Before digital cameras became readily available, using photography to help sell a home was time-consuming and relatively impractical. While the increased availability of inexpensive digital cameras has made real estate photography more practical, it is the increased use of the Internet by potential buyers that has made photographing home listings a necessity.

For the professional real estate agent, a digital camera allows you to do the following:

- Show prospective buyers photographs of properties online via a web page, e-mail, CD, or even promotional DVD.

- Prepare photos of properties for your web page, listing services, newspaper ads, and highlight sheets.

- Create online virtual tours of homes. This takes more time and effort to create, but many agents that I have worked with use virtual reality (VR) images to show panoramas of a home's setting, including its exterior and interior layouts.

- Produce photographs of a property for buyers to take with them.

- Provide photographic answers to out-of-town buyers regarding specifics of a property.

Photograph Your Home

If you're not a professional real estate agent, you can still do a lot of cool things with photographs of your home. Here are just a few ideas:

- Create "we moved" postcards containing your new address and a photo of the new home.

- Send photos of your new home (interior and exterior) via e-mail or post them on your personal web page.

- Take photos of your yard and other landscaping to the nursery to assist them in helping you either identify existing plants or for making recommendations concerning changes to the landscaping.

- Make a visual inventory of your home for insurance purposes.

17

Tips for Photographing Your Home

When taking pictures of your house, whether you are selling it or sending the photo to some friends, you want it to look as good as possible. Some novice photographers might assume that you should always take outdoor photos on a bright, sunny day because a blue sky always provides a strong contrasting background, making your house look better.

However, the ideal photo can be taken on an overcast day, which produces diffused light and reveals more details. You can then use your computer to replace the background, like the before and after shot shown in Figure 17-1. In Chapter 20, you'll learn how to replace an overcast sky.

FIGURE 17-1 Original photo (A); after the sky is replaced (B).

A.

B.

The problem with taking your photo on a bright sunny day is that it produces harsh shadows. Shadows can be a distraction in the photo, such as the tree shadow on the garage door in Figure 17-2.

FIGURE 17-2 An otherwise good photo has a distracting shadow across the garage door.

Take Interior Photos of Your House

Fill the frame of your camera with your subject. You want to show as much of the house/room as possible. The orientation of your camera will affect how the room appears. The dining room shown in portrait orientation in Figure 17-3 was also shot in landscape orientation in Figure 17-4. You can see how different orientations produce very different shots.

FIGURE 17-3 This photo makes the dining room appear to be very narrow.

FIGURE 17-4 Changing the orientation of the camera makes the room appear larger.

17

Get the Best Photo

Emulate professional architectural photographers as much as possible:

- Set your camera to its widest zoom setting.

- Use a tripod and cable release.

- Before taking your photos, study the room and see what time of day produces the most pleasing light. Often, you can match the exterior light that shines through the windows with the interior light by shooting late in the day.

- You can use an external flash that isn't attached to the camera to *paint* the room with light. Use a very small aperture (such as f:22), and then bounce the flash off the ceiling while the shutter is open.

- Keep the lens perpendicular to the floor to avoid the *falling* aspect of your room's vertical lines.

The portrait orientation of the first photo in Figure 17-3 makes the dining area appear narrow, while moving just two feet to the right and changing the camera orientation to landscape make the same room appear much larger. The light from the window has caused the area around the window to be blown-out, which is technically a no-no, but since the rest of the room is properly exposed, and that's what we care about, it is acceptable.

 Take photos of your home from different angles so potential buyers have a way to judge the size of the home and property.

It is usually best to use available light from windows or open doors to illuminate the room. This makes the room appear light and airy. If you use flash when taking indoor photos when the room doesn't have outdoor light sources, you should turn on every light in the room (and possibly bring in some free-standing lights for additional illumination) before using a flash. If you photograph a dark room using only a single flash, the corners of the room will appear dark, giving the room a cave-like appearance. Also be cautious when using a flash, as objects (such as light polished surfaces) in the foreground will produce a distracting glare.

The digital camera is a marvelous tool, not only for artistic work, but also to help accomplish the mundane chores of daily life.

Jim Patterson, digital photographer and writer

Visually Inventory Your Home

In Texas, we experience two basic types of natural disasters: floods and tornados. I have conducted photo assignments after both, and as I talked with the victims afterward, I realized how impossible it is for people to remember everything that they own (which is essential to get the fairest settlement from the insurance company). All homeowner and renters insurance brochures advise you to create a thorough inventory of your household possessions. When most of us think about that, we reassure ourselves that we really ought to do that some day. With a digital camera, you no longer need keep written records and save those records in a safety deposit box. You can create a visual inventory of your possessions, and save your photos on a CD or DVD and store them in a safe off premises.

How to Manage a Home Inventory

One of the problems with owning a lot of stuff is that the task of making an inventory can seem overwhelming. Here are some suggestions for how to approach this task:

- **Take it one room at a time.** "How do you eat an elephant? One bite at a time." Keep this in mind as you take inventory of an entire home. Doing the entire house can seem overwhelming, but you can shoot stuff in a single room in a reasonably short time.

- **Create a list.** Begin your inventory by creating a written list of the valuables located in the designated room. Move from one wall to another in an organized

17

pattern, making note of anything that would have to be replaced if it were lost or stolen.

- **Photograph the items on the list.**   As you photograph each item, check it off the list.

- **Repeat this pattern in the other rooms of your house, photographing each wall individually, and finishing with the center of the room.**   Remember that as you store completed rolls to label your film canisters with their respective room assignments.

Adding Audio Notes to Supplement Your Inventory

If your camera supports audio notes (many cameras now offer this feature), use it to add details of when each item was purchased and for what price. When you're finished with your home's interior, photograph the exterior, an exercise that verifies the general condition in which you've maintained your property.

Did you know?

How to Create a Visual Inventory

I am a big fan of PBS's *Antiques Road Show* (especially the original BBC version) and it has made me realize that some old stuff is worth a lot of money. If you have old silver, china, vases, painted dishes, and other antiques, you should make detailed photographic records of each item.

Don't just take a general photograph of your open cabinet containing the family heirlooms. Remove all of these pieces, because they likely rank among your highest-valued possessions. Arrange them on a table; this saves you time and provides a much better view of their detail, size, and estimated worth. Take two photographs of each item, front and back, enabling a view of the underside. This is important to capture any markings. It's a good idea to place each item either next to a ruler or some other object that provides some basis for gauging relative size.

When you're finished, put the photos onto a CD and store it in a safe place—not in the same place where the articles are kept. As you find or acquire more possessions, don't forget to add their photos and videos to your collection.

Photograph Stuff for eBay

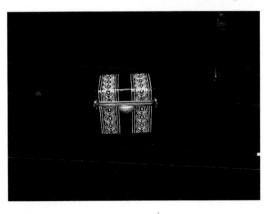

FIGURE 17-5 This is a photo of a blue enameled box—at least, that what it is supposed to be!

FIGURE 17-6 This photo could be improved to make the item more saleable.

I use eBay way too much; maybe I could start a support group. Bottom line, if you want to sell stuff on eBay and get a good price, you need to include photos of the stuff you want to sell with the ad placement. Unfortunately, a lot of the photos that show up on eBay are too dark, and the subject being sold is almost unrecognizable—like the item shown in Figure 17-5.

On the other hand, when photographing items that are relatively close to the camera, use of the flash has a tendency to produce bright spots, like the one shown above the glass sugar bowl in Figure 17-6.

The photo shown in Figure 17-6 could be improved in several ways. First, instead of using a single sheet of paper as a background, the seller should have covered the entire table with a white or light-colored cloth. Another option would have been to buy a large poster board and place the object on one end of it, and then bend the other end of the poster board up against a wall, producing a seamless background for the item. The bowl is also slightly out of focus, making it difficult for potential buyers to see the details. Lastly, the flash made a large blowout above the bowl.

Figure 17-7 shows a much better example of how to photograph a glass object. Using available light coming in from the window to backlight the object brings out the patterns in the glass.

To show details, include additional photos like the photograph shown in Figure 17-8. This was shot in macro mode and was lit by the same available light. To get a clear photo, you'll need to use a tripod.

17

FIGURE 17-7 Using backlight from a window provides an excellent light source for photographing glass objects.

FIGURE 17-8 Macro mode and a tripod allow the use of available light to illuminate an object.

Photograph Your Car

Most folks give little thought to photographing a car for sale, and their photos show it. Study some automobile magazines such as *Road & Track* to see how the pros do it. Do not study *Auto Trader* because their professionals have one idea in mind: get the picture and get on the road.

In preparation of photographing your car, you should do the following:

- Clean your car and tires thoroughly; give your tires a rubdown with a tire dressing.

- Plan on taking your photos either very early or very late in the day. If it is a cloudy overcast day, anytime will work.

- If you plan to photograph your vehicle in a public place, get permission from the owner or proper authority.

- Park your car on (clean, unstriped) pavement, not parked on grass. Clean asphalt looks better than concrete. A vehicle on grass appears to be abandoned.

- Hose down the pavement on which your car will be parked. Having wet pavement (even concrete) darkens it, providing excellent backdrop. If you have any doubts about the wisdom of this, watch a car commercial on TV. Nine out of ten cars that are parked on pavement are parked on wet pavement. Use can use your garden hose or take along a five-gallon jug of water to wet the pavement. An extreme example of this concept is shown in Figure 17-9.

- If you are taking photos of all sides of your car, you should rotate the car and not the camera so that you've got evenly-distributed sunlight on the surfaces of your car always coming from the same direction. Don't forget to include a 3/4 view (front and one side).

- The car doors should be closed.

- The sun should be directly behind you unless it is an overcast day.

- Check your results to make sure the reflection of you or your equipment is not visible in the glass or chrome.

- Don't include people in the photo. While the major car vendors may enhance the appearance of their vehicles by placing a model in a skimpy bathing suit in their cars, these are professional models being photographed by professional photographers. Your cousin may look great in a bathing suit, but I promise you she will make your car photo look really cheesy.

Once you are ready to photograph the car, here are some suggestions to follow. Shoot from many angles. If you are showing the car to potential buyers on the Internet, they are going to want to see as many angles as possible. Here are a few positions/angles to try:

- Crouch down and shoot at headlight level.

- Use a step ladder to get a shot from a higher elevation.

- If you're shooting at or near sunset as the light begins to fade, take some photos with your headlights or parking lights on.

17

FIGURE 17-9 Wet pavement always makes car photos look better.

▪ Use a "normal" focal-length lens or set your zoom lens accordingly (avoid wide-angle settings except for engine, cockpit, and luggage-compartment shots). Avoid extreme telephoto views of the car as these will foreshorten the vehicle and make it look squatty.

▪ Zoom in. Fill the frame with automobile, *not* real estate.

▪ Bracket your exposures. Often, an image made at 1/2 to 2/3 of a stop overexposure reveals more detail on dark cars.

Chapter 18

Photographing a Panorama

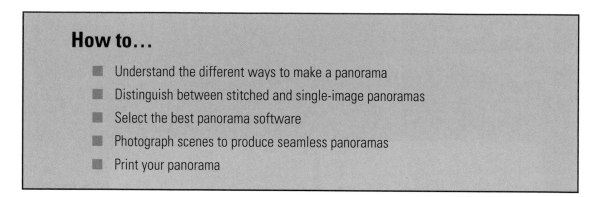

How to…

- Understand the different ways to make a panorama
- Distinguish between stitched and single-image panoramas
- Select the best panorama software
- Photograph scenes to produce seamless panoramas
- Print your panorama

Digital Photography Myth Number 18: It takes a large and expensive camera to photograph panoramas.

Fact: True, but false. From the first panoramas until those created around 1980, it *did* take a special (and expensive) camera to create a panorama, but that's not the case today.

In this chapter, you will discover how a series of photos can be stitched together to make a *panorama*. You will also discover that panoramas are not limited to photos of grand and majestic landscapes but can be used for any subject that would normally be crowded if you attempted to squeeze it into a normal-sized camera frame. You will also learn how simple it is to shoot the photos necessary to create a panorama. Some of equipment that you need—and some that you don't need—may surprise you.

Why a Panorama?

Panoramas are not a new thing. Soon after the invention of photography in 1839, the desire to show the broad expanse of both cities and landscapes—or large groups of people— prompted photographers to begin creating panoramas. (See the Did You Know box "The Fascinating History of Panoramas.") Say the word *panorama* and most people envision a wide, full-color photograph of some majestic landscape such as the Grand Canyon or a tropical paradise. But back in the early days of photography, because of the limited quality of the photographic process, panoramas were most often used to document people, places, and events.

Figures 18-1 through 18-4 show examples of the many types of subject matter that have been used for panoramas.

FIGURE 18-1 A California bathing beauty pageant in 1918 (courtesy of the Library of Congress)

Beauty pageants (Figure 18-1) were one of the more popular panorama subjects as well as cityscapes of well-known cities such as New York (Figure 18-2 shows the city in 1931). Group

FIGURE 18-2 A view of the New York skyline in 1931 (courtesy of the Library of Congress)

photos of everything from fire departments to political conventions and sporting teams were also routinely photographed and sold. Figure 18-3 shows the entire Chicago Cub baseball team, which won the National League pennant in 1929.

FIGURE 18-3 The Chicago Cubs after winning the National League pennant in 1929 (courtesy of the Library of Congress)

Historic moments in time, such as the aftermath of the great San Francisco earthquake of 1906, were captured in panoramas to

18

convey the scope of the cataclysm. The panorama shown in Figure 18-4 represents only a third of the original panorama.

The desire to capture the entire scope of the world as we see it no longer requires a custom camera and the many hours it used to take photographers to create these images.

FIGURE 18-4 A view of the aftermath caused by the great San Francisco earthquake of 1906 (courtesy of the Library of Congress)

Note   *Since it's not difficult to do so, should we shoot all of our photos in panorama? Absolutely not. Almost all photo opportunities are more than adequately satisfied using the standard photo ratio of 3:2.*

Did you know?

The Fascinating History of Panoramas

Panoramic photos began to be created almost as soon as people figured out how to use cameras. One of the earliest panoramas in the U.S. Library of Congress archives was made in 1851 using five plates. Although the photographer did not attempt to make a seamless panorama, the photos were placed side-by-side.

During the Civil War, panoramic photos of terrain, battle aftermaths, and fortifications were greatly valued by both Union engineers and generals. (The South would have valued them as well if photographers had taken any, but it seems that all photographers were Yankees.) While the process of making the panorama into a single seamless (or almost seamless) photo in the darkroom continued to improve, the photos were still being taken using a standard view camera. Many old panoramas from this period are distinguished by solid white vertical lines that mark the points at which the negative plates were fitted together.

The year 1898 saw the first camera designed specifically to photograph panoramas, and within a few years several companies were selling panorama cameras. Mass-produced panoramic cameras worked on the "swing-lens" principle (which is a camera that has a slit that rotates which exposes a wider size negative than possible with a fixed lens), used roll film, and made small panoramas measuring no more than 12 inches long with a field of view of almost 180 degrees.

Kodak tried to revive the panorama format as part of the introduction of APS (Advanced Photo System) film in 1996. APS doesn't take a true panorama but instead crops the top and bottom off of a standard image. Today several companies manufacture panoramic film cameras for professionals. These cameras are typically expensive and only semi-automatic in their operation. With the continuing improvements in both digital cameras and panorama creation software, most of the panoramas of the future will probably be created digitally.

How Panoramas Are Made

Today's panorama shots are made in two ways: you can use a camera that takes panoramas or stitch the individual photos together using software designed for this purpose. Two types of film cameras produce panoramic photos: consumer and professional. The consumer cameras use standard 35mm film and essentially cut off the top and bottom of the frame, which produces a small, squat image like the one shown in Figure 18-5 that cannot be enlarged to any significant size without serious quality issues.

FIGURE 18-5 Panoramas made with consumer cameras result in small images that cannot be enlarged much.

The price of a professional panorama camera starts at $2000 USD—which explains why you probably haven't seen them for sale in your local superstore. Enough said.

Stitching (Panorama) Software

If you are going to create a panorama with photos you take with a digital camera, you need software to do the job right. Digital cameras have wide lenses that result in distortion around the

18

edges of the photos. If you were to attempt to stitch photos together manually using a photo editor, the edges where the photo overlap wouldn't match up properly.

An example of this is shown in Figure 18-6. I used Photoshop to stitch two photos together manually. The top overlap layer was at a reduced opacity so I could see through the two images to align them. The result was that objects near the edge are misaligned, which is very apparent in high contrast objects like the water towers.

Misalignment

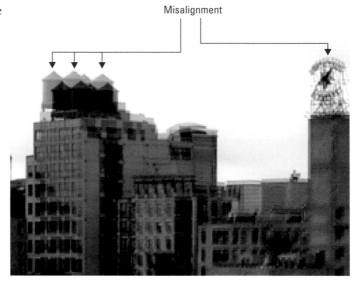

FIGURE 18-6 Misalignment caused by wide-angle lens distortion.

Stitching the Photos Together

After you take the photos for your panorama, how you create the panorama depends on the stitching software that you use. Every software is a little different, but they work in about the same way. I used Photoshop CS's Photomerge tool to create the panorama from the photos shown in Figure 18-7.

Here's how this was done in Photoshop:

1. Choose File | Photomerge.

2. In the Photomerge dialog box, select the photos that you want to merge together. You don't need to open the files; each file that is open consumes system memory, and using too much system memory can slow down the panorama process.

FIGURE 18-7 Five photos were used to create a panorama in Photoshop.

3. A dialog box like the one shown in Figure 18-8 opens and the program attempts to put the photos in the correct order. If the order is incorrect, you can drag the thumbnails around in the dialog box until they are correct.

4. Clicking the OK button starts the process of creating a panorama. Depending on the size and number of the photos, the process may take from a few minutes up to 15 minutes.

FIGURE 18-8 Photomerge's panorama

You can create two types of flat panoramas: Normal or Perspective view, as shown in Figure 18-9. The Normal view tends to be distorted (pushed out in the center), making straight horizontal lines appear to bend away from the camera. The Perspective view attempts to correct the horizontal distortion at the expense of extreme distortion on the ends.

FIGURE 18-9 Normal view (A) and Perspective view (B)

A.

B.

18

Selecting the Best Panorama Software

A lot of software applications on the market today will stitch your photos together to make a panorama. Some of these stitching programs are included with such programs as Adobe Photoshop Elements 2, Photoshop CS, or Jasc Paint Shop Album, and other programs were created only for stitching. Most of these panorama programs are available online.

Two Kinds of Panoramas

When you begin looking for panorama software, you will discover that two different kinds of panoramas can be created. The type that we have been looking at so far in this chapter is called a flat or a 2D panorama, which can be printed or viewed on any computer.

The other type of panorama is called QTVR (Quick Time Virtual Reality), or just VR. This type of panorama cannot be printed and can be displayed only on a computer screen using proprietary software. The advantage of the VR approach is that the resulting panorama provides the viewer a window in which the viewpoint can be altered by moving around a hand cursor inside the image, offering a the viewer a 360-degree view of the subject area. This offers the viewer the ability to change the view virtually to any point on the compass, as if the person were standing in the same spot as the camera that photographed the image.

VR panoramas are becoming popular with real-estate agents who want to allow customers to view property from their computers. If the agent has taken the time to shoot and build a QTVR file of a room in the house, a perspective buyer can open a window that shows the room and then use a cursor to change the view. The room view in the window changes just as if the viewer were standing in the room and turning around.

Holding the camera vertically for horizontal panoramas gives you more height in the images but requires more images to cover the same horizontal area.

—*Dennis Curtin, photographer and author*

Panorama Software Choices

The following is a short (opinionated) list of panorama software that I have used. This is not a definitive listing, and new programs and improvements on existing programs occur all the time.

Photomerge

This feature is built into all versions of Photoshop Elements and Photoshop CS, and you can get a 30-day trial of these programs from http://www.adobe.com. Photomerge automatically attempts to place the individual photos that make up the panorama in the correct order to create a single, seamless image. When it cannot figure out either the order in which the photos should be placed or the correct amount of overlap necessary to align the photos, it gives you the option of determining the order of the panels. This is called *manual intervention,* and it is a great and necessary feature when the panorama doesn't come together correctly, like the image shown in Figure 18-10.

FIGURE 18-10 Sometimes a panorama program cannot automatically make the photos align properly.

Paint Shop Album

The panorama feature in this program allows you to select and organize the panels that you want to use in your panorama. The program is totally automatic, offering no manual intervention except to allow you to determine the order of the photos, but the automatic features are strong and it rarely stitches the images incorrectly. The only limitation it has occurs when you're working with large images. If you attempt to make a panorama

18

using files that are too large (greater than five megapixels), the program may halt. If you use the default settings, this is not a problem as the program automatically resizes the images, making them (and the resulting panorama) significantly smaller. You can get a 30-day trial of this program at http://www.jasc.com.

Panorama Factory

This program has been around for a long time and is a full-featured application. It used to be challenging to use, as it offers lots of controls and adjustments and therefore is rather complicated. The company has now added a wizard-like interface that takes you step-by-step through the process of creating a panorama. A 30-day trial of this application is available at http://www.smokycitydesigns.com. Panoramas made with the trial application put a small watermark in the center of the finished panorama, which encourages you to buy the program.

Photovista Panorama

One of the better applications for natural subjects such as clouds and hills, Photovista does the best job of blending lighting of different photos of any I have tried. It can be used to make flat (2D) and 360-degree (VR) panoramas. A slick interface offers view adjustments. It also allows you to select the digital camera you are using from a drop-down list to assist in correction of lens distortion. A 15-day trial of this application is available at http://www.iseemedia.com.

PixMaker Value

This is my favorite panorama program. It is fast and almost totally automatic. The more expensive version has additional manual controls that I rarely need to use. A 30-day trial of this application is available at http://www.pixaround.com.

Taking Pictures for a Panorama

To take the best possible photos to create a good panorama requires quite a bit of preparation on the photographic side. Taking photos to be used in a panorama isn't that difficult—it

Did you know?

Where to Find Panoramas

A great collection of old panoramas can be found on the Library of Congress web site (http://www.loc.gov). All the old panoramas in this chapter were selected from the library's archive of more than 4000 panoramas. When you get to the home page, use the search feature to look up the word *panorama*. The excellent search engine uses keywords (such as *ship*, *baseball*, and so on) to find and show all of the matching images. Because hundreds (if not thousands) of panoramas of cities and towns were taken between 1910 and 1950, it can be fun to see if an old photograph of either your hometown or the city in which you currently reside exists here.

just takes some practice. My dad was a cook, and he had a sign in the kitchen that read "Even my failures are edible." When it comes to shooting and stitching a panorama together, even your "failures" will look cool, and if you catch the panorama bug, you will just keep trying to improve them.

What You Need to Take Panoramas

Probably the most important item that you need to take panoramas is a tripod. I interviewed several programmers who write these panorama programs, and they believe that the biggest single problem encountered when people attempt to use the application is that they try to stitch together photos that don't have enough overlap or for which the camera changed relative position as it was rotated to take the photos.

Note *Having said that, some of my best panoramic shots were taken without using a tripod. I always try to find something solid upon which I can place the camera, and when I rotate the camera, I made a conscious effort to move the camera in a straight line relative to the horizon. The resulting panoramas work out because the alignment was close enough for the stitching software to be able to correct for the multitude of imperfections.*

Be Aware of Your Light Source

Depending on where the sun is located in relation to your subject, your photos on one side of the panorama can be much lighter

18

than photos on the other end. To fix such a problem, you can lock the automatic exposure (AE) settings on your camera, and every book I have read on the subject encourages this approach. In theory, when you begin taking a series of photographs, if the camera's automatic exposure system is continually adjusting between the individual photos, it will produce nonuniform exposure in each photo you take as you rotate the camera.

It has been my experience, however, that locking the AE can sometimes create the same problems. For example, if I begin shooting the first photo at the bright end of the series and lock the camera's AE, as I rotate away from the lighter part each progressive photo will still be using the same settings and the photos are darker, and so I've ended up with light and dark lines of demarcation, as shown in Figure 18-11. Because the idea is to create the sense of the photo being one continuous picture, this problem definitely takes away from the effect.

FIGURE 18-11 The position of the sun may produce dark and light panels in the finished panorama.

Most digital cameras have an AE lock feature that is enabled by pressing the shutter halfway down.

The ideal solution for shooting in the outdoors is to shoot with the sun to your back, which causes each photo in the panorama to be more or less uniformly exposed. When the sun isn't in a cooperative mood, you can always use the Gamma control (*not* brightness) of your photo-editing software to adjust the overall brightness of the images so that they appear to have the same overall brightness.

Don't Get Too Close

When taking panoramic pictures, you want to get as far away from the subject as reasonable. The closer you are to the subject,

Did you know?

What Is Gamma?

In very simplistic terms, gamma is the measure of the contrast—brightness of the midtone values—captured by a digital camera. The advantage of adjusting gamma is that when an image is brighten using a gamma setting the brighter area won't blow out. Likewise, you can darken an image using gamma and not lose details in the shadows.

the wider the setting on your zoom lens; this produces greater barrel distortion on each panel. If there's too much distortion, even the best panorama stitching program cannot avoid weird-looking gaps between each panel. Try to position the camera a good distance away from your subject and set your zoom lens so it is closer to either wide or mid-point.

The panorama shown back in Figure 18-10 shows the old entrance to the Houston Museum of Fine Arts. Because several trees were blocking the view of the entrance, I had to get too close to the building, and regardless of which stitching software I used, the result was ugly.

Control Overlap

Overlap is the next aspect that you must consider. Overlap refers to the amount that each succeeding photo overlaps the previous one. You need to shoot just enough overlap to get the job done. With too much overlap, the file becomes huge and the program doesn't do a good job in auto-matching the edges of the photos together. How much is enough? Most stitching programs want an overlap of 20–30 percent.

So, how do you calculate a 20–30 percent overlap? If your tripod has a head that indicates the rotation in degrees, you can calculate how many degrees are necessary to achieve the necessary overlap. My tripod shows degree markings, and after shooting digital photographs for a year and a half, I have yet to use it.

18

Here is the method I use, which seems to work. When I take the initial photograph, I make note of some point of reference in the LCD frame of my digital camera. As I rotate the camera (more on that in a moment), I try to make sure that the reference point remains in the right or left third of the frame (depending on which way I turn the camera).

FIGURE 18-12 (A) The right side of the frame serves as the reference for the next photo; (B) rotate the camera until the reference appears in the leftthird of the photo.

In Figure 18-12 (A), the right side of the frame serves as the reference point. Rotating the camera to the right, the reference point ends up in the middle of the left half of the frame (B).

A.

When you rotate the camera, make every effort to have the camera lens rotate around an imaginary axis going through the center of the camera lens. When I first started taking panoramic photos, I held the camera and turned my body. By doing that, I changed the angle of the camera in reference to the scenery that I was photographing. This is less important when the subject is a great distance away, but it becomes important when the subject matter is close.

B.

The best panorama images result when you hold the lens level and perpendicular to the subject. This is where a tripod comes in handy. If you don't use a tripod, try lining up the images using the viewfinder's center focus spot to keep a point in the image level.

If you have your camera tilted away from level (up or down), you'll see converging angles at the edges of the images that make it more difficult to stitch smoothly.

Taking Vertical Panoramas

Not all panoramas are horizontally oriented. Most panorama stitching programs have the ability to make vertical as well as horizontal panoramas, because lots of things in this world are taller than they are wide— Michael Jordan comes to mind. The panorama in Figure 18-13 was stitched from three photographs. The challenge faced when using vertical panoramas is that they can be difficult to lay out in a publication like this book.

A Different Way to Make a Panorama

In the panorama shown in Figure 18-14, the lens was kept level. However, to include all of the visual elements the photographer desired, the finished panorama was assembled in stair steps.

FIGURE 18-13 Not all panoramas have to be horizontal.

When it comes to making panoramas, the most frequently asked question is "How wide should a panorama be?" There's no good answer to that question. If you make a panorama that is too much wider than it is tall, when you attempt to print or place it in a document, its height may be so small that it will be difficult to see.

Printing Panoramas

Because I like to print my panoramas, I like to make sure that the width is usually 20 inches or less so it fits into my printer.

18

The trick with printing panoramas is to use a printer that can print on panorama-sized paper or a printer that accepts roll paper. This typically means that the printer accepts paper from the rear of the unit.

FIGURE 18-14 Assembling a panorama in stair steps

If your panorama image is larger than the paper on which you are printing, you should resize the image using your photo-editing software. Do not let the printer software do it, because the quality of the resized image will not be good.

Epson offers panorama paper in a single fixed size, but if you use this paper, of course, you must make sure that your panorama fits the paper before you print. If you are using roll paper, theoretically you can make your panoramas any size you want—just keep in mind that if you want to frame your print, panorama frames are not common and custom frames are expensive.

Part V

Professional Tips, Tricks, and Other Stuff

Chapter 19

Fixing Photo Goofs

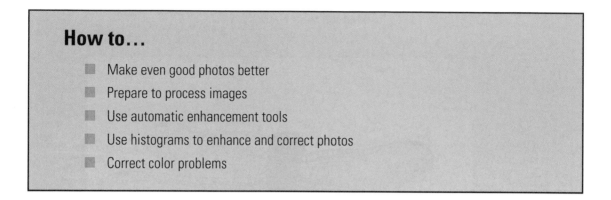

How to...

■ Make even good photos better

■ Prepare to process images

■ Use automatic enhancement tools

■ Use histograms to enhance and correct photos

■ Correct color problems

Digital Photography Myth Number 19: Problems with photos made with digital cameras can be easily corrected.

Fact: True. If you read, learned, and followed all of the material in the previous chapters, you should have very few photographic goofs to fix. Still, even the most experienced photographer uses the wrong setting or forgets some important photographic concept once in awhile. In digital images, just about any photographic sin can be fixed (except an out-of-focus shot can never be corrected). In this chapter, we will discover how to correct common photographic goofs using a couple of popular photo editors.

Make Good Photos Better

While most of the photos that you take with your digital camera look good, most users are surprised to discover how easy it is to make them look even better. A TV commercial that was shown about 10 years ago displayed a bar of soap that looked normal until an off-screen hand dragged a squeegee across the glass in front of the soap, and you realized that the original glass had been covered with a slightly opaque film. Many digital photos are like the soap behind the filmy glass. They look good, but with a little effort they can look better.

The unaltered photo in Figure 19-1A was taken in an old Texas cemetery covered

FIGURE 19-1 Original unaltered photo (A), and the photo after applying photo correction tools (B).

A.

B.

with bluebonnets. Photo B shows how it looks after I applied a few automatic tonal and color correction tools. Photo B looks like a layer of filmy opacity has been cleared away.

Sorting Before You Start

Because you can (and should) take many photos with a digital camera, before you begin to apply corrections to your photos, you should sort through them, setting aside the keepers. If you don't do this, you may spend a lot of time applying corrections to duplicate or less than desirable photos.

Over the years, I have developed a system: I create a new folder called Keepers within the folder containing the photos. Using a slide viewer/album program, I run a slide show to view all of the images using the full screen. I tag the best photos and place a copy of each one in the Keepers folder. These are the images that I will work on. This way, the original photos remain unaltered in the primary folder, and I can work on the copies.

You can even use Windows to help you do the initial sort—just change the view button to Thumbnails, and you'll see something similar to that shown in Figure 19-2.

Tip   *With programs like Photoshop CS, Photoshop Elements, and Paint Shop Pro, the file browser can be used to sort and create a Keepers folder. The advantage of using these applications for sorting is that because you are already working in your editing application, you don't have to quit one application and open another.*

A powerful feature of Adobe Photoshop Elements is the File browser. It can be used along with the Batch command to process images from a digital camera, automatically, with a single push of the button, saving a lot of time and effort.

Kathy Fisher, Barton Photo Labs

19

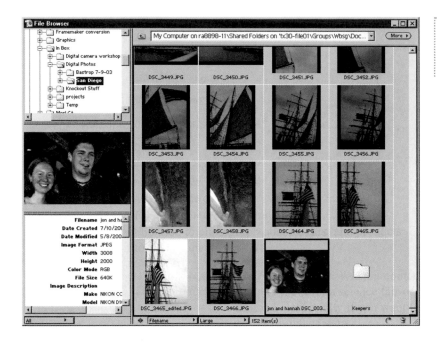

FIGURE 19-2 Sorting your photographs is the first important step to improving your photos.

While most images can be improved using a photo-editing application, it's still a good idea to work on duplicate images to avoid the chances of ruining the originals.

Use Automatic Tools

The automatic features that are available depend on the program that you use for your photo-editing work. Since I can't cover all of the photo editors in a single book, I focus on two of the most popular ones—Jasc Paint Shop Pro and Photoshop Elements 2. Though the terminology may be different among applications, the concepts used by these features generally apply to all photo editors.

Automatic photo-correction features are generally available in two configurations: the all-automatic, hold-your-breath-and-hope-for-the-best function, and what I call the "smorgasbord style" that uses a dialog box in which you can choose from the several types of corrections. The problem with automatic tools, however, is that they work from a given set of default factors, some or all of which may not apply to your photo.

For example, most photo-editors offer a tool that expands the tonal range of an image. In Photoshop Elements it is called Auto-Levels and in Paint Shop Pro it is called Histogramic Equalization. Both programs distribute the pixels in an image so that they are evenly spread out between the darkest and the lightest parts of the spectrum. The automatic tool is based on the belief that if there is even tonal distribution in an image, it looks better.

For some photos it works wonderfully but, in many cases, the automatic tool will cause an image to experience a serious color shift (usually toward blue). So, just because it is automatic, it doesn't mean it will fix the image you are working on.

A.

B.

FIGURE 19-3 Original photo (A); after applying automatic correction (B).

Go Fully Automatic with Paint Shop Pro 8

The latest version of Jasc's Paint Shop Pro has a feature called One Step Photo Fix. Clicking the One Step Photo Fix button runs a script that applies a large number of correction tools. On many photos, this feature does a bang-up job of correcting may problems, like the one shown in Figure 19-3.

Sometimes a photo, like the one shown in Figure 19-4A, is made worse by using the automatic features, as shown in Figure 19-4B. The problem with Figure 19-4A occurred as a result of the camera's flash not firing.

 If your external flash takes more than a minute to recharge between flashes, it's time to replace its batteries.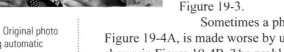

While the subjects need to be lightened, the background doesn't need it; Paint Shop Pro's One Step Photo Fix, however, has no way of knowing what does and does not need to be lightened. As a result of the automatic attempt to adjust the lighting of the background, the color of the mother's and daughter's faces in the foreground gets hammered pretty hard, as evidenced

19

in Figure 19-4B. By using the individual image correction tools in Paint Shop Pro instead of the automatic fix, however, it is possible to correct the image, as shown in see Figure19-4C, so that the subjects can be seen and the colors look correct.

Add Zip to Your Photos Using Photoshop Elements 2

Photoshop Elements 2 offers many similar tools for enhancing photos. One of my favorites is called Quick Fix, and the dialog box for this feature is shown in Figure 19-5.

The advantage of using the Quick Fix approach is that the user can selectively apply each photo enhancement feature and preview the results in the Before and After preview windows. If after applying one of the enhancements the photo looks worse, you can undo it and try another enhancement. When the After preview looks the way you want it, you click OK to apply only the enhancements you selected.

Figure 19-6A was taken on an overcast day in San Diego (the locals call it the "June Gloom"). Quick Fix took less than a minute to enhance the photo, as shown in Figure 19-6B. The only complaint I have about this particular feature is that the preview windows are very small, making it difficult to see some of the changes produced, and while the changes also are previewed on the actual image, the dialog box fills most of the screen so you can't see the entire image.

FIGURE 19-4 (A) This would have been a good photo if the flash had fired. (B) Using an automatic photo fixer lightens the overall image, but the colors look poor. (C) Using individual photo adjustment tools allows the image to be recovered without too much damage.

FIGURE 19-5 The Quick Fix dialog allows selective application of many photo enhancements.

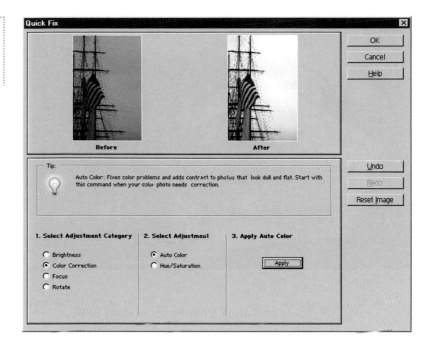

Photo Editors Have Similar Features

FIGURE 19-6 (A) An overcast day makes photo look downright drab; (B) applying the Quick Fix feature brightens photo considerably.

While each photo editor excels with one feature or another, with the increasing popularity of digital photography, each offers comparable photo-enhancement features. Regardless of which photo-editor you use, you will discover that it features automatic tools to enhance or correct the following:

A.  B.

- Contrast
- Levels
- Color

Although applications may include many other photo-enhancing commands to restore faded photos or compensate for back-lit photos, the contrast, levels, and brightness fixers are the common denominator of all of the photo-editing programs and produce the greatest effects.

19

Contrast: Instant Zip for Your Photos

The effect of contrast can be dramatic when applied to photos that for one reason or another appear dull. In the case of the sailing ship shown in Figure 19-6, the original photo was taken on a day with a heavy layer of clouds hanging over the harbor with little light, resulting in a low-contrast image. We talk about contrast a lot but few understand what it is. See the Did You Know box, "Contrast Essentials," for more information about this subject.

Most photo editors have some sort of auto-contrast feature that automatically adjusts the overall contrast and mixture of colors in an image. Unlike auto-level commands (which we will learn about next), the auto-contrast should not introduce or remove color casts. Instead, it should change the lightest and darkest pixels in the image to white and black, respectively, which makes highlights appear lighter and shadows appear darker.

 Auto-contrast improves the appearance of many photographic images. It does not improve high-contrast or flat color images, however.

Did you know?

Contrast Essentials

What about contrast makes dull, flat images come to life? To understand this, you must first know what contrast is. The contrast of a digital image is basically a measure of the difference in brightness between adjoining pixels. For example, suppose a line of light gray pixels is surrounded by dark gray pixels in an image; the difference between the two hues are not great, and visually the edge formed by these two colors appears "soft." If you were to make all of the light gray pixels white and turn all of the dark gray pixels black, you would increase the contrast, and the edges would appear much sharper and distinct.

In a nutshell, increasing contrast makes the brighter colors brighter and darker shades darker (sounds like an ad for a laundry detergent, doesn't it?). The increased contrast can create new problems, however. While the brighter pixels get brighter, they also begin to lose detail as they approach pure white. Conversely, as the darker pixels get darker, any detail in the shadows is lost. The trick is to find a happy medium between the benefits of increased contrast and loss of image detail.

Using Contrast with Restraint

The effects of increasing a photo's contrast can be dramatic. The photo of a sunflower taken on a bright sunny day in Kansas (Figure 19-7A) has little contrast because it was brightly illuminated by the midday sun.

FIGURE 19-7 (A) A slightly washed-out, low-contrast photo is transformed into (B) a much more desirable image by applying contrast.

A.

B.

FIGURE 19-8 Detail loss caused by increasing contrast is apparent when the original photo (left pane) is compared to the finished photo (right pane).

By increasing the contrast in the Figure 19-7B, the darker areas become darker and the lighter areas appear brighter. As mentioned earlier in the Did You Know box, the increase in overall contrast can come at a price. Figure 19-8 shows a close-up, before-and-after comparison of the sunflower petals. Notice how the detail in the petals has been lost when the contrast is increased.

Some photographers and graphic artists believe that the sacrifice of detail does not justify the overall improvement, much in the same way that antique appraisers encourage owners of antiques not to clean or polish their heirlooms for fear of reducing their

19

value. So should you apply contrast to your washed-out photo? Yes, usually.

Consider your viewing audience. If you think that your Aunt Bertha or a coworker will pull out a loupe to examine the photograph, looking for tiny detail loss, you might choose not to apply contrast. However, if most viewers will just look at a photo and say, "What a lovely photo of a sunflower," why not make the adjustment?

Tip *If you need to preserve detail for some future application, you can do what I do: keep the original of every photo in your originals archive. Apply the contrast to the copies in your Keepers folder.*

Unleash the Power of Levels

Probably the most powerful tool for enhancing or applying correction to photos is the levels command. The term *levels* was coined by Adobe for Photoshop to describe changing the tonal range and color balance of an image by adjusting intensity levels of the image's shadows, midtones, and highlights; other photo-editing programs have adopted the term. Levels use the *histogram* as a visual indicator of the adjustments being made to the image.

A Crash Course in Digital Images

To understand the levels method of adjustment, you need to know a little bit more about the composition of a digital image.

All digital pictures are made of building blocks called *pixels*. Your digital camera displays how many millions of pixels its sensor captures each time you press the shutter. Color stuff aside for the moment, each pixel in the image has a brightness value. These levels of brightness are divided into three regions:

- ■ Shadows
- ■ Midtones
- ■ Highlights

Examples of pixels of each region are shown in Figure 19-9.

FIGURE 19-9 The brightness levels of the pixels in this image range from dark shadows to pure white.

Demystifying Histograms

A *histogram* is a graph that shows the distribution of pixels in an image. It shows you how many pixels fall in each brightness level, but not where in the image they are located. A perfect histogram would resemble a mountain with a peak (middle grays) in the middle and consistent slopes to the black and white ends of the scale. Just because an image has a "perfect" histogram doesn't make it a good photo; it means that there is no clipping of the highlights or shadows (which is a good thing).

The histogram shown in Figure 19-10 shows how the brightness values in a photo relate to the histogram.

Specular highlights/blowouts

Shadow region

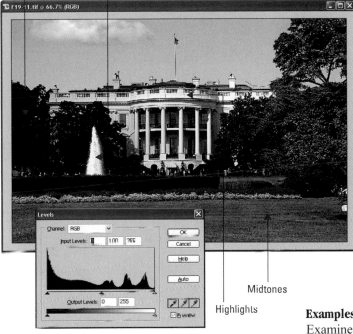

Midtones

Highlights

FIGURE 19-10 A histogram provides a lot of information about a digital photo.

Examples of Real-World Histograms

Examine the following photos, shown with their histograms, so you can see how the histogram changes with each type of photo. The photograph of an old telegraph pole and the associated histogram (see Figure 19-11) show how the pixels in the photo are concentrated in two areas, the gray background and the darker pixels of the wooden pole.

An example of an image with most of the pixels in the shadow region is shown in Figure 19-12. Notice how the pixels are up flat against the left side of the histogram. This is an indication that part of the detail in the shadow region has been lost, and it's called *clipping*.

The overexposed photo in Figure 19-13 has most of its pixels concentrated in the highlights region of the histogram. Like the image shown in Figure 19-12, the histogram for this image shows that the photo also has clipping, but it is in the

19

FIGURE 19-11 Pixels in this histogram are concentrated in two areas.

highlight region instead of the shadows, which means that areas of the photo are blown out and the detail is lost with no hope of recovery.

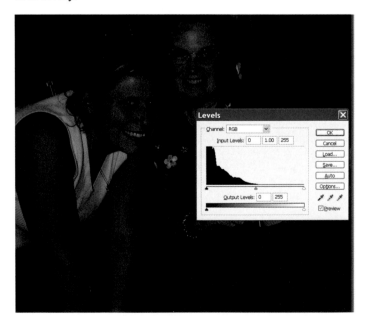

FIGURE 19-12 The histogram shows what we can see visually, that parts of the photo are underexposed and the shadows are clipped.

Histograms and Underexposed Images   Now that you are a little more familiar with histograms, let's see how you can use them as a visual indicator when correcting problems with photos. First, we'll look at the underexposed photo shown in Figure 19-14 and learn how to correct it. In this case, the flash went off, but like many built-in flash units, it was a little too far away to illuminate the subject properly.

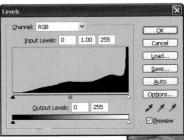

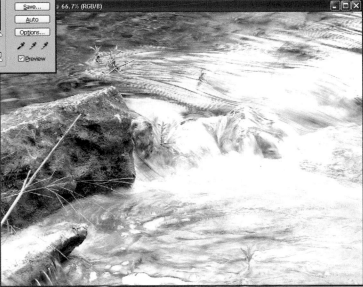

FIGURE 19-13 The histogram shows that this photo has clipping in the highlights region.

Look at the histogram shown in Figure 19-14. You can see that no pixels are brighter than the center of the midtone of the curve. Earlier in the chapter, you saw what happened to an image when an automatic contrast was applied. Figure 19-15 shows the effect of auto-contrast on the photo and how the distribution of the pixels is changed in the histogram.

In the original photo (Figure 19-14), all of the pixels were concentrated in the shadow and the lower portion of the midtone region. What does that mean? The brightest pixels in the photo are no brighter than half as bright as they can be. Auto-contrast reassigns (remaps) the brightness values of the pixels so that the brightest pixel now approaches white. Notice in Figure 19-15 that the pixel distribution is no longer close together, appearing as a solid curve; instead it is spread out across the contrast range.

19

Problems of Underexposed Images

You can recover a lot of detail in underexposed images with a photo editor, but recovery can introduce other problems. The photo shown in Figure 19-14 is underexposed because

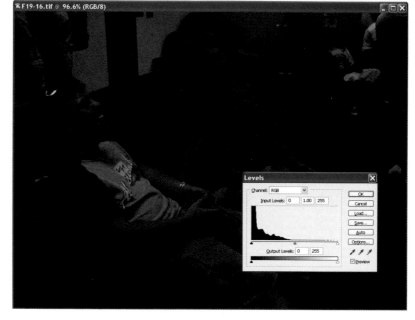

FIGURE 19-14 An underexposed photo is a common photo problem.

the subjects were too far away for the camera's built-in flash.

Applying an auto adjustment tool (see Figure 19-15) makes the photo look brighter, but if you look at a close-up of the image (Figure 19-16), you will see that remapping the pixels introduces "noise" in the photo that appears as blotchy areas. The resulting histogram looks like a picket fence. This demonstrates that, when it comes time to recover an underexposed photo, you should know in advance that you will have to make a tradeoff between the amount of brightening you want add and the amount of noise you are willing to tolerate.

Tip

Spikes or vertical lines in a histogram usually indicate that a photo has already been modified in a photo editor or that the digital camera that took the photo has a lot of noise, which is a common occurrence with photos taken under low-light conditions.

Working with Overexposed Images

Overexposed images can be corrected using the same tools used to fix underexposed images. When working with overexposed images, you need to remember something from earlier in the chapter: you cannot recover detail in any areas of a photo that

FIGURE 19-15
Applying an auto adjustment tool makes the underexposed image much brighter.

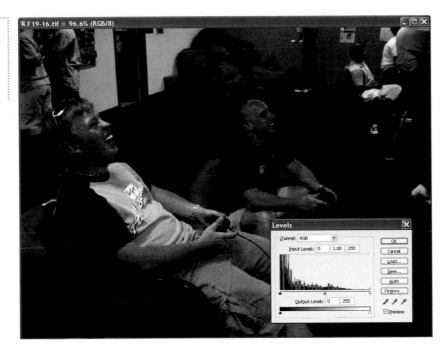

FIGURE 19-16
Recovering detail from shadows usually introduces noise into the photo.

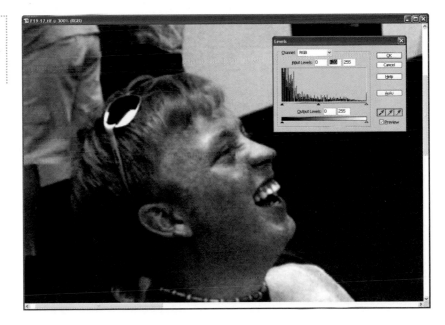

19

have gone pure white (called *specular blowouts*), such as those shown in Figure 19-13.

Even though you can't recover lost details in blowouts, you can make the photos look a lot better by using the Levels command in Photoshop Elements or the histogram adjustment in Paint Shop Pro.

For example, the photo shown in Figure 19-17 was taken at an air show in Texas around noon in the middle of summer, and even though the camera's metering system did its best to compensate, the photo ended up being mildly overexposed.

FIGURE 19-17 Bright sunny days can create overexposed photos.

By moving the middle slider (also called the *gamma* slider) of the histogram to the left, just the pixels in the midtone region are remapped toward the shadow region. All of the pixels in the shadows and the highlight region are uneffected, as shown in Figure 19-18. If all of the pixels were shifted to the darker side by the same amount, details in the shadow region would be lost.

 Some photo editors offer the ability to adjust only the gamma without ever opening a histogram.

FIGURE 19-18 Adjusting the pixels in the photo can turn slightly overexposed images into much better ones.

Color Correction

Sometimes the problem with your photo is that the colors are slightly wrong. This slightly off-color problem is called a *color cast*. The most common color cast problem with photos taken with a digital camera is a blue cast. Most photo editors offer several types of automatic color correction tools that work in roughly the same way. The computer attempts to determine which pixels in the image are neutral colors in an image and then analyzes them to determine the color cast to correct them.

FIGURE 19-19 The original photo (A) is mildly overexposed and has a blue color cast; after adjusting the exposure, the color improves the final photo (B).

A.

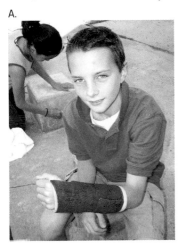

B.

On occasion, these color cast removal tools actually work—it's not that they are poorly designed, it's just that it is difficult for any software to know what colors in the photo were neutral when the photo was taken. Typically, when the tool is applied to a photo and it doesn't work, the colors tend to shift toward blue. When this happens, use the Undo feature of your program and manually correct the colors.

The photo shown in Figure 19-19A is slightly overexposed and it has a slightly blue cast. After correcting the overexposure using levels, the color in the photo was corrected by adjusting the individual color channels shown in Figure 19-19B.

Color Correction and Color Channels

The color photos made by your digital camera are composed of three channels: Red, Green, and Blue (RGB). Until now, when the histogram was used to adjust exposures, it adjusted all three of these color channels simultaneously. You can a lso adjust color channels individually, which may sound complicated but isn't.

Color Correction by the Numbers   Here is a step-by-step personal recipe for tweaking colors in photos:

1. Open the photo in your photo editor and evaluate it to determine what needs to be changed. The photo of a field of sunflowers shown in Figure 19-20 is overexposed, causing a blue cast. We'll fix the exposure and color cast.

FIGURE 19-19 The original photo (A) is mildly overexposed and has a blue color cast; after adjusting the exposure, the color improves the final photo (B).

FIGURE 19-20 Sunflowers are overexposed, resulting in a blue color cast.

2. Apply the automatic correction tools to see if they are of any help. Using the Auto Levels of Photoshop Elements produces an even worse color shift, as shown in Figure 19-21. (See the Did You Know box, coming up, "Auto Levels and Color," to learn why.) Because this didn't work, undo it.

FIGURE 19-21 Auto levels creates even a worse color cast.

3. Use the levels (or equivalent) command to adjust the midtones (gamma) to correct for the overexposure (see Figure 19-22). You can't correct color until you have the exposure right. Look how much the blue color cast was reduced by adjusting the exposure.

FIGURE 19-22 Correcting the exposure reduces the color cast.

4. Still, a slight blue color cast dominates the photo, and you can correct it by adjusting the individual color channels. Figure 19-23 shows the final image.

FIGURE 19-23 The final image looks more like sunflowers.

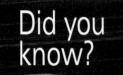

Auto Levels and Color

Most programs offer an automated version of levels that redistributes the pixels in all three color channels. About half the time this works great, but since each color channel individually has its pixels redistributed, the blue channel (typically the weakest of the three color channels) tends to become dominant. You may notice that after you have applied auto colors, the photo has developed a slight bluish color cast.

Hopefully, you have learned a few tricks to fix common photo problems. In the next chapter, you will learn how to do some pretty fancy photo magic.

19

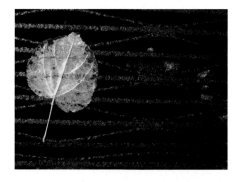

Chapter 20

The Magic of Digital Photography

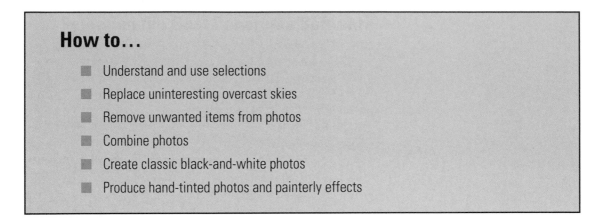

How to...

■ Understand and use selections

■ Replace uninteresting overcast skies

■ Remove unwanted items from photos

■ Combine photos

■ Create classic black-and-white photos

■ Produce hand-tinted photos and painterly effects

Digital Photography Myth Number 20: You need costly professional photo-editing software and an equally expensive computer to achieve special effects with your digital photos.

Fact: False. Many popular photo-editing applications that sell for less than $100 offer a number of sophisticated, professional-level capabilities and effects.

In this chapter you will learn about a broad selection of professional tricks and tips to help improve your digital photographs. All of the topics covered in this chapter have one thing in common: the techniques are all done on a computer after the shoot. You will discover how to expand the dynamic range of your camera, remove and replace someone or something from a photo (such as a time-date stamp from a photograph), combine photos, and add effects to your shots.

FIGURE 20-1 This is a great photo, except for the fact that the background is somewhat mundane.

One of the really cool things that you can do with digital photographs is create a montage by merging different photos together, rearrange objects within a photo, or—even better—add someone or something from one photo into another.

Most of us have some favorite photo that looks really cool—except, perhaps, it has a cluttered or uninteresting background. The photo in Figure 20-1 is a classic example of a young man posing in his kitchen. I thought the pose was great, but the

FIGURE 20-2 Using your computer, you can change the background to something more interesting.

background makes a lame backdrop. Using a photo editor, it is possible to select him and extract him from the photo for placement in a different photograph, like the one shown in Figure 20-2.

Doesn't that look cool? You'll learn how to create images like this later in the chapter in the section "Moving a Subject from One Photo to Another."

Wouldn't it be nice if the computer could automatically outline the subject by your pressing a button? The truth is, it takes a little effort to do this, but most photo editors do offer a few options that can help. You use a *selection* to isolate the subject; then you can move it into whatever other image you want.

Using the Power of Selections

The secret of combining parts from different photos into the same image involves using techniques called *selections*. As we humans look at Figure 20-1, we see the young man and the background in the photo. To the computer, though, shapes don't register; it sees only binary data. To isolate a subject from the rest of the photo, we need to define an area using a selection, which we use to group together the binary data. The shape of a selection can range from the simple, such as the rectangular shape of a building, to the complex, such as the boy and the busy background.

Because complex-shaped selections require more control than is possible with selection tools that make only geometric shapes (such as a Rectangle selection tool or a Ellipse selection tool), most photo editors provide an assortment of selection tools that allow you to select precisely that portion of the image that you want to work on and protect the other parts of the image. To be able to use these tools effectively, we are going to spend a little time learning just how selections work and how you use them.

20

Understanding Selections

In this chapter, I will demonstrate techniques using two of the most popular photo-editing applications: Photoshop Elements (http://www.adobe.com) and Paint Shop Pro (http://www.jasc.com). Both Adobe and Jasc offer free 30-day trail versions of these programs, which are available for download from the manufacturers' web sites.

Did you know?

What's In a Name?

Most photo-editing software programs feature similar selection tools, but each application uses its own names for these tools, which makes it difficult to talk about them all at once. The tools used to select part of an image using Paint Shop Pro are called *selection tools*. In Photoshop Elements, these same tools are called *Lasso* and *Marquee tools*, so named because you select an area by encircling it with a lasso-like tool, and the selected area is indicated by a marquee of dots—sometimes called "marching ants" because, well, they look like little bugs moving on the screen; you'll recognize them when you see them. Both types of tools work essentially the same way.

In Corel PHOTO-PAINT selections are also referred to as *masks*. This is because making a selection excludes the area beyond the selection—in short, it "masks off" a selection from its surroundings. After a selection is made, changes can be made only within the selected area.

You should get familiar with the names of the particular interfaces and their functions in the photo-editing application you use. If you switch to another application, even though the names may change, the functions remain pretty similar.

What a Selection Does

The purpose of a selection tool is to define the part of the image on which you want to work. If this is your first time using a photo editor, don't let the large number of selection tools (most applications have from six to eight different tools) with their strange-sounding names overwhelm you.

Isolating and protecting an object using selections is a concept we all have used at one time or another in our lives.

A.

Although I have heard many analogies to selections and their uses, here are a few popular ones that might clarify this concept:

If you have ever used a stencil, you have used a selection. The stencil allows you to apply paint only to part of the background material and it protects the rest.

Another example of a selection that is closer to home (maybe even literally) occurs for you careful painters when you're painting the trim or walls. You may use masking tape to mask off the parts of a room on which you don't want to get paint. Photo-editing selections act just like a stencil or masking tape when it comes to isolating or applying any effect to part of an image.

Let's look at the most basic selection tools.

Using Basic Selection Tools

The selection tools shown in Figure 20-3 appear in the toolbars of Photoshop Elements and Paint Shop Pro. These selection tools can be used to create selections in the shapes of rectangles, ellipses, polygons, and other nondescript shapes. If you access the Options palette in Paint Shop Pro you can also create unique selections in fixed shapes.

B.

Before we get into making complicated selections, let's see how basic selection tools can be used to create some cool stuff.

Expanding a Photograph Using a Selection

Here is a great trick using a *floating selection* with Photoshop Elements to expand the photograph shown in Figure 20-4. This photo is almost square, but because I want to use it for a title page, it needs to be widened to allow room for title text.

FIGURE 20-3 Selection tools are the basic building blocks for isolating and protecting parts of an image. Image A displays the tools for Photoshop Elements and Image B shows the tools for Paint Shop Pro.

1. Many commonly used tools and features have shortcut keys that you can use instead of menu selections, which are indicated in parentheses here. Learning to use these keyboard shortcuts saves you from having to select features and tools using your mouse.

20

In Photoshop Elements, use the Canvas Size (choose Image | Resize | Canvas Size) to extend the right side of the photo 2 inches, as shown here:

Selection marquee

2. Choose the Rectangular Marquee selection tool (press M) and drag a selection over the part of the photo you want to duplicate to add it to the right edge of the photo. The edge of the selection is marked by a flashing marquee, or "marching ants," as shown at left.

3. Change to the Move tool (V), and while holding down the ALT/OPTION key, drag the selection (so that it becomes a floating selection) over the new extension of the image, as shown below.

4. The added area is obviously a duplicate. You can use the Clone Stamp tool to remove the seam, but we can be a little more creative. Holding down the ALT key, click the middle control on the left side of the floating selection and drag it to the opposite side. This action (called a *free transform* in Photoshop Elements) flips the selection horizontally, as shown next. When you have finished flipping the selection, double-click it to complete the transformation.

20

Control

5. Delete the selection (CTRL-D/COMMAND-D), and the floating selection is merged into the photo. Now you can crop the photo to the desired size and add a title like the one shown in Figure 20-5.

FIGURE 20-5 A rectangular-shaped floating selection is used to expand a photo so it can be used as a title page.

Adding Text to a Photo

When you use the Canvas Size feature (either in Paint Shop Pro or Photoshop Elements), you are adding area to one or more sides of the existing image. The color of the new area is determined by the currently selected fill/background color. The photo of the little toy pig on the motorcycle, shown in Figure 20-6, is a good candidate for making a poster, but there's

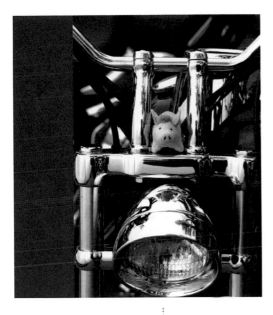

FIGURE 20 6 Preparing to create a poster

not much room here to add text. We can use Photoshop Elements to change the background color and add text to create a poster.

1. Change the background color to the desired color. A good way to get the desired color is to use the Eyedropper tool and click on a color within your image.

2. Use the Canvas Size (Image | Resize | Canvas Size) to extend the left side of the photo 2 inches.

Most photo editors enable you to add text to an image. Both Photoshop Elements and Paint Shop Pro also let you orient the text either horizontally or vertically. In Figure 20-7, I used the Vertical Text tool to add the text. I then distorted the text horizontally by dragging the middle handle before applying one of the metallic text styles.

Using Selection Shapes for Emphasis

When you need to place a large amount of text over a photo, you can add a solid block of a contrasting color and place the text on it. Here is a trick professionals use to emphasize text on photos.

1. Use one of the shaped selection tools and select an area of the photo. Any effect applied to the photo will now be applied only to the area within the selection.

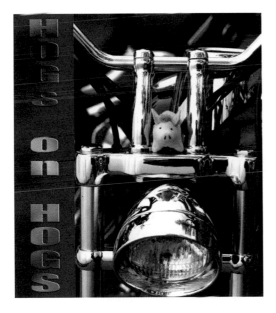

FIGURE 20-7 This photo's background was changed, and it was widened to add text to make a poster.

20

2. Use either Gamma adjustment or Brightness to lighten the area inside the selection, as shown here:

3. Delete the selection (CTRL-D/COMMAND-D).

4. Add text and adjust it so that it fits into the area defined by the selection. The finished results are shown in Figure 20-8.

FIGURE 20-8 Using a selection restricted the image brightening so that only the area behind text would be effected.

The history of cattle tipping dates back to 1254 AD when Sir Reginold Tipum asked Sir Charles Buba on the plains of Beevus "What shall we do this evening?" Cattle tipping soon became the national sport of Tipinstan. Countless numbers attended both local and national tipping events. When Tipinstan applied to the Olympic committee to have cattle tipping introduced as an event in 1924...

(continued on page 834)

Did you know?

Adding Text Using a Photo Editor Has Its Limitations

Adding text to an image using the Type tool in your photo editor has some limitations of which you should be aware.

When it comes to adding paragraph text like the kind shown in Figure 20-8, you are required to adjust the line breaks manually so that the paragraph fits in the area as desired. Last, and most important, when you add text in a photo editor in most all applications, the text is *rasterized*, which means it is converted to pixels, so the text may not appear sharp when the photo is output to a printer.

To my knowledge, no photo editor currently offers spell checking, which is a serious consideration as we become more and more dependent on computer programs to check our spelling. Physically proofreading the copy before you rasterize the text is a habit you'll never regret.

Feathering the Selections

Until now, we have been considering selections that have hard and defined edges, but you'll often find that you want to make a selection that has a soft edge. For example, if you are moving an image from one photograph into another, you can use a feathered selection to make the moved image blend into the new picture more smoothly.

You need to be careful with the amount of feathering you apply to the mask, however. Usually, you add feathering details in an Options dialog box (you can find out how to do that in your photo editor by reading the manual). Using just a few pixels (1 to 2 pixels) of feathering is usually sufficient. If you add a large amount of feathered pixels, the object looks like it is glowing or is furry.

While many things can be done with the selection tools to produce a defined geometric shape, when you need to create an irregular shaped selection, you need to use the Lasso tools.

Rounding Up the Lasso Tools

Photoshop Elements offers *Lasso tools,* because you encircle the subject with a selection that looks like a lasso. Paint Shop Pro offers the same tools, but they're called *Freehand selection tools*.

You can use three basic kinds of Lasso/Freehand tools to draw both straight-edged and freehand edges when making an

20

irregularly shaped selection. In Photoshop Elements/Paintshop Pro, they are as follows:

- Lasso tool/Freehand tool
- Polygonal Lasso tool/Point-to-Point tool
- Magnetic Lasso tool/Smart Edge and Edge Seeker tool (Paint Shop Pro has two versions of this tool)

Unlike the selection tools that produce closed shapes, the Lasso tools let you draw a meandering path around a subject. When you have selected what you want, you either let go of the mouse button or double-click it (this depends on which tool you are using) and the application will make a straight line back to the starting point to complete the selection.

Creating a Selection Manually

All selection tools act in a similar fashion. In the grand scheme of things, the Lasso/Freehand selection tool is designed to draw freehand selections and the Polygonal/Point-to-Point tools are used to create a selection made out of a lot of straight lines. The one problem with the Lasso/Freehand selection tool is that the moment that you let go of the mouse button (usually by accident), the application completes the selection, which can be frustrating. Drawing intricate lines with a mouse is difficult for several reasons. The mouse was never designed to replace the pencil— for example, if you can sign your name using a mouse, you probably need to get out more! It is difficult to follow an irregular line using only a mouse.

If you find you are making a lot of selections, you should consider getting a pressure-sensitive stylus like the one shown in Figure 20-9. Wacom styluses and tablets have become the industry standard for this type of device, and its product comes highly recommended, especially for its ergonomic design.

The *pressure-sensitive* part means that your photo editor can be configured to read the amount of pressure that you're exerting on the stylus and change a setting, such as tool brush width or opacity, based on the amount of pressure you apply. Does this

FIGURE 20-9 A stylus and tablet like this one made by Wacom don't cost much and make creating selections much easier.

mean you can't use Lasso Selection tools without a graphics tablet? Of course not; but it's a lot easier if you use a tablet. With that matter settled, let's consider some ideas on how to make better selections.

If you don't have a stylus, here are some suggestions when using a mouse to make selections.

Break up the Selection into Parts   Rather than try to make a complex selection all in one go, you can outline part of the area and save the selection to combine with other selections. Since all selection tools offer the ability to modify selections, you can change the selection mode to the Add To mode. If you don't change modes, the original selection disappears when you begin to outline the next part of the selection. After you outline the next part of the selection, you must add it to the original when you save it. In Photoshop Elements, you can add to a selection by holding down the + key and subtract from a selection by holding down the ALT/OPTION key

Zoom in Close   This is important when you're working with a mouse. The closer you zoom in, the easier it is to follow the outline of your subject. Don't worry about running off the screen. All applications will move (pan) the image as you approach the edge of the current window.

Use Polygon/Point-to-Point Tools   Even if your image doesn't have flat edges, you can still use these tools. By definition, even a *circle* is just a polygon made up of an infinite number of line segments. The advantage of using these tools it that when you release the mouse button, the application doesn't close the selection automatically. These tools offer a great way to rest your hands during a long and complex selection. If you zoom in close, you can use these tools effectively even if your subject is all curves.

Using Automatic Edge Detecting Tools

These selection tools act like their Lasso/Freehand selection tool cousins, except they have the ability to detect the edge automatically (in most cases), which can save you a lot of work. Most folks use a combination of automatic tools and the Lasso/ Freehand selection tools to isolate the part of a photograph that they want.

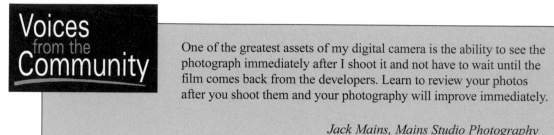

One of the greatest assets of my digital camera is the ability to see the photograph immediately after I shoot it and not have to wait until the film comes back from the developers. Learn to review your photos after you shoot them and your photography will improve immediately.

Jack Mains, Mains Studio Photography

Controlling the Auto Edge Detection Tools

The automatic tools (Magnetic Lasso and Smart Edge) are great timesavers when it comes to making selections. Essentially, as you move the tool along an edge you want to select, the tool "looks" for the edge. On a high contrast, well-defined edge, automatic selection works better than advertised. On edges that are poorly defined, though, such as when the colors inside and outside the edge are nearly the same, the tools can need a little help from you.

Using automatic tools is quite simple. Click once on the point where you want to begin the selection. This point is called a *fastening* point. Now move the tool (slowly, and with or without holding down the mouse button) along the edge. Fastening points will appear along the edge of the selection as the computer tries to determine where the edge is. At some point, the computer will guess wrong; when it does, stop and press the BACKSPACE key. Each time you press the key, your application removes the last point on the selection. Continue to do this until you get to a point on the selection that is on the actual edge. You can try the automatic process again, but usually, when the magnetic tool is guessing wrong, it means that it's encountering either a low-contrast edge or something nearby (not on the edge) is pulling the tool away from the edge.

When you hit a rough patch, if the edge is irregular (lots of ins and outs) you can click on each of the points that define the edge, making them very close together. Another option is to switch to the Lasso tool temporarily by holding down the ALT/OPTION key and dragging the mouse along the edge with the mouse button depressed. If the edge that is confusing the Magnetic Lasso tool is basically composed of straight lines, you can temporarily switch to the Polygon tool by holding down the CONTROL/ COMMAND key and clicking from point to point.

Get the Best Selections (in the Least Amount of Time)

Whether I'm doing art layout for work or for community projects (read: free), I have spent the past 10 years making composite images by using selections. In that time, I have come up with a short list of dos and don'ts that I share here to help you make great selections.

First, Make a Rough Cut Selection   If the image is so large that it does not fit on the screen when viewing at 100 percent, you should change the zoom level to Fit On Screen so that the entire subject you are going to isolate fits into the image window.

Next, make a rough selection. It doesn't matter which selection tool you use; you just want to get as close as you can but not spend a lot of time doing it. This rough selection just gets you in the ballpark.

Next, Add Some and Take Some   Using the Add To Selection and Subtract From Selection modes, begin to shape the selection to fit the subject you are trying to isolate. Here is a trick that will save you time when doing this part. First, rather than clicking the buttons in the menus to change modes, use the keyboard shortcuts to change between modes. Pressing the SHIFT key changes the selection mode to Add To, and pressing the ALT/OPTION key changes it to Subtract From for most programs. Just remember that these modifier keys must be pressed *before* you click the mouse.

Finally, Get in Close   On some areas, you may need to zoom in at levels even greater than 100 percent. (Photoshop goes up to 1600 percent, which allows you to select microbes and stray electrons.) Now and again you should change the image so that it fits in the image window, just to keep a perspective on the whole image.

Speaking of keeping a perspective, all the time you are improving the selection, keep in mind the ultimate amount of tweaking you want to make for the image you are selecting. Here are some questions that should help you adjust the degree of exactness you want to invest in your selection.

- How close is the background color of the image you are selecting and the current background colors? If they are roughly the same colors, investing a lot of time producing a detailed selection doesn't make much sense, since a feathered edge will work just fine.

20

- Will the final image be larger, smaller, or the same size? If you are going to be making the current image larger, every detail will stick out like the proverbial sore thumb, so any extra time you spend to make the selection as exact as possible will pay big benefits. If you are going to reduce the size of the subject, a lot of tiny detail will become lost when it is resized, so don't invest a lot of time in the selection.

- Is this a paid job or a freebee? Creating a complex selection is a time-consuming process. If perfection is not required, maybe you don't need to make a perfect selection.

Did you know?

The Alpha Channel

How do you save a selection? If you invest a lot of time making a selection, you might want to save it to use again. The process is simple, but before I tell you how to do it, I must introduce a term that you may have heard before: the *alpha channel*. Sounds like the name of a science-fiction channel on your local cable TV. The alpha channel is not a channel at all, but the name assigned by Apple (who created it) for additional storage space in a graphics file format called TIFF (Tagged Image Format File).

Why is it called alpha channel? The truth is, when Apple created the concept of the channel, it wasn't sure what the tool was going to be used for until Adobe latched onto it and made it the general-purpose storage for selections. While it is still technically referred to as *alpha channel* to differentiate it from the red, green, and blue channels, Adobe and the others working in the graphics industry just call it a *channel*.

How many alpha channels can fit into a Paint Shop Pro file? Good question, how big of a file can you live with? For all practical purposes, there is no limit to the number of additional channels that can be included in a TIFF, a Paint Shop Pro, or a Photoshop/Photoshop Elements file.

Using the Magic Wand Tool to Make Magic

The Magic Wand tool is a great tool for making selections of areas containing similar colors. Both Paint Shop Pro and Photoshop Elements have a Magic Wand tool and both operate in the same fashion. Unfortunately, because many users have no idea how to use this tool, they are disappointed when the magic doesn't work.

The first fact about the Magic Wand tool—there's no magic (surprised?). Up until now, all of the selection tools we have discussed involved either closed shapes or lassos that surround the subject to be selected. The Magic Wand tool acts a little like dropping a stone in a calm pool of water. The selection, like ripples of water, spreads outward from the starting point. It continues radiating outward, selecting similar (and adjacent) colored pixels until it reaches pixels whose color/shade is so different from the starting point that they can't be included.

Tips on Troubleshooting the Magic Wand

When working with the Magic Wand tool, you may click in an area and find that it does not produce a uniform selection, but instead creates a bunch of little selections. These little selection "islands" are caused when the difference between the color value of the starting point is greater than the pixels that make up these "islands." You can resolve this issue in several ways.

You could hold down the SHIFT key and click all of the individual points with the Magic Wand tool until they are all gone, but that's not the smart way to do it (and I am embarrassed to admit how many times I have done just that). Here is the best way to fix this problem: If the colors you are selecting are very different from those in the rest of the image, you can either choose Select | Similar or try increasing the Tolerance setting and try reselecting the same area again.

The problem with both of these approaches, however, is that many times the selection begins to appear in the part of the image that you do not want selected. If the selection goes too far into the part of the image that you don't want selected (especially at the edge), here is another trick you can try. You can use the Select | Similar command, in which Elements uses the current Tolerance setting, to determine which pixels are included in the selection. This means that after you do an initial selection with the Magic Wand tool, you can lower the Tolerance setting to a low value, such as 4–8, and when you choose the Select | Similar command, it will add only colors that are closer to the original starting point.

Still, sometimes the selection islands appear because the selection contains areas of vastly different colors. In this case, select a Selection tool and, holding down the SHIFT key (Add To

20

selection), drag a selection shape over the islands; that should resolve the issue.

 You can add a small amount of feathering to the selected islands. A feather amount of two to five pixels often smoothes out the selection.

Selection marquee

Moving a Subject from One Photo to Another

Now that you know a little about the selection tools of your photo editor, let's see how they can be used to take someone out of one photo and put him into another. Remember the photo of young man back in the beginning of the chapter, in Figure 20-1?

Here is how you can move a subject from one photo into another.

1. Outline the subject with a selection tool, as shown in Figure 20-10.

2. Copy the selected area to the clipboard (CTRL-C).

3. Open the photo into which you want to place the subject—see the photo in Figure 20-11.

FIGURE 20-10 The selection marquee shows that the subject in this photo is selected.

FIGURE 20-11 This photo could make a good background for the subject copied from the original photo.

FIGURE 20-12 The subject is now floating in a layer and can be moved anywhere in the photo.

FIGURE 20-13 This background photo was shot near sunset.

4. If you're using Photoshop Elements, you can paste the image into the existing photo by using CONTROL-V/ (Paste). For Paint Shop Pro, use CONTROL-L (Paste New Layer). The contents of the selection will be floating on top of the original photo, as shown in Figure 20-12.

5. When you look at Figure 20-10, you will notice that the subject is a lot larger than the photo in which he has been placed. You can correct problems with comparative size issues in two ways: You can undo the previous paste and resize the background photo before again pasting in the Clipboard contents. Since the subject is now a layer, you can also resize, rotate, flip, and otherwise distort the layer using the Transform (Photoshop Elements) or the Deformation (Paint Shop Pro) tool.

Refer to Figure 20-2 and you can see the original subject was made small enough to fit the frame. He was flipped horizontally to improve the overall composition, and his color temperature was made cooler to match the overall cool colors of the background photo.

In Figure 20-13 we have the opposite color problem. The photo was taken near sunset, so the colors are warm and there are a lot of shadows.

In the original photo the young man was illuminated by a flash, which is rather cool, while the background photo to which he was added was taken near sunset. In addition to the different color temperature of the lighting, his face in the original is uniformly illuminated by the flash and so there aren't any long shadows across his face, which would be there as the sun was coming in low from the right (his left).

So, to prevent the photo from appearing as a composite image, after using the Hue/Saturation/

20

Lightness controls to correct the color temperature (or using Color Balance if the control is available) the Burn tool (which is a brush that darkens the pixels) I darkened the side of this face that would have been away from the sun had he actually been standing near the marina. The resulting composite photo is shown in Figure 20-14.

By applying color correction only to the layer containing the new subject (the young man), it is possible to match the color "temperature" for all of the subjects in the photo, as shown in Figure 20-14, so it isn't so apparent that they are actually two different photos.

FIGURE 20-14 Correcting the color balance of each layer allows you to make parts from different photos blend together.

Replacing an Overcast Sky

Taking photographs on an overcast day is always a mixed blessing. Because of the clouds, the illumination is diffused—and that's good. Because of the clouds, the horizon on a landscape photograph is uninteresting, at best— that's not so good. For example, if you are taking photos of a house that you are planning to sell, the house will always appear more appealing with a blue sky to provide sharp contrast and define the outline of the house.

Using the Magic Wand selection tool allows you to replace overcast skies using your photo-editing software and another photograph of a sky with clouds taken on a clear day.

Here is how it is done:

1. Open the photograph that needs its sky replaced.

2. Choose the Magic Wand tool.

3. Change the Tolerance setting so that is high enough to ensure that all of the areas of the overcast sky around the branches will be tightly selected. If you're using Photoshop Elements, uncheck the Contiguous box in the Options bar. If you're using Paint Shop Pro, you must choose Selection | Modify | More to include all the sky area.

Incorrectly selected areas

Selection marquee

4. To ensure you select all of the sky, even the tiny portions among leaves, choose Select | Similar.

5. The only drawback to using the Magic Wand is that it selects everything that contains the same color as the overcast sky. In this case, the selection includes a bright spot on the sidewalk, the roof on the left side of the house, and other small areas. If this happens, change the mode of your Lasso/Freehand selection tool to Subtract mode and circle all of the unwanted selection areas until they are gone.

6. Open the photo containing the replacement sky you intend to use, like the one shown next. Select the entire image (CONTROL-A/) and copy it to the Clipboard (CONTROL-C/). Close the photo without saving it.

7. Back in the original image, choose Edit | Paste Into (SHIFT-CONTROL-V/SHIFT-) and the contents of the Clipboard appear in the selection, as shown in Figure 20-15.

20

The marching ants selection marquee can be a little distracting, so all photo editors allow you to turn off the display. These controls are typically found in the View menu.

Removing and Replacing Objects in Photos

One of the real benefits of digital photos is that you can remove unwanted objects from photos, such as the time-date stamp in the lower-left corner of the photo shown in Figure 20-16.

If your digital images include the time and date information on the image, look in your camera manual to find out how to turn off this feature.

Time-date stamp

FIGURE 20-15 Now a new sky replaces the original overcast one in the photograph.

FIGURE 20-16 This photo would be a lot cuter if the time-date stamp weren't in the corner.

Removing Unwanted Stuff from Photos

The quickest way to remove small items from a photo, such as the time-date stamp, is to use the Clone tool (the Clone Stamp tool in Photoshop Elements). The Clone tool is a brush that paints using another part of the photo as a source. In other words, you use the Clone tool to select a part of the photo that you want to copy, and then when you drag the Clone brush, the source material is pasted to where you are painting.

Let's use it to remove the time-date stamp from Figure 20-16.

1. Zoom in on the part of the photo that's to be modified with the Clone tool.

2. Select the Clone tool (Clone Stamp brush) and locate a part of the photo that is similar in appearance to the area containing the part you want removed. This area will be the *source* for your clone brush. In Photoshop Elements, hold down the ALT/OPTION key and click the spot; in Paint Shop Pro, you need to right-click an area to establish the source point.

FIGURE 20-17 Find a spot to use as a source for the replacement materials.

Clone brush replaces
pixels as it moves up

Select this as the source

3. To remove the time-date stamp on the blanket, we can use the area to the immediate right of the text as the source. Placing the Clone brush to the immediate right of the red time-date stamp, as shown in Figure 20-17, right-click or ALT/-click to tell the program that it is to use this as a source. Note that if you just drag the Clone brush across an offending area, you may see a repeating pattern in the cloned area. This can be avoided by selecting several source points and using short and small clone strokes.

4. The key to removing the entire time-date stamp (or any other object) is patience. We can zoom in as far as possible and use a much smaller clone brush setting when working on the area around his hand.

20

The Clone Brush tool is also handy for removing little distracting details like the stain (all baby blankets have stains) and the blanket tag on the right. The finished image is shown in Figure 20-18.

Switching Faces with the Clone Tools

The Clone tool is not limited to paintcopying the pixels from one part of the image to another. You can also use it to paint part of one photo onto another photo. This is handy for creating a "group photo" when you actually have only photos of single people, or when you take group shots in which individuals in one shot look better than they do in the other. You can add the people to a single photo so that it looks like the photo was taken of the group at one time. Figures 20-19 and 20-20 show two family photos. Each photo has both good and bad expressions.

FIGURE 20-18 Using the Clone tool allows you to remove just about anything from a photo.

FIGURE 20-19 Nice group shot, except some of the expressions aren't as good as those in Figures 20-20 and 20- 21.

FIGURE 20-20 Another nice shot, especially of the ladies on the right.

FIGURE 20-21 The Clone tool moved the desired expression from one photo to another.

Here is how to get all the good expressions onto a single photo:

1. Determine which photo will serve as the photo that will receive the cloned expression from the other photo.

2. Select the source photo, and pick a spot on the part of the image that you want to clone to the other photo. In this example, I want the young ladies on the right side of Figure 20-20 cloned to replace their duplicates in Figure 20-19.

3. Select the source photo, and set the starting point of the part you want to clone. In this case, we'll replace the face of the young lady on the far right.

4. Select the destination photo and pick roughly the same point, and then begin applying the Clone brush. Figure 20-21 shows the face replaced.

5. Repeat steps 2–4 until all of the parts from the other photos have been moved. The final photo is shown in Figure 20-22.

FIGURE 20-22 Using the Clone tool let me combine the best of several photos into one.

Creating Classic Black-and-White Effects

Black-and-white photography was the norm until the 1950s. Before then, color was expensive and not very accurate. Your digital camera probably has a feature that lets you take black-and-white photos. Kodak is now selling disposable film cameras that take black-and-white photos, called "classic" photos.

Using your photo editor, you can turn color photos you take with you digital camera into black-and-white photos in a single step.

If you change the color mode of an image to Grayscale, you end up with a classic black-and-white photo like the one shown in Figure 20-23. While this is a cool trick, it is only the tip of the trick iceberg.

All photo editors (and some digital cameras) offer a feature that turns a photo into a sepia-toned image like the one shown in Figure 20-24. In Photoshop Elements, you use the Colorize command; in Paint Shop Pro, you can use one of several filters that are available.

FIGURE 20-23 Classic black-and-white photos can be made in an instant in your computer.

FIGURE 20-24 Converting a photo to a sepia tone gives it an old look.

Creating Hand-Tinted Photos

Until the 1950s, a popular technique that was used to give photos the appearance of color was to tint the photo with colors applied with a brush. Hand-colored photos had a distinct appearance, and that style of photo is becoming popular once again. Using your photo-editing software makes it easy to convert a color photo, like the one shown in Figure 20-25, into one that looks as though it were hand-tinted.

20

Here is all that you need do to create this appearance:

1. Locate the Hue-Saturation-Brightness controls (these are almost always located together) in your photo-editing software.

2. Drag the Saturation level down and watch as the colors fade in the image (make sure your software's Preview capability is turned on while doing this, or you won't see anything as you move the Saturation slider).

3. Start with a 70 percent reduction in the saturation, and adjust the Hue slider until the color appears the way you want it.

4. Click OK, and you'll create a imitation hand-tinted photo, like the one shown in Figure 20-26.

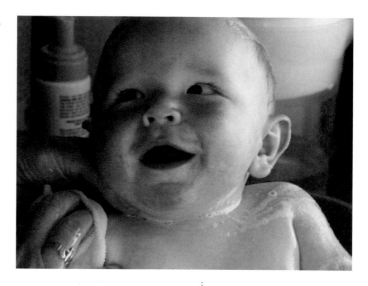

FIGURE 20-25 The original color photo looks great.

FIGURE 20-26 Reducing the saturation gives the appearance of hand-tinted photos.

For a finishing touch, you can always use your photo editor's saturation tool (called a Sponge tool in Photoshop Elements) and increase the saturation on parts of the photo. In the baby photo, saturation levels can be increased in the lips and the blush on the cheeks (see Figure 20-27). The difference is subtle, but this really gives the impression that it is an antique photo.

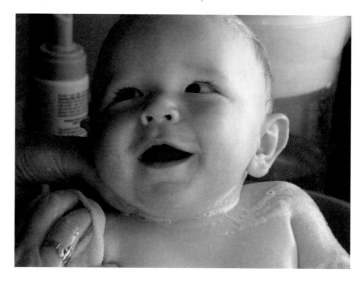

FIGURE 20-27 Using increased saturation on parts of the image heightens the impression the photo has been hand-tinted.

Achieving Painterly Effects with Photos

Several programs out there claim to be able to change any of your photos into "paintings." Some work well, but others don't. The best program for these effects is Virtual Painter from Jasc Software (http://www.jasc.com). It works as a plug-in to your photo-editing software. (A plug-in is software that operates within your photo editor.)

The advantage of using Virtual Painter is that the size of the brush strokes varies with the physical size of the image. Most of the painterly programs use only a fixed brush size, which means that when they are applied to a large image, you cannot see the brush strokes, and when applied to a smaller image, the brush strokes are so large the image is unrecognizable.

Photoshop Elements is supplied with a number of plug-in filters that can achieve a painterly effect. They are found under the *artistic* and *brush stroke* categories.

An example of how image detail can be preserved is shown when you compare the original photo in Figure 20-28A with the colored pencil effect shown in Figure 20-28B.

Always work on a duplicate of your original image or at least a separate layer to avoid losing, or defacing, the original image.

A.   B.

In this chapter, you have learned how to use the selection tools to isolate parts of an image so that you can remove or replace them with something else. It may take some practice to get good at making selections, but the time that you invest in this important skill will help you make better compositions and montages with your photographs.

You also discovered that you can move objects from one place in a photo to another and from one photo to another. It's all part of the magic that is digital photography and digital photo editing.

FIGURE 20-28 (A) Here is the original digital photo of my friend and technical editor, Jim Patterson. (B) Applying a colored pencil effect from Virtual Painter gives it just enough of a painterly effect without losing detail.

Quick and Easy Ways to Take Better Photos

FIGURE
1

FIGURE
2

FIGURE
3

Why the Optical Zoom Ability of Your Camera Is Important

Digital cameras offer zoom lens with different magnification factors (that's optical zoom; digital zoom doesn't count in magnification) that range from 2X to 10X. How important is a camera's zoom factor to you? Take a look: **Figure 1** was taken with a camera using a 2X zoom. **Figure 2** was taken with a camera with a 10X zoom. **Figure 3** was shot with the same 10X zoom camera using a 2X telephoto add-on lens. Besides the impact of optical zoom on photographs, Chapter 2 outlines many factors to consider when selecting a digital camera.

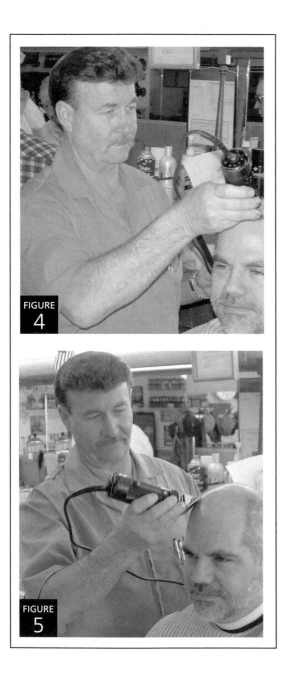

FIGURE
4

FIGURE
5

Use Your Flash Effectively

The internal flash of your camera can wash out the color in your subject if you stand too close to it (see **Figure 4**). However, if you step back a few feet and use your camera's zoom feature, the colors in the photo will appear richer and more vivid, as shown in **Figure 5**.

FIGURE
6

FIGURE
7

Get Close To Your Subject

Digital cameras have a wide lens. Standing the same distance from your subject as you would using your film camera (see **Figure 6**) usually results in lessening the photo's impact. You need to use your camera's zoom feature to get in close (see **Figure 7**).

FIGURE 8

FIGURE 9

FIGURE 10

The Importance of White Balance

The white balance (WB) setting is unique to digital cameras. It controls how the camera renders colors in photographs. Here are some examples of photos taken with different WB settings. The photo in **Figure 8** was taken on a bright, sunny day but the camera's Automatic White Balance (AWB) didn't adjust the color temperature correctly, resulting in a bluish cast. In **Figure 9** the WB setting of the camera was set for an overcast sky, rendering the colors too warm. A proper white balance setting will give you a vivid image like the one shown in **Figure 10**. Also, there won't be a color cast on the photo that you'll need to remove, via a computer.

FIGURE
11

FIGURE
12

How Metering System Choices Effect Your Photos

Digital cameras offer several types of light metering systems to ensure the camera achieves the best possible exposure. In **Figure 11**, using the Average (Matrix) metering system, the camera attempts to adjust for the brightly lit sky in the background. This literally leaves the subjects in the dark. Using a spot metering system ensures the subjects are properly exposed (see **Figure 12**).

FIGURE
13

FIGURE
14

FIGURE
15

Discover The Wonder In The Details

Nearly every digital camera has an excellent macro mode that lets you explore the beauty of objects and creatures around you. This macro mode lets you catch the intricacies of the green glass doorknob shown in **Figure 13**, the curious grasshopper on my finger in **Figure 14**, and the detail of an elaborately decorated wedding cake, shown in **Figure 15**.

Quick and Easy Ways to Take Better Photos

FIGURE
16

Create Special Effects With Your Camera

You don't need a computer to create distinctive looking photos with your camera. **Figure 16** is an example of placing an object in the foreground to block the sun while creating an interesting effect.

Quick and Easy Ways to Take Better Photos

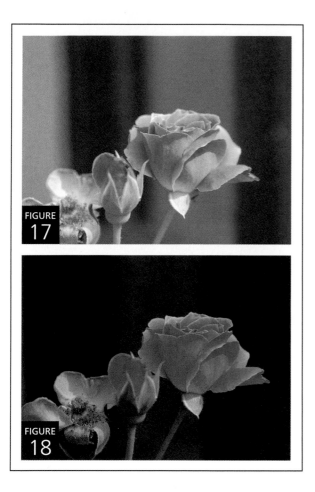

FIGURE 17

FIGURE 18

More Special Effects

Just by changing your camera's metering system selection, you can take an extraordinary close-up of a rose. **Figure 17** was taken with the default metering selection; changing over to spot metering gives us the effect seen in **Figure 18**.

Index

INTERNATIONAL CONTACT INFORMATION

AUSTRALIA
McGraw-Hill Book Company
Australia Pty. Ltd.
TEL +61-2-9900-1800
FAX +61-2-9878-8881
http://www.mcgraw-hill.com.au
books-it_sydney@mcgraw-hill.com

CANADA
McGraw-Hill Ryerson Ltd.
TEL +905-430-5000
FAX +905-430-5020
http://www.mcgraw-hill.ca

GREECE, MIDDLE EAST, & AFRICA
(Excluding South Africa)
McGraw-Hill Hellas
TEL +30-210-6560-990
TEL +30-210-6560-993
TEL +30-210-6560-994
FAX +30-210-6545-525

MEXICO (Also serving Latin America)
McGraw-Hill Interamericana Editores
S.A. de C.V.
TEL +525-1500-5108
FAX +525-117-1589
http://www.mcgraw-hill.com.mx
carlos_ruiz@mcgraw-hill.com

SINGAPORE (Serving Asia)
McGraw-Hill Book Company
TEL +65-6863-1580
FAX +65-6862-3354
http://www.mcgraw-hill.com.sg
mghasia@mcgraw-hill.com

SOUTH AFRICA
McGraw-Hill South Africa
TEL +27-11-622-7512
FAX +27-11-622-9045
robyn_swanepoel@mcgraw-hill.com

SPAIN
McGraw-Hill/
Interamericana de España, S.A.U.
TEL +34-91-180-3000
FAX +34-91-372-8513
http://www.mcgraw-hill.es
professional@mcgraw-hill.es

UNITED KINGDOM, NORTHERN,
EASTERN, & CENTRAL EUROPE
McGraw-Hill Education Europe
TEL +44-1-628-502500
FAX +44-1-628-770224
http://www.mcgraw-hill.co.uk
emea_queries@mcgraw-hill.com

ALL OTHER INQUIRIES Contact:
McGraw-Hill/Osborne
TEL +1-510-420-7700
FAX +1-510-420-7703
http://www.osborne.com
omg_international@mcgraw-hill.com